Organizational Membership

SUNY Series in the Sociology of Work

Richard H. Hall, Editor

Organizational Membership
Personal Development in the Workplace

Howell S. Baum

State University of New York Press

Parts of Chapters 1 and 2 and the Appendix are reprinted by permission of the publisher from Schön, Donald, *The Reflective Turn: Case Studies of Reflection in and on Practice*. (New York: Teachers College Press, ©1990 by Teachers College, Columbia University. All rights reserved.)

Figure 5 is reprinted by permission of the publisher from Baum, Howell S., *The Invisible Bureaucracy; The Unconscious in Organizational Problem Solving* (New York: Oxford University Press, ©1987 by Oxford University Press. All rights reserved.)

Published by
State University of New York Press, Albany

©1990   State University of New York

For information, address the State University of New York Press,
State University Plaza, Albany, NY 12246

Library of Congress Cataloging-in-Publication Data

Baum, Howell S.
  Organizational membership: personal development in the workplace
/ Howell S. Baum.
      p.   cm—(SUNY series in the sociology of work.)
  Includes bibliographical references.
  ISBN 0-7914-0385-8.—ISBN 0-7914-0386-6 (pbk.)
  1. Organizational behavior.   2. Organizational change.
3. Initiations (into trades, societies, etc.)   4. Work—
Psychological aspects.   I. Title.   II. Series.
HD58.7.B38   1990
302.3'4—dc20

10 9 8 7 6 5 4 3 2 1

To Madelyn, Elena, and Maya
In the hope they have good work
In their own good time.

Work without Hope draws nectar in a sieve,
And Hope without an object cannot live.

> —Samuel Taylor Coleridge,
> *Work Without Hope*

Every really able man, in whatever direction he work . . . if you talk
sincerely with him, considers his work, however much admired, as far
short of what it should be.

> —Ralph Waldo Emerson,
> *Letters and Social Aims*

Work keeps us from three great evils, boredom, vice, and need.

> —Voltaire,
> *Candide*

Life grants nothing to us mortals without hard work.

> —Horace,
> *Satires*

I don't like work—no man does—but I like what is in work—the chance to
find yourself. Your own reality—for yourself, not for others—what no
other man can ever know.

> —Joseph Conrad,
> *Heart of Darkness*

In that dark night which shrouds from our eyes the most remote antiquity,
a light appears which cannot lead us astray. I speak of this incontestable
truth: the social world is certainly the work of man.

> —Giovanni Battista Vico,
> *Scienza Nuova*

And now I have finished a work that neither the wrath of love, nor fire,
nor the sword, nor devouring age shall be able to destroy.

> —Ovid,
> *Metamorphoses*

Never have I thought that I was the happy possessor of a "talent"; my sole
concern has been to save myself by work and faith.

> —Jean-Paul Sartre,
> *The Words*

Contents

Introduction

ORIGINS OF THE BOOK

When I started teaching, I worked for administrators who were not very good at what they did. They were anxious about exercising authority, and they often reacted by being dictatorial when they should have been directive. They quickly let others understand that they did not want to discuss policies or problems and that their orders should be unquestioningly, or at least silently, followed. The results were what could be expected: the suppression of conflict aroused anxiety; faculty members avoided saying what they thought and were ashamed of their timidity; and meetings became characterized by the most tensely circumspect nondiscussion imaginable.

One dean, to keep a record of what faculty members said, as well as to intimidate them, taped meetings. He also circulated attendance sheets, to identify those who seemed to act in good faith by coming. However, once someone signed "Mickey Mouse," and the dean made several false accusations about who had pretended to be a rodent. This pleased the faculty immensely.

Whatever the competence of these administrators, exercising authority is not an easy matter. Because managerial acts echo so widely, each step or misstep is quickly heard and often distorted, and the reverberations may scare managers from acting decisively or else frighten them into trying to deaden others' ability to respond. The problems of leading people in large organizations are a subject for another time. Here, I want to focus on what is involved in entering a work organization and how the actions of managers and other workers affect newcomers who think about joining.

I had two typical experiences during those early years. First, I gradually realized that at many meetings people acted so as to avoid making decisions. They were comfortable enough with prevailing arrangements, and they did not want to create problems. Revising even a single course could mean submitting a well-considered proposal to two or three different committees where members would think in terms of protecting their turf and talk in terms of academic integrity. The end result, months later, would be a political and intellectual compromise. After participating in many such meetings, I became curious about why action in organizations is so difficult, what real and imagined dangers make people so anxious and defensive.

On another occasion, I was spending many weekend hours finishing a proposal for a new program involving the cooperation of six departments. As I pored through books for documentation of the need for such a program, I suddenly let myself think that it was clear from the inter-departmental committee meetings of the past half year that no one wanted such a proposal, that I was preparing it only for the record, because the dean wanted something to show for my time on the committee. In other words, I couldn't find a single good reason for finishing the report. I realized that this wasn't the first time I found myself in such a situation, and I began to ask why people do things at work that make little or no sense to them.

One answer to both questions is fear: people are afraid of being punished for doing or not doing something that would displease their boss. This is certainly true, but people may distort a manager's request and often exaggerate the likely consequences of acting. I asked workers about these things in an earlier research project, and they talked about how bureaucratic relationships with authority make them feel afraid of being ashamed before a powerful boss. My book, *The Invisible Bureaucracy*, describes how real inequalities in power and workers' unconscious needs and anxieties combine to create the experience of work organizations as alien institutions. People feel that working *in* organizations requires working *against* them as well.

Bureaucratically induced feelings of shame disable people by mak-ing them doubt their efficacy, value, and ability to get jobs elsewhere. Nevertheless, people have opportunities to leave, but they stay. They are not simply frightened. Whatever pushes them away, something draws them to an organization as well. They get—or, at least, want—something from being part of an organization. People often participate in meetings in good faith. They expect—or would like—something to come of them. People push on with seemingly senseless projects not simply out of fear or inertia. They want to create something. This book explores these attractions to work organizations.

This book is about how people experience becoming members of work organizations. My thinking reflects my appreciation of the duality of workplaces. When I began, I considered organizations alien places and asked what people feel they lose or are asked to give up in order to become part of them. Still, there was the question of why people want to enter at all; money was a weak answer. My colleagues and I often righteously proclaim that we could certainly make more money working somewhere else, and I have heard many others outside academia say the same thing. We want to do or be something in our work.

My bias in thinking about organizational life has for some time been psychoanalytic. Simply put, people have unconscious wishes and intentions in addition to conscious purposes, and their actions and lives express the interaction of the two realms. Hence, in asking what draws people to work organizations, I wondered about unconscious motives in addition to conscious ones. In looking for a way to understand these connections, I settled on Erik Erikson's developmental framework. Not only is Erikson one of the few psychoanalysts who talk about work and consider it important, but he also writes about the ways in which people try to satisfy their personal needs in the social world. A number of my sociologist-friends say that Erikson's descriptions of people's motivation makes sense to them. Erikson suggested that people go to work — and work organizations — in order to carry out a series of developmental tasks.

I was thinking about entering an organization, joining it, or becoming a member of it in more than the superficial sense of getting a paycheck. I was puzzled about the psychological experience of feeling somehow different as part of a new social unit. Surely, many people are on the payroll and don't feel part of the workplace. How, then, did people become members? What happened to them, and who did it to or with them?

One afternoon, when I must have been thinking about these things, I went to see an exhibit of African masks at the Baltimore Museum of Art. The masks intrigued me. How did they work? What did they do to the wearer? Who was the wearer while wearing the mask? Was he someone else, was he still himself acting as if he were someone else, or was he, perhaps, a bit of both? And if he was in any way someone else, why did he ever take the mask off? I began to formulate my own theory as I walked through the exhibit. It seemed that someone wearing a mask must be in a transitional state of existence, simultaneously himself and someone else, able momentarily to take on another's powers or responsibilities while taking his own life journey. Did people always voluntarily put on masks, or were there instances when they were unwillingly changed in these ways?

All at once, it seemed to me that these masks were like social roles, such as organizational roles. People put on these roles in order to become part of collectivities, and yet they always keep a separate identity behind the roles. What is the power of roles? And how do they, like masks, work? In what sense do people experience roles as transitional states, somewhere ambiguously between an organization and themselves?

And then it seemed that these questions were related to those I had been asking about organizations for a long time. How do people become members of organizations? How do they experience themselves on the inside as opposed to the outside? What do people feel happens to them as they pass through an organization's boundary? And how do they manage to move through the boundary safely? In trying to make sense of roles and masks, I began to think about initiations, as well as rituals and play as ways of dealing with alien or injurious experiences. In the end, I haven't said anything about masks here, though the original encounter with them was crucial in formulating this book.

SOME BIASES

I want to make explicit my bias about work which became clear to me in the most interesting surprise of the research. I interviewed a state agency employee who, after talking emotionally about his job for nearly two hours, suddenly exclaimed that if he won the lottery, he would quit work the next day, because it didn't mean anything to him. He only worked as hard as he did because he was supposed to work hard, not because he cared about his job. Two days later, I talked to another staff person in the same organization who said almost the same thing. After talking with pride about how he had completed several analyses that had shaped departmental policy, he commented that if he won the lottery, he would quit his job the next day. He did his job creatively, because that made it interesting, but it didn't mean anything to him; everything in life, after all, is a game.

I was surprised at how angry these comments made me. How could these people say that work meant nothing to them? Arguably, their words were paradoxical and puzzling: Didn't their evident engagement in their work mean that their work did matter? Weren't they, perhaps, just ambivalent about their work? Probably, I would say now, they had conflicting feelings about work, but there they were, insisting work was meaningless.

My work matters to me, I thought, pleading with some unknown adversary. *Does* it? I quickly doubted. If so, why did I avoid so many meetings at the university, for example? Why did I feel like such a bad organizational citizen? On the other hand, I spent many enjoyable hours interviewing people, analyzing the interviews, and struggling to write them up sensibly. *That* was certainly work, and it brought me considerable pleasure. Then it seemed to me that I had fallen again across the conventional distinction between "work" and "job," where doing the former is often difficult because of conflicts with organizational conditions for carrying out the latter.

But, still, what stuck with me is my conviction that I creatively put myself into my work and that it reflects well on me when I am done. At least for an unforgettable moment, I found these people's comments threatening: perhaps work is not as important as I imagine. But, finally, my feelings about my work have, before I realized it, shaped this study. My work is good, and I want to believe others can have good work. Do they?

But more than that, can people find good work within organizations? I have done my work as much outside or, even, against the organization as in it. Are there people who find places where they can do good work in community with others? And, if so, how does it happen? These questions have led me to do this research and write this book.

THEMES IN THE BOOK

I interviewed people about their experiences in becoming, or trying to become, members of the organizations they worked in. I asked them to construct an account of their organizational careers, including the emotional events in their relationship with the organization. What did they want from the organization? What did they get? How did their satisfaction or frustration affect them? When, if ever, did they feel like members of the organization, somehow part of it? Did they ever identify with it?

People rarely talk deeply about their work, perhaps because it is so intimate an expression of their longings. However, my questions about the emotional meanings of work made sense to most. Some people did offer little more than the facts of a résumé or carefully delimited accounts of their past. A few told obviously one-sided accounts of grudges. But most seemed to talk openly, often enthusiastically, frequently with humor, sometimes with evident hurt. They talked not only of acceptance and triumph, but also of needs for friendship and romance, alcoholism and incarceration, family problems, and depression about work. Several said the interview helped make sense of their careers. One man, imagining college teaching could be more gratifying than public policy-making, asked for career advice. I think my tacit guarantee never to bother these people again encouraged them to trust me with some of the best stories they could tell.

Many of their accounts appear in their own words. The most important theme is that people try to use work organizations to grow. Consciously and unconsciously, they expect the workplace to provide social relationships enabling them to move ahead through a sequence of developmental steps. However, trying to get in, they encounter people in the organization who want them to give up some of their identity in return for membership. Veterans submit newcomers to an initiation ritual with this purpose. In response, the newcomers design their own self-initiation. Through these two rituals, veterans and newcomer negotiate the terms of membership. If social and psychological compromises are possible, a new employee becomes a member. If not, the worker, though on the payroll, remains an outsider in the organization.

This book shows the centrality of play in self-initiation. Psychologically, play is a process of symbolically repeating something painful in an effort to gain control over it and to neutralize the injury. New workers are hurt by veterans' demands that they give up an old identity in return for membership. They play with the role they are given—thinking about different ways of interpreting it and experimenting with some of them—in order to pacify it, control it, and make it their own in a way that will be acceptable to the veterans as well.

Workers measure an organization from their very first contacts with it, to see whether it will satisfy or frustrate them, and their initial judgments shape the rest of their reactions to the organization. In particular, until workers become members or give up on the prospect, they organize their activities to let them play with early disappointments This may go on for years. Hence, a great deal of organizational behavior consists of play with the purpose of becoming a member. For them, much organizational work is, in this special sense, play.

Some people who become members go on to identify with their organizations and feel close to coworkers. Only these workers can respond to organizational cultures that encourage cohesion. Whether workers succeed in becoming members or identifying with organizations has to do with what they expect initially, as well as how veterans react to them. People in some developmental stages have better chances than others. But this is all part of the story of this book.

AIMS OF THE STUDY

The Appendix will discuss the methodology, sample, and analysis in detail, but a few comments about the aim of the study are in order here. The people interviewed were selected randomly from lists of professional and managerial staff in several public agencies. Arguably, they represent their counterparts in these organizations, and the organizations are typical of public agencies at various governmental levels. People in Maryland do not obviously differ in basic ways from people elsewhere in the United States. Finally, the experiences of these people are similar to those reported in the literature on private sector workers.

I am interested in understanding the distribution of phenomena I have found, but I am interested, before that, in understanding what they are. I want to understand what people's expectations are, how they are related to one another, and how particular expectations may be received by organizational veterans. The data of the book are people's stories, and they offer "specimens" of organizational experience. The challenge is to try to ascertain when specimens are distinct, what their relationship is, and, at all times, what they are specimens of. Only after we have seen and analyzed many specimens can we begin the important work of generalizing about the distribution of organizational experiences.

I believe the people interviewed are representative enough of professional and managerial workers and their stories are familiar enough to warrant taking them seriously as common examples of what people want of the workplace and how they react to what they get. Where reasonable, I have generalized about proportions of people holding certain expectations or attaining organizational membership. However, getting caught up in sampling arguments would be an unfortunate digression from taking people's experiences seriously and trying to understand what they tell us about organizations and membership.

ACKNOWLEDGMENTS

I would like to acknowledge others who have helped to shape the framework of this study and to interpret people's stories. I have been immeasurably supported by members of the International Society for the Psychoanalytic Study of Organizations. Not only have they given specific comments on early presentations of material in the book, but they have sustained my belief in the value of psychoanalytic ways of understanding organizational life. Michael Diamond has consistently encouraged me, and he generously read an earlier draft of the book. He offered a number of helpful suggestions for thinking about membership and intimacy. Howard Schwartz has developed the important concept of organizational ideal. His writing, presentations, and personal conversations have helped me think about the risks in identifying with an organization and tensions between individual and organizational interests. Larry Hirschhorn has contributed a special understanding of workers' anxiety about aggression and of their needs for reparation. He was particularly helpful in developing some ideas about organizational culture. Harry Levinson, who has done pioneering work in the field, showed by example that a psychoanalytic orientation can help understand organizations. Along the way, he caringly offered support and suggestions. Michael Hofmann encouraged me to take Erik Erikson's thinking seriously. Abraham Zaleznik presented a paper introducing the useful concept of "specimen" for thinking about the status of case material.

Donald Schön gently pushed me to think more explicitly about how I have interpreted people's stories. He raised issues about the validity of interpretations, and some of the remarks in the Appendix respond to his questions. William Torbert, commenting on my earlier writing about bureaucracy, helpfully suggested that I consider how differences in personal development shape people's actions in organizations, and his questions encouraged me to think in the directions of this book. A number of people have commented on earlier drafts of the material. Among them are Seth Allcorn, Gilles Amado, Leonard Duhl, Thomas

Gilmore, Davydd Greenwood, Lawrence Jacobson, Donald Levine, Rose Mersky, Kathryn Moore, Evelyn Rodstein, Glenn Swogger, and Benjamin Zablocki.

John Forester has been a close friend and unambivalent supporter. We started out in city planning together, and each chose his own way of making sense of what he saw in planning agencies and other organizations. He has initiated himself into critical theory while I have gone to psychoanalysis. Speaking different but not incompatible languages, we have agreed and disagreed with increasing usefulness over the years. My wife, Madelyn, is a psychiatrist. From different origins years ago, we each became interested in psychoanalytic ways of understanding human activity. While she works with individuals, I study organizations. She has provided important encouragement to continue my explorations.

Part One
Experiencing Organizational Work

Organizational Experience:
What People Expect of Work Organizations

We often speculate on whether people would work if they could otherwise pay for life's necessities. We ask ourselves what we would do if tomorrow we became financially independent. Many of us ponder whether we should retire early.

Surely, money is a strong bond to work, and yet most of us want to work for other reasons as well. Work enables us to feel competent—to express ourselves in shaping materials or people. Moreover, when we work with others, and when the results of our efforts are visible, work incorporates us in a community: others appreciate us. Thus competence and community membership are closely linked by a work role.

Still further, the social character of work provides us with an opportunity to express various needs. For instance, being recognized is a fundamental human wish, and work offers a setting in which adults may get recognition. Similarly, work presents ways of exercising authority and of mentoring others.

Thus, work may have many meanings, even for those of us who insist that we do it only—or mainly—for the money. Although we may take the social character of work for granted, it is central to the personal meanings of work. Moreover, today most people work in particular types of social settings—formal, usually bureaucratic organizations. These organizations provide their own peculiar opportunities for expressing personal needs—and present typical obstacles to satisfaction.

With fewer and fewer exceptions, work is work in an organization, and questions about the meanings of work are inevitably questions about the meanings of organizational life. What happens to people when they join work organizations? How do they feel different? What kind of a deal do they make in return for membership? Above all, does organizational membership add meaning and stimulate growth, or does it confuse and disable people? This book is an inquiry into the experience of organizational membership. I have talked with people about what happened to them when they became part of their organizations and how organizational membership has affected them. One man commented that "talking about work is a turn-on." He meant that work is intimate and exciting, that in discussing it we reveal our private truths. He might have added that some of the power of these discussions comes from their infrequency. Most everyday questions about work are superficial; we rarely talk deeply about it.

These people wanted to talk about their work, and they have strong feelings about how their organizations have touched them. They carried hopes and ambitions into these organizations, and they have kept their own reckonings of whether the organizations have enhanced or diminished them. Their stories reveal that organizations provide much more than just an income.

The people who speak in this book are professional staff or administrators in public agencies. They hold relatively high-skill, high-status, and high-pay positions. Nevertheless, their needs are fundamental—for responsibility, recognition, authority, competence, and the like. They may differ from others in their organizations—for example, clerical and maintenance workers—not so much in their needs, as in what their class position leads them to expect from work and enables them to get there.

Their organizations range in size from 60 to 15,000 and are located at all levels of government. Some of these organizations carry out staff functions for elected executives, others deliver services, and some do both. The 50 people interviewed were randomly selected from agency lists of professional and administrative personnel. About three-fifths of the people interviewed are professional staff, with higher proportions in local and state than in federal agencies. Administrative personnel manage units ranging from four persons to several hundred; some do technical work as well. The average age is 43 years, with entry at 30, and with 13 years in the organization.

Thus these are people who have settled into their organizations. They have advanced in rank, and some have moved from technical to managerial work. They have been in their workplaces long enough to come to terms with them. They fit these organizations better than others who have come and gone. At the same time, they are approaching or are in the middle of life. This is a time when people begin to examine what they have done and measure its meaning. On the one hand, they are inclined to look carefully at how they started out in their organizations. At the same time, they may find that their expectations have changed, that what once satisfied them and enabled them to stay so long is challenged by other needs, which may move them on or out.

Interviews with these workers lasted two to three hours. Open-ended questions asked people to recount their organizational careers—

events, thoughts, and feelings from the first organizational contact to the present. They were asked what they expected of their organizations, what they found, and how they reacted to their satisfactions or disappointments. A general interest was exploring how each person felt affected by becoming part of a work organization. This book is based on the transcripts from these interviews.

Because of the number of organizations represented, it is impossible to say that the interviewees constitute representative samples of professionals and administrators in their agencies. Instead, they provide a sample of the experiences of workers in large and small organizations at three different levels of government. The similarities in their reports support the view that organizational membership presents common challenges regardless of organizational size or jurisdiction.

There is no reason to suspect that these public agency workers are inherently different from others in the private sector. They confront similarly demanding tasks in equally complex environments. Most are highly educated, with at least two college degrees. Their formal responsibilities—planning, research, public relations, and management— have clear counterparts in private business. The main difference between public and private workers, the former would say, is that they suffer from uncharitable public perceptions. For more than a decade now, people inside and outside the government have attacked public activity as unnecessary and inefficient and have ridiculed public servants as cushioned and lazy. In the end, public workers want much more than a paycheck and job security—many of the same things, in short, that their private sector counterparts wish for.

THE POSSIBILITIES OF WORK

Bellah, Madsen, Sullivan, Swidler, and Tipton (1986), describe three subjective experiences of work

In the sense of a "job," work is a way of making money and making a living. It supports a self defined by economic success, security, and all that money can buy. In the sense of a "career," work traces one's progress through life by achievement and advancement in an occupation. It yields a self defined by a broader sort of success, which takes in social standing and prestige, and by a sense of expanding power and competency that renders work itself a source of self-esteem. In the strongest sense of a "calling," work constitutes a practical ideal of activity and character that makes a person's work morally inseparable from his or her life. It subsumes the self into a community of disciplined practice and sound judgment whose activity has meaning and value in itself, not just in the output or profit that results from it. (1986:66)

These three conceptions imply progressively deeper personal investment in work activities. Work that is just a job is something one does mainly for the money. It is an external, instrumental activity. When work is a career, one identifies with the activity and regards achievements as reflections and measures of the self. The person who regards work as a calling experiences these activities as a collective responsibility and accomplishment. Success or failure is communal in the dual sense that cooperation is both essential to achievement and builds and strengthens ties among colleagues.

This book will say a great deal about organizational membership, and it is important to fit that concept in with these conceptions of work. As an example, a state highway administration may employ someone as an engineer. If he thinks of his work as merely a job, he may say that it provides him with a reasonable income for supporting his family, sailing a boat, taking vacations, and sending children to college. But being an engineer—or becoming a better-trained engineer—means little to him in comparison with the private rewards of his job. His work is not a career. Furthermore, he cares little about his organization, other than that it continue to pay him and that working conditions be pleasant enough. He may have close friendships at work, and he may have job security or even high status, but subjectively, emotionally, he does not regard himself as a member. His work is not a calling.

A second example illustrates these meanings further. Another engineer in the same agency has similar family interests but sees his work as a career. He thinks of himself as an engineer. He wants to become the best engineer he can be, learning state-of-the-art methods, and advancing into more and more prestigious positions. Still, he may be indifferent to the organization that employs him. He uses it for his personal advancement, and he cares only that it continue to pay and support him in his independent efforts. Subjectively, he does not feel that he is a member of the organization. His work is not a calling either.

A third engineer in the same agency regards his work as a calling. He shares the others' family interests and professional ambitions. In addition, he thinks of himself as part of a community of engineers, bound not only by personal relations, but also by a commitment to solving human problems. This community also includes other staff members at the state highway administration. He associates his work there with a collective effort to do good engineering and to improve citizens' opportunities to travel in their daily lives. In identifying his competence and professional role with the mission of his organization, he experiences himself as a member of the organization. Its challenges, risks, and accomplishments are his, and he grows as it grows. This association enhances his sense of work as a calling.

These three examples illustrate different subjective experiences of work and relations with a work organization. Self-perceptions and others' perceptions may be related, but they need not be. Thus, although only the third engineer thinks of himself as a member of the state highway administration, coworkers may see all three similarly as members of the organization. This book is concerned with the subjective experience of membership and its consequences for individuals and organizations.

The book also examines what it takes for people to think of themselves as members of a work organization. Under what conditions is a worker willing to join an organization? Answers to this question can be conceptualized in terms of a "psychological contract" (Levinson, Price, Munden, Mandl, and Solley 1962) between an individual and an organization. Conventional formal employment agreements cover responsibilities, compensation, accountability, and promotional opportunities. In addition, workers may be at least as concerned about what they can get with and from coworkers in interpersonal relations. For example, someone concerned about authority may want to be sure that others will defer to him on specific matters. Another, concerned about getting recognition, may want to get continual compliments and reassurance. These issues cannot be negotiated in any formal way. Rather, they emerge and may be resolved in interactions over time. Yet matters like these may be the most important ones for workers in their "psychological contract" with organizations. If they can get the organization to satisfy these demands, they will join and think of themselves as members. If not, they may take home a paycheck but give little thought to the organization.[1]

THINKING PSYCHOANALYTICALLY ABOUT WORK AND ORGANIZATIONS

Yankelovich and Immerwahr (1983) find that many contemporary workers, particularly those with college educations, expect their jobs to help them develop. Moreover, when asked what they want in a job, people speak of not only what will enable them to work competently, but also supportive social relations. When Porter, Steers, Mowday, and Boulian (1974) analyzed why some workers stayed in their jobs while others quit, they found that satisfaction with wages and other job conditions mattered less than commitment to the organization.

People want coworkers to recognize, respect, and support them for the same reasons they like feeling attached to an organization: these relationships satisfy developmental needs. The studies just cited touch the surface of a world explored in depth by psychoanalysis. This book presents a psychoanalytic perspective on individuals' entry into organizations and how they try to become organizational members. In analyzing how people experience organizations, it complements mainstream organizational studies in two ways.

First, sociological research identifies the social structures of the families, groups, associations, and formal organizations in which people live and work. People in these relationships make demands on, and have obligations toward, one another, and the networks of authority and responsibilities order people's activities. Studies of job turnover, for example, emphasize a social definition of an organization, with the boundary defined by attachment to a payroll office.

Psychoanalytic research, in turn, asks how individuals experience and make sense of social relations such as those in the workplace. For example, people react differently to others' demands and exercise authority with varying degrees of comfort. As a result, they may define the organization in different ways. Economically, they may identify it with everyone on the payroll. Emotionally, they may include only those persons whose requests they consider legitimate or only those they care about. The everyday expression that someone may be "in" an organization but not "of" it acknowledges this difference between social and psychological membership.

Second, cognitive research also explores the subjective meanings of organizations. Different individuals may act similarly to serve different motives and with different satisfaction. Studies of job satisfaction and organizational commitment, for example, ask workers what they want from work generally or why they acted in some particular way. This research assumes that people act only for conscious reasons and that they are aware of all these reasons. For example, if someone says that he wants coworkers who will give him authority, a cognitively oriented researcher would take this statement at face value, expressing a reasonable wish for authority in getting a job done.

However, depending on the individual, there could be other interpretations. Perhaps this person wants to dominate others because he enjoys controlling people. Or maybe, just the opposite, he wishes he had power over others because he usually feels unable to influence anyone. Both possibilities suggest motivations that are unrelated to work requirements *per se*. Furthermore, these interests could interfere with work by diverting attention, instead, to setting up situations where others could be controlled or avoiding others where they could not. On the other hand, this person might find ways of satisfying his interests in authority while also getting his work done. Supervising others could be such a compromise.

These questions can be answered only with respect to specific individuals, but they point to intentions that lie beneath and go beyond simple conscious interests. Such aims are normally unconscious: people are not aware of trying to serve them. Overt actions express some combination of conscious and unconscious purposes. Psychoanalysis adds to cognitive research by explicating the unconscious meanings of actions and by examining the interplay between these meanings and conscious thoughts.

Psychoanalysis sheds light on organizational behavior from two vantage points. One looks at the distinctive social relationships created in formal organizations and considers the typical psychological responses they encourage. Research with these interests has grown in recent years. Some studies have examined how people react to hierarchical structures and subordinacy (e.g., Levinson, Price, Munden, Mandl, and Solley 1962; Hodgson, Levinson, and Zaleznik 1965; Zaleznik 1965; Schwartz 1985, 1987a, 1987b; and Baum 1987). Others have looked at how working relations in groups affect workers (e.g., Jaques 1951 and 1955; Rice 1958 and 1963; Miller and Rice 1969; Menzies 1975; and Hirschhorn 1988). Still other studies have analyzed the influence of managers' personalities on organizations (e.g., Zaleznik 1967; Levinson 1968; and Kets de Vries and Miller 1984).[2]

A second viewpoint looks at how individuals try to use organizations to satisfy their needs and wishes. This perspective complements the first in that any organizational behavior represents a commingling of individual and organizational purposes. Whereas the first orientation looks primarily at the influence of organizations on individuals, the second emphasizes the converse. The first body of research may be thought of as offering psychoanalytic interpretations of phenomena reported in a broad organizational literature. This second set of studies look at how the range of human needs and aims reported in the psychoanalytic literature may be expressed in work and in organizational settings. For example, Diamond (1984 and 1985) examines the ways people create organizational structures and routines to reduce their anxiety.

This book is in the latter tradition. It explores how individuals' conscious and unconscious plans for personal development lead them to use work organizations—for example, as places where coworkers may lend support or as entities to feel committed to. In examining organizational membership, five basic psychoanalytic assumptions will be important.

First, human beings want to elaborate and preserve a coherent identity. This means they want to act in ways that are simultaneously congruent with their self-perceptions and with others' expectations of them. In addition, they want to act in ways consistent with their past actions. One consequence of this interest is that earlier experiences, such as those of infancy and childhood, shape later, adulthood perceptions and intentions. Adults may even repeat specific earlier actions, because they were successful or at least because they are familiar.

Second, the effort to keep a coherent identity is developmental. While maintaining a distinct personal orientation toward the world, people expect to confront and master a series of increasingly complex challenges. Each task draws on earlier accomplishments, and success lays the groundwork for later ones. In approaching each test, the child or adult has some ideas about what success requires and actively tries to get others to act in ways that would allow it.

Third, people react to others in terms of this dual wish to develop while maintaining their integrity. They consider each new situation as one that may help them grow and calculate what they would have to do to master their current developmental concerns. At the same time, whenever a situation threatens their identity, they attempt to work with the experience to repair any damage. Specifically, when people are hurt, they try to repeat the injurious experience in a symbolic way that is safe and that does not harm them. By actively repeating something unpleasant experienced passively, people can treat themselves for the earlier damage and continue to grow. Some injuries may be easily compensated; others, including some from childhood, may take years or a lifetime to overcome.

Fourth, developmental striving and efforts at treatment are both partly conscious and partly unconscious. People are aware of some of their aims and injuries but not others. The balance of awareness changes over a lifetime. Whereas the infant initially is not conscious of anything, the developing human becomes increasingly conscious of his* purposes and calculations. Nevertheless, some intentions remain or become unconscious because thinking of them arouses anxiety. For example, someone may consider acting aggressively toward another and fear reprisal; he can protect himself from worrying about retribution by keeping the idea unconscious. Conscious thoughts and overt actions represent compromises between conscious ideas and intentions and unconscious wishes and considerations.

---

*For stylistic simplicity, masculine pronouns have been used in theoretical discussions of development and intrapsychic processes. This convention is not to imply that gender differences do not matter, and variations are described in the text. Although both boys and girls, men and women go through the same developmental stages, their aims and choices, as the discussion shows, can differ significantly. The men and women in the case examples illustrate some of these differences.

Fifth, these principles obtain everywhere. People think and act the same, for example, inside organizations and outside. There are no distinct psychological principles for organizations, any more than organizations have unique sociological principles. Rather, organizations create typical situations that present particular developmental opportunities or that pose particular threats. Adults, seeking to maintain their identity and to grow, try to use the workplace as other situations. This means that the child who is present in the adult elsewhere, also enters the work organization. It also means that unconscious motivations affect people's actions at work as in other places. In short, organizational behavior is continuous with the rest of human behavior.

WHAT PEOPLE WANT FROM WORK ORGANIZATIONS

The following vignettes illustrate the variety of people's expectations of work organizations. Each person is reasonably successful at formal assignments, and yet each hesitates to identify with the organization. Even those who have continued to rise or who remain in high positions do not consider themselves full members. Despite organizational rewards, work does not give them what they want. These examples suggest the range of conscious and unconscious demands people bring to work, in terms of which they evaluate organizations before committing themselves to join.

Ambivalence About Joining an Organization

Organizational membership is formally sealed with a paycheck. Socially, membership requires that a worker be included in others' activities. Psychologically, a worker feels like a member when he identifies with some part of the organization. The worker may collaborate with, and feel close to, coworkers and associate their relationship with the organization. In addition, the worker may identify with management actions or with an organizational mission. In these cases, the worker thinks of coworkers', managers', or the organization's welfare as his own.

Psychological membership requires the wish and security to become intimately attached to an organization. It entails a willingness to compromise independence and accept collective norms. Some may find the rewards of affiliation, such as inclusion and even warmth, sufficiently satisfying to warrant exchanging autonomy for membership. Others may hesitate about making such a deal, perhaps drifting from job to job, perhaps hovering on the periphery of an organization, or perhaps painstakingly negotiating entry into an organizational role. Charles Latham[3] offers an example of the third response.

Ten years ago he graduated from a professional program in city planning and took a job with a county planning department. He had interned there while in school and concluded that it would be a good place to begin his career. He wanted to become a planner in order to promote urban development and to help reduce poverty. Furthermore, the job offered the chance "to deal with people directly." What he wanted from work was "more on the noble ideals side of the ledger than making money."

He liked his first supervisor, and yet, in describing his initial position, he emphasizes his separateness. He was hired to do social planning in a traditional physical planning agency, and his small section was located in a nearly inaccessible corner of the building. He felt others were "officious and aloof," that they considered themselves "a club you had to graduate into." He and other staff members spoke different professional languages and rarely consulted on substantive matters. He felt they regarded the social planning section as "a bastard child." They considered him "an outsider, a frill," and were "unaware of what we were doing." At the same time, he "felt deficient in physical planning areas" and "didn't know what a whole lot of maps were for."

Although he says he wanted to settle into the planning department, he spent more and more time with staff members of other, human service, agencies. While continuing to complain about his exclusion from the organizational mainstream, he increasingly cherished his independence. He spoke of his identity as a social planner, in contrast with the physical planners of his department. He distinguished traditional planning's support for business interests from social planning's concern for minorities and the disadvantaged. He prized his outside contacts and valued their rewards more highly than departmental relations. Other agencies implemented some of his proposals, but that recognition did not improve his standing in his own department. As time went on, he lost interest in the projects of the planning agency, and other staff members questioned his commitment to the organization. This situation continued for a half dozen years.

At last, he "decided to transfer into a recognized section." When a position opened up in community planning, he applied for it, successfully. The job required him to work with citizen groups, helping them prepare proposals for problems they identified and getting their responses to development plans. He had to represent residents' positions to the department and present the agency's position to neighborhood groups. This role transformed his relations with the rest of the staff.

At once, he was central to the department. Not only was the community planner involved in physical planning, but he was the gatekeeper for other staff members when they contacted neighborhood businesses or citizen groups about plans or proposals. Others began to talk to him, both to inform him about their actions and to ask his opinions about community reactions. "All of a sudden," he says, "I was immediately connected to every section. I felt a little ridiculous, because here they were asking me all the questions, and I was new on the job." To his pleasant surprise, he found "there was no mystique" in the physical planning methods or maps he could not understand before, and he "learned all this quickly."

He sums up the crucial social and psychological meaning of this change. "It happened very dramatically and all at once. From the day I became a community planner, I was a member of the club—that simple." He became "an integral part of the department," "the eyes and ears of the department in the community." After six years of standoff, community planning provided an organizationally legitimate role for Latham to be both an outsider and an insider. He could throw himself into departmental work because it did not require surrendering his autonomy.

He continued in community planning for three years, until an episode where his work with a community put him into conflict with the county council. Several council members pressured his director to replace him. The director kept him but moved him to another position. Although his next role was not as central to the department, and even though he left community planning under fire, his tenure there irreversibly led him and others to consider him a member. At last he identified with the organization. After all this, he says, "I feel very much part of the In Crowd. I feel my opinion is respected."

Latham shows how people can equate joining an organization with giving up their independence. Even if they succeed at their work, they may resist identifying with others in the organization. Latham joins the organization emotionally only when he finds a formal role that simultaneously offers autonomy as well as membership.

Being a Special Assistant

As Latham shows, people may consider relations with coworkers more important than the substance of work in making a commitment to an organization. People may also look for a special relationship with the boss, whom they equate with the organization. They enter work seeking recognition from the top, and if they get it, they are loyal to the boss and identify with the organization. Barry Landsdowne provides an example.

For the past year he has been a senior advisor to the secretary of a state social service agency. He has worked for the department for approximately twelve years. He first came when someone with whom he worked elsewhere was appointed department secretary and invited him along as special assistant.

He helped his boss get to know the organization, which, despite its high professional reputation, both found disappointingly parochial. Shortly after they arrived, Congress enacted a major new program that they had to implement. Thus Landsdowne had the dual excitement of being at the top and creating something big from scratch. He observes that he enjoys solving problems. His position enabled him to shape his role and work relationships to fit his emotional needs. He wanted to be authoritative without being authoritarian, to see his views accepted because they were reasonable, not because he wielded the boss's power.

As point man for the secretary's policies, Landsdowne tried to negotiate collaborative relationships with career middle management staff. Although, he notes, "in one sense they had to accept me," he did not want to push his views on others. He "worked very hard to establish relations nonthreateningly." In part, political wisdom dictated this position.

> Coming in with the secretary, it was clear to all concerned that I was a confidant of his, and, therefore, I was treated warily and with some deference. I had to play a role which was—or at least the way I chose to play it—not very authoritarian. I made suggestions.

Acknowledging his personal motivations, he adds, "My personality—I don't feel comfortable in an authoritarian mode." His emotional needs supported a management style of eliciting discussion and seeking consensus. He believes that he "was able to carry that off [by the end of] probably a year."

Landsdowne and his boss consolidated the new federal program over the next seven years, and then the boss left to head another agency. Landsdowne stayed on. He had "fun times" with the acting secretary who succeeded his boss, but the new permanent secretary "looked at me with a jaundiced eye, and I looked at him. . . . I had had enough." At the time, his old boss was looking for a deputy for planning in the new agency, and Landsdowne jumped at the opportunity. However, the agency turned out to be "a screwy world" with "a very political atmosphere" requiring a lot of "diplomacy." Within a year, the boss decided the job was untenable and left to become vice president of a major private corporation. Landsdowne stayed on but could not make much headway in the politicized setting.

After a while, a friend directing policy analysis at the old state agency called him and invited him to return as his deputy. Landsdowne went back, but soon afterward a new governor appointed a secretary who disliked the policy staff. Landsdowne essentially ran the policy office for three years but had no influence on decisions. Upset at his isolation, he left to try a position in policy analysis with the state police. He had little interest in the field itself, but found the opportunities for solving problems "fun."

Ten months later, the governor appointed a new secretary to the social service department, someone Landsdowne had known for years, and she urged him to return. "She brought me back," he notes, "not as her primary special assistant, but as a special assistant to her"—not as *primus*, but as one of *pares*. However, his new work was not very exciting. After a year, a change in administrations brought in still another secretary. Landsdowne was doing little, and he was mainly involved in personnel matters. Unlike formerly, when he could effectively tell others what to do, now he had to negotiate painstakingly with people who did not give him much authority. He finally urged the secretary to appoint him to an appropriate position, involving more analytic work. She made him a senior advisor to herself, an associate secretary, and a deputy secretary, but the position carried little prestige or authority. He "was the old hand who knew the organization," and he now serves others in positions lower than where he started out. Not only does he rarely see the boss, but he spends his energy maintaining old programs, rather than creating new ones.

Landsdowne's career has followed a downward trajectory. He says of himself,

You sat at the top of the agency for seven years and really had a major hand in running things—in contrast with what I am doing now. And I say, "Gee, you have really come down in the world." . . . I have been there.

Now fifty, he thinks about changing careers, but he lacks the confidence to move. "The idea of teaching appeals to me," he says, but "I am not sure I have anything to teach."

One might argue that Landsdowne suffered the normal afflictions of those who start out at the top and must compete with challengers from new political regimes and administrations. However, he did not really start out at the top; he was special assistant to the man at the top. A special assistant is always dependent on someone wanting a loyal deputy; moreover, the intimacy between executive and advisor is a special personal relationship, not easily cultivated anew with a succession of bosses.

Landsdowne's organizational career can be seen more clearly as a product of his early emotional choices. He wanted to wield the authority of an expert without seeming autocratic. Closeness to the boss gave him power he could exercise without seeming to do so. He could consult with middle management and conclude that their cooperation was intellectual commitment, and not simply acquiescence. He succeeded in finding a good fit between these needs and an organizational role for seven years. He identified more and more with the organization that he had originally criticized as being too parochial. However, once his first boss left, he never managed to create another privileged relationship, and he has become disenchanted and disappointed with the organization.

Landsdowne shows how expectations of a work organization may center on relations with the boss. He had extensive responsibility, even considerable authority, but no amount of programmatic success compensated for his failure to find continuing intimacy with the men and women at the top.

Passing Something On

People not only want certain relationships at work, but they also want to be able to take something from the job to build relationships on elsewhere. They want to see their efforts reflected in the surrounding world, and many want to pass the fruits of their labors on to their children. David Ryan complains that his work lets him do none of these things. He says the bureaucracy that regulates workers' activities prevents them from having much control over the products of their efforts. He is one of a number of public employees who see private entrepreneurship as a more rewarding antithesis of government. Although he is still rising through senior management in a federal welfare agency, he talks of going into business on his own.

Ryan portrays himself as a self-made man. Right out of high school he began working in a technical section of a large private corporation. He became interested in computers and concluded that they were a growth field. Even then, he notes, "I wanted to work in an organization where ultimately I would have a chance to run it." He worked in the corporation for four more years, getting a good technical education, but he decided to leave when he realized that all the positions ahead of him were filled by people his own age. He had never wanted to work in the public sector, but he found an opening in a federal agency with a good reputation, where he has worked for the past twenty years.

To his pleasant surprise, not only was morale good, but management was "enlightened," and people had a "can-do attitude." Fortuitously, the agency was automating its information system, and he knew more about software than most others in the organization. This was his break.

> I guess the guy who was *the power* in information systems—a very results-oriented guy—one of the three or four persons in my life that I respected most. . . . I had been following a series of articles about certain software items that would be useful. I thought about them as if I ran the place. The word came down that Harry was

interested in this, and did anyone know about them? I said I did; so they arranged a presentation to the top people. A nerve-wracking experience. I just went in and gave the pros and cons. Harry asked me what my recommendations were, and he agreed with that. I got a call from him directly, six pegs up the chain from me. I went to my boss and asked who he was. My boss said I had better talk to him: he was the boss of us all. From that day on, he took a personal interest in me, which was interesting. He laid another project on me ... asked if I would give the guy a hand, and I took over and got it going. He had an interesting idea about how to operate. A minor mentor. A lesson in motivation: the personal touch and an interest in activities of people who do things is time well spent. Which is what I have always done. So that gave me a good feeling of belonging.

This Horatio Alger-like episode convinced him that the organization rewarded competence.

He completed a college degree at night and rose from hands-on computer work to manage increasingly larger units. More and more, he ran up against bureaucratic procedures that unnecessarily complicated requisitions and reports.

If I were running my own business, I would not have tolerated it. But in the bureaucratic environment that is the way it is. The process I became comfortable with after a year or two. Adjusting to the way it is—I don't know if I ever adjusted to it.

Still, he enjoyed recognition and promotion. However, as he moved into higher management, he encountered "the political people." They held jobs only because they served the current administration, they had little programmatic knowledge or respect for professional staff, and they used their positions to block technically sound initiatives.

In the middle of his life, Ryan was no longer so willing to wait on others as when he was younger.

In retrospect I feel I unnecessarily narrowed my focus to this place. What is the best you can do at this place? You can make only 65 to 70 grand, and that is all she wrote. You can get six more promotions, and yet ... I might have been better off getting into other activities at an earlier age. Not only money, giving my kids some options I didn't have. That is more important than being a successful bureaucrat. I want to have things to pass on to them. What am I going to do? Bring them into government? But that isn't all there is to go after.

His current position has influence, and he has plenty of work, "but you feel like you would be better off running an organization or something. That would be at this stage in my life what I am looking to do."

His ideal job, he says, would be President of the United States, so he could put his ideas into practice, but his entrepreneurial interests are not fantasies.

When his brothers retired, he told them:

"Let's buy a business and run the goddamned thing." So I bought a service station, and we have two or three good mechanics, people pumping gas. It is clear it could be profitable. [I could retire in 2½ years.] I want to be in a position where I can make decisions.

Ryan's career in the department has two stages. As a junior staff member, he was pleased to be recognized and rewarded for his competence. But in midlife he confronted the mediated character of bureaucracy. He felt that, no matter how hard—and intelligently—he worked, there were limits to what the organization would let him accomplish.[4] Moreover, at a time when he thought of creating a heritage for his children, the agency gave him nothing he could pass on. Hence, despite his success in the organization's terms, he did not feel successful. He planned to go into business for himself.

Ryan shows how people's work expectations can include the wish to own work products and part of an organization. These aims may become especially salient at certain life stages, and they can be stronger than interests in money, upward mobility, or organizational membership.

Something to Believe In

Another way to describe Ryan's expectations is that he wants work to make sense by offering rewards commensurate with his efforts. He thinks instrumentally of the results of work, in terms of the outside social relations they support: he wants to develop a heritage to pass on to his children. Other people expect work to make sense intrinsically and more abstractly. They want to find rational, fair relations at work, as evidence that the world itself is reasonable and just. Mary Beecham, for example, demands that her organization give her something to believe in.

Beecham is a policy analyst in a state community development agency, where she has worked for fifteen years. Now in her forties, she still measures much of what she does in terms of her childhood heart disease, which set the tone for her adolescence and later life. For years she was severely incapacitated, and her survival itself was in question. Her condition was eventually stabilized surgically. Still, despite career successes, even now she finds humor in the fact that she just bought a house with a fifteen-year mortgage, because she never expected to live so long.

After her surgery, she left years in a sickbed to go to college, where she studied mathematics. She had planned to teach on the university level, but she grew impatient with the years of study required, and she began to look for a job while she was still in graduate school. She says, "I was not interested in going back to school, but I was interested in getting away from home with my parents." However, in a tight economy she found few choices. Eventually, someone she knew suggested she apply for a position in the community development agency. "Very desperate" for "anything," she interviewed for a clerical position. The man she talked with recognized her potential and created a new position in order to hire her. However, as soon as she arrived, he left for several months without giving her any assignments.

The precariousness of her earlier life distinguishes her from others, but made her keenly sensitive to a general, existential concern: work should endow life with meaning. She says the hardest part of the early days in her first position was trying to look busy when there was nothing to do. In recounting that period, she says,

> There were just some bureaucratic ways I was not used to. The first letter I was asked to draft was in response to a legislator. When I wrote it, I wrote, "Thank you for your interest" at the beginning and the end. My boss took out one of them, and his boss took out the other. My father [a federal employee] said you do this for Congress, but apparently that was not the attitude in the state. And the body of the letter said we can't tell you now—but when the survey is done.

Beecham calls the incident typically "bureaucratic." Originally simply a sociological description, the term subsequently became a moral judgment.

She describes her organizational career as one in which she formed illusions and then became disillusioned. At first, she came to accept bureaucratic ways; later, she found them senseless and painful. "I suppose that when I came, mere survival was all that I looked for. I never had any notion that I would attain any role of relative prominence in the organization." And yet her first supervisor recognized her ability. He taught her bureaucratic procedures and eventually promoted her to an administrative position supervising grants. "And later on," she continues on the topic of relatively prominent roles, "I assumed I would take on such a role and would be disappointed if I stopped taking such a role."

Higher departmental administrators began to recognize what she could do, and after eight years she was appointed director of institutional research. She made contact with outside funding agencies, universities— and politicians. People put pressure on her to undertake certain research and to make particular findings. Unlike her previous work, a great deal was subject to negotiation. She felt her existence was precarious.

> I went up to a level where I was fairly prominent and vulnerable in the organization. People perceived that I had power—though it is clear that you have the power you take in this organization! I learned very clearly that it was not worth it. I would not accept a position if I had a chance again. I would prefer to remain anonymous, or semianonymous. . . . But that position got into a lot of controversy at that time. . . . You may have power, but you are very vulnerable. Unless you are very, very smart, and get out at the right time, you have a risky existence. I am not much for a risky existence.

Finally, not only battered, but also bothered by the compromises she made, she resigned to take her present position, shielded from political pressures.

She acknowledges that others are temperamentally better suited to organizational politics, and yet her complaint about "politics" goes far deeper than comfort in personal relationships. If her own best-considered judgments are routinely overruled because she lacks power, how can she consider herself competent? And, more troubling than that, what sense can there be in the bureaucratic world?

Her disillusionment proceeds first to a rejection of the organization as meaningless.

> I don't necessarily find the bureaucracy a terribly challenging place to exist. I think it is mostly the feeling that little of what I do makes a difference in the real world. I try to convince myself that if you don't have bureaucracies and monitoring systems, things would be different. But if you are only part of bureaucracy and monitoring systems, you don't feel you make a difference.

In addition, because she depends on the organization to give her something to believe in, disenchantment with it touches her self-esteem. "They also give you a feeling that if you died tomorrow, nothing would change in the world." Consistently, she says she would tell others

considering joining the organization, "Take
ously!" She wanted to use the work organizatic
herself seriously, and when she could not take it ..
taking herself seriously. Although management cont..
her work, she regards the organization as alien. It has
means to other ends.

> I suppose at this point I value it mostly economically and thro...
> personal relations. There are some very satisfying personal rela
> tions through the workplace—more so than in my previous jobs
> in the [agency].

Beecham's life is extreme in that she confronted the power of death
early and then insisted that an organization show her meaning equal in
greatness. Perhaps no organization could meet that demand. And yet her
example vividly illustrates a more ordinary expectation that a work organization provide an orderly world in which one can act effectively and
with dignity. Neither pay nor position compensates for meaninglessness.

WHAT THESE CASES TELL ABOUT WORK EXPECTATIONS

These examples show that people expect work organizations to
provide things that have little to do with formal or conventional terms of
employment. These professionals are well paid and highly regarded, and
they have various amounts of influence. But money, status, and power
are not enough. They want work organizations to allow them to be
competent, to affiliate with colleagues in specific ways, to see results of
their efforts, and, above all, to maintain their self-esteem.

Beecham speaks for all when she says that an organization must be
believable before she considers joining. She wants rules and relations
that make her daily activities meaningful. Ryan emphasizes that this
means that actions must be consequential. He will not commit himself
to an organization unless it gives him free rein to create as much as he
can. Landsdowne shows one of the ways in which people think of
organizational membership in terms of relationships with coworkers. In
order to identify with an organization, he needs a specific personal
connection with the boss. Latham stresses that work relations must be
safe. Like others, he will accept organizational membership only when
he is certain that it does not cost him his autonomy.

These stories offer four lessons for understanding the experience of
organizational membership. First, entry into work organizations is a
complex negotiation, in which individuals bring a number of demands
and measure organizational offerings before deciding whether to become

Organizational Membership

ers. People may become employees, even be regarded as integral members, without ever considering themselves part of an organization, and they may cease regarding themselves as part even while continuing on the formal rolls. They are less concerned about whether they fit into an organization than whether the organization fits into their lives. When workers are not satisfied with what an organization can give them, they may give little of themselves in return.

Second, workers' demands come from expectations that the workplace provide opportunities and relationships to help them develop personally. Work is only one of a number of domains in which they live, and they want it to serve their overall growth. They want to be competent not for the sake of organizational productivity, but to feel they are creatively efficacious. It is not enough for them if organizational affairs make sense to top management; they must find their own meaning in what they do.

Third, some of workers' most urgent demands are often only tacit. They are not the formal or conventional terms of employment. Not only are they often difficult to express (e.g., a wish that activities feel meaningful), but they may also seem excessively selfish or altruistic (e.g., a wish to serve the boss), or they may sound disloyal (e.g., a wish to stay outside an organization while working for it). Often, workers are not conscious of their most pressing expectations. They may be aware of a wish to feel part of an organization, but they may not recognize all they are asking in return (e.g., autonomy or the boss' special favor). Even if they do, they may not understand why these things are so important to them. In either case, they still may not know what actions or signs from coworkers would satisfy these needs. Although they may sense that they have a "good deal" or a "bad deal" with an organization, they may not be aware of all the negotiations that led to such feelings.

Finally, these negotiations may go on for years before workers decide whether they are satisfied, and negotiations may start anew as workers' expectations change. Crucially, this means that a lot of organizational behavior represents tacit efforts to determine whether organizational membership is worthwhile, and whether acceptable psychological contracts are worthwhile. Furthermore, workers' conclusions—that they will become members or that they cannot—shape much of their subsequent actions in the organization. In short, organizational behavior is intimately linked to organizational entry.

THE BOOK

This book examines the unconscious connections between organizational entry and organizational behavior by exploring the organizational experience psychoanalytically. This means taking seriously what people say about what they wanted when they first entered their organization, and how they reacted when they did or didn't attain their aims. It means looking for underlying themes that tie specific organizational expectations to earlier and broader life experiences, conflicts, and efforts to deal with them. It means searching for common conscious and unconscious aims that help explain why some of us more easily join work organizations than do others.

Chapter 2 introduces the psychoanalytic perspective and uses Erik Erikson's developmental framework to conceptualize work expectations. That chapter reexamines the cases just presented to show the underlying developmental logic in each set of work demands.

Part 2 analyzes organizational entry as an initiation process. Chapter 3 looks at organizational demands of the new worker. It draws on sociological and anthropological material to show how veteran organizational members attempt to change a new worker's identity through a deliberately structured initiation ritual.

Chapter 4 examines the new worker's response. It makes use of psychoanalytic studies to show how workers unconsciously negotiate with organizations. Newcomers develop self-initiation rituals intended both to defend themselves from veterans' demands, and to establish relationships that permit them to advance developmentally. The self-initiation rituals follow childhood patterns of play.

Part 3 analyzes the initiation process using material from interviews. Chapter 5 looks at work expectations most likely to lead to successful initiation—and growth: work ability, work identity, and organizational affiliation. Case examples illustrate successful initiations, successful self-initiations, and unsuccessful self-initiations for each of these stages.

Chapter 6 looks at "postwork" expectations: mentoring and making sense of life experiences. These expectations come at a time of life when work loses its centrality, and when personal growth may or may not contribute to organizational membership. Case examples illustrate successful and unsuccessful self-initiations for these developmental stages.

Part 4 examines disappointment with organizations, where neither initiation nor self-initiation leads to membership or growth. Chapter 7 focuses on "prework" expectations: recognition, autonomy, and power. These are difficult demands for organizations to satisfy when newcomers hold them foremost. Case examples show failed initiations and self-initiations for each of these developmental stages.

Chapter 8 analyzes the preceding three chapters for lessons regarding the consequences of disappointment in entry negotiations. Workers may successfully respond by initiating themselves through play. However when they cannot do so, they engage in compensatory or escapist play and withdraw from the organization.

Part 4 draws conclusions from the study. Chapter 9 looks at the connection between two findings: workers' dislike for organizational politics and their hesitation to affiliate deeply with coworkers or with the organization. Unconsciously, conventional politics make intimacy difficult.

Chapter 10 examines implications of the study for organizational theory and organizational reform. It considers an alternative style of organizational politics that would promote workers' development. It concludes with guidelines for organizational management.

The Developmental Meanings of Work

What is striking about the examples in the first chapter is how strongly these individuals want what they want, even when their wishes make it harder to join or stay in a work organization. Satisfying these expectations matters more than being paid well or being promoted. What accounts for the centrality of these wishes in workers' encounters with organizations? Where do these wishes come from? If we sense that there is something "basic" about them, we have a clue: these needs are tied to our nature as human beings.

Psychoanalysis helps understand these connections because it is concerned with how people express their inner needs in social relationships.[1] Erik Erikson's writings are particularly useful because he is one of the few analysts to write specifically about work.[2]

ERIKSON'S DEVELOPMENTAL FRAMEWORK

Erikson (1963 and 1968) has studied how people react to, and make use of, the social world in order to develop. Like other psychoanalysts, he believes that human beings normally progress through specific stages in the course of development. Each stage involves a challenge that must be mastered in order to advance to the next. Gradually maturing biological needs and potentials lead the growing individual to attend to a sequence of bodily zones and functions. Erikson emphasizes that the infant, child, or adult thinks of each set of challenges in terms of social relationships that it permits and requires. Success at any stage entails establishing an at least tacit agreement with significant others regarding reciprocal biological and social aims, intentions, and obligations.

Also like other psychoanalysts, Erikson believes that perceptions of the social world and actions in it reflect a combination of conscious intentions and unconscious wishes, that everyday activities represent compromises between these two sets of aims. However, while the infant is born as an unreflective biological organism, it immediately begins a lifelong project of increasingly consciously thinking about and conceptualizing the world. The ego is that largely conscious mental aspect that is concerned with mediating external relations, and Erikson emphasizes that the human biography can be seen as the unfolding and increasing mastery of the ego.

One of Erikson's basic arguments is that individuals actively manipulate the world in order to establish social relations that will satisfy specific developmental challenges and make it possible to grow further. In contrast with traditional psychoanalytic views that individuals primarily avoid stressful situations, Erikson emphasizes that individuals act with positive goals in mind. Both unconsciously and, increasingly, consciously, they plan actions that will enable them to develop.[3]

Erikson's most important contribution is to show that the goal guiding human plans is the establishment and maintenance of a personal identity. He describes "the sense of ego identity" as

> the accrued confidence that the inner sameness and continuity prepared in the past are matched by the sameness and continuity of one's meaning for others, as evidenced in the tangible promise of a "career." (1963:261-262)

Although he finds that securing a personal identity is the special challenge of adolescence, he observes that from birth, humans aim at developing meaningful, cohesive relations with others.[4]

Erikson's thinking about work illustrates his point of view. He finds it is a normal part of growth for contemporary Western children between about six and eleven to try to develop a sense of "industry" (1963). Young people discover skills and tools valued by the larger culture and attempt to master them so that they may shape the world themselves. Centrally, they must learn that work is a social activity. "Industry involves doing things besides and with others, a first sense of division of labor and differential opportunity" (1963:260). In this process, the nascent worker "learns to win recognition by producing things" (1968:124). The challenge is actively to confront the world and to gain the feeling that one can form it to one's own ends. This is "the *sense of industry*. Without this, even the best entertained child soon acts exploited" (1968:123) A young person who remains a passive observer and fails to develop this confidence ends up feeling his or her tools and skills are inferior to the world. Erikson characterizes the young person's experience of this developmental stage as a challenge of "industry versus inferiority."

Success—development of a sense of industry—makes it possible to move on to the next developmental challenge, "identity versus identity confusion." A stable sense of personal identity, Erikson observes, depends on confidence in one's work ability. Someone feeling inferior about his work effectiveness cannot develop a strong adult identity. Consistently, a young person can face the test of industry versus inferiority only after having mastered the previous developmental challenge of "initiative versus guilt." Acquiring a sense of industry depends on being able to act appropriately aggressively in relation to other people and inanimate objects in order to make things and get work done. It may mean bending or breaking physical materials, and it may mean telling other people what to do. Success depends on the ability to act aggressively, to take initiative, without feeling guilty about the consequences. Hence, the prior sense of initiative is a prerequisite for the sense of industry, which, in turn, sets the groundwork for a sense of identity.

These brief examples illustrate the nature of developmental stages. The interaction of biology and social history requires that human beings grow by mastering tasks in a specific sequence. Success at one stage is necessary for advancement to the next. In addition, mastery of any challenge depends on continued competence at all preceding tasks.

When someone cannot master a particular developmental test, he normally remains competent at preceding tasks but has difficulty advancing. This person may have partial success at later tasks, but most of his effort remains concentrated on the unmet challenge. If someone works on a developmental task without success for a long time, the dilemma presented at this stage may become a central life concern. Erikson would say that this person's identity is focused on these issues. For example, someone who never succeeds in taking initiative without feeling guilty not only will have difficulty developing a sense of industry, but he may come to see most new experiences as challenges to exercise his initiative, even when this perception is unrealistic.

Although Erikson calls this the individual's "sense of identity," a traditional psychoanalytic term, "character" (which he rejects [1968:324]), conveys a similar meaning. Fenichel writes, "The term character stresses the habitual form of a given reaction, its relative constancy. Widely differing stimuli produce similar reactions. . . ." (1945:467). Psychoanalysts speak, for example, of the "oral character" of someone who unconsciously approaches the world as if it were all something to eat. Analogously, one might use Erikson's terms to describe the phenomena he writes about, although the resultant language is not his. For example, we could speak of an "initiative versus guilt sense of identity," or an "industry versus inferiority sense of identity." The language is awkward, but the meaning is important. Someone who fails to master the tasks of any stage experiences many subsequent events in terms of the related developmental dilemma.

Sometimes a person who has passed a particular developmental stage encounters a situation that presents a challenge corresponding to that stage and that he cannot readily master. When this happens, the individual "regresses" to a concern with the dilemma of that stage, almost as if he were confronting it for the first time.[5]

While this person again struggles with the developmental test, he loses some of his prior success at subsequent stages. In addition, he may focus on situations that allow him to express the accomplishments of the preceding stage, momentarily his last arena of success. For example, someone who has developed a secure sense of personal identity may encounter a situation that calls his sense of industry, or competence, into question. As a consequence, he may feel less confident of his identity, and he may repeat earlier efforts to establish a sense of industry. In addition, he may look for situations where he can demonstrate his success in taking initiative without guilt.

This brief example illustrates Erikson's framework, and begins to show how concerns with work ability reflect basic human developmental concerns. The following section describes all eight of Erikson's developmental stages and shows how each may find expression in adults' expectations of work organizations.[6]

DEVELOPMENTAL STAGES AND WORK EXPECTATIONS

1. Basic Trust versus Basic Mistrust

An infant's first challenge, crucial for both physical and emotional survival, is to find the world trustworthy. This means learning that the mother can go out of sight without going out of existence. It entails developing an inner image of her that substitutes for her when she is physically absent. In addition, the infant must learn that he can trust his own body and impulses, that he can satisfy his urges without repelling or harming the mother. By experimenting with different actions toward the mother (with the mother's tacit cooperation), the infant may develop confidence in the basic trustworthiness of the external world, as well as his own sensations, images, and motives. If the infant fails at this, he sees the world with basic mistrust and is unlikely to develop further.

These infantile preoccupations have a counterpart in adult thinking about work organizations. This does not mean those work expectations are childish or immature. Nor does it necessarily mean that they are foolish or unrealistic. Rather, it means that, first, adults consciously or, more often, unconsciously, find many contemporary situations reminiscent of earlier situations. In particular, adults draw analogies from past experiences in order to interpret new conditions. Some of these prior experiences come from infancy and childhood.

Second, adults deliberately or, frequently, unconsciously, attempt to use current situations and relationships in ways like they used the related situations in the past. They continue to seek a variety of satisfactions they have enjoyed earlier in life, either because the rewards have been inherently pleasurable, or because they have provided relief from stressful situations. These activities may include efforts to repeat past developmental achievements.

Third, although the adult meanings of contemporary situations are related to prior experiences, they are not the same. Socially, cognitively, and emotionally, the adult world is far more complex than the infantile or childhood world. A situation that holds out dangers or satisfactions related to earlier life is still different from prior situations, just as the consequences of actions are different. Simply put, if current situations had no specifically adult meanings, adults would not participate in them.

The following example illustrates these relationships for the trust-mistrust dilemma. An infant whose mother unaccountably leaves is preoccupied with controlling her comings and goings, understanding them, and developing an internal image of her that keeps her symbolically within reach. He wants a reciprocal relationship, in which he can both see the mother and be assured of her recognition in return. Analogously, adult workers in large organizations are often concerned about what their bosses do when they don't see them. In particular, they may worry about what their supervisors think about them, how they evaluate work assignments, or even whether they care how they are doing.[7] In this situation, adult workers want *recognition*—at least of their work, but also of their existence and good intentions.

However, although adult workers and infants may both expect recognition, they are different entities and confront different significant others. Moreover, the consequences of recognition are different. A nursing mother nourishes and sustains an infant, whereas a supervisor commends, promotes, and financially rewards a worker. Nevertheless, unconsciously, adults may associate aspects of the work situation with elements of the infantile or childhood condition.[8]

For example, positively, a worker who seeks recognition from a supervisor may take great pleasure from being seen. Some of this gratification relates to realistic contemporary gains. Some of it unconsciously repeats the infant's joy in receiving the mother's glance. This association may encourage a worker to do things that are likely to be recognized and rewarded. Negatively, a worker who associates a boss' reciprocation with the mother's attention, may unconsciously seek the boss' acknowledgment with an intensity that accurately repeats the infant's urgency, but is inappropriate to the work situation. Not content with normal signs of

recognition, the worker may continually create situations that demand—
and dare—the boss to appear and acknowledge the subordinate.

Workers vary both in the value they give to recognition as an expectation of the work organization and in the specific contemporary and
past meanings recognition has for them. For example, some other work
expectations are also analogous and may unconsciously be related to
infants' wishes in the trust-mistrust stage. *Reciprocity* is a more complex
variation of recognition, whereby a worker may expect a supervisor's
continuing recognition in return for acknowledging him. A wish for
responsibility is a wish for recognition, in that having responsibility makes
one visible to others with respect to a specific task or domain. When
professionals say they want *credibility* for what they do, they are talking
about recognition of certain inherent abilities, prior to any actions they
take. Wanting *supervision* may include a wish for continuing recognition
and support from someone who is stronger or more powerful. Concerns
about *pay* have realistic bases but may also express a wish to get as much
nurturance as one feels necessary for survival.

All these expectations ask whether the worker can trust the organizational world, through its representatives, unfailingly and unequivocally to
acknowledge his place and value. Satisfaction with an organization's offerings permits a worker to look for things related to the next or later developmental stages. Otherwise, a worker remains focused on these concerns.

2. Autonomy versus Shame and Doubt

The gradual development of infants' musculature presents them
with a new dilemma: If they assert themselves, holding on and letting go
on their own terms, will the world they basically trust support them or
resist and drop them? A child around the age of two considers this
question in the light of a particular image of the parents. Unconsciously,
the child associates the parents with the "ego ideal," an image of everything perfect the child would like to be.[9] They seem omnipotent and
omni-competent, and the child imagines they can flawlessly do everything they ask of him. Moreover, the child assumes that they unceasingly
sit in judgment of his performance.

Hence a child's question about the consequences of acting autonomously involves anxiety about behaving improperly and seeing parents
withdraw their love as a result. For the child, the loss of parents'
love amounts to annihilation, because it can conceive of no other
support for life. Thus any misstep leads to the extremely painful experience of shame: the child feels exposed as having acted out of place
and is abandoned. Shame, in turn, makes the child doubt it can ever
act independently and acceptably.[10] Success in developing a sense of
autonomy depends on the child's collaborating with parents in learning

ways of acting that satisfy both his impulses toward independence and the external demands of a trustworthy world.

Adult workers commonly insist on having *autonomy*, or *independence*, to do their job. They want to be able to *control* the people and materials needed to get it done. Although these demands rest on considerably more knowledge than the urges of a two-year-old child, they express similar sentiments. If one has ability, one wants to use it; self-respect comes from a sense of efficacy. In contrast, many people find merely doing what others ask shameful. When their bosses evaluate them, they assume the bosses could do the job perfectly and will judge shortcomings harshly. In fact, the longer subordinates continue just taking orders, the more they doubt they could act on their own, and this doubt, too, adds to their shame. If doubt and shame continue to reinforce one another, people may cease expressing their opinions, uncertain whether they even know anything.[11]

Adults' expectations of exercising control at work, just as wishes for recognition and responsibility, may express two sets of meanings. Realistically, workers may know how to do their jobs and want to do them. They may regard constraints as ridiculous and insulting, as well as shameful. Unconsciously, their encounters with supervisors may evoke memories of earlier parental confrontations, in which they were intent more on asserting their independence than on accomplishing any coherent project. Such connections may increase workers' motivation by giving them special pleasure in controlling things, and in doing assignments on their own. However, there is a danger that workers making these associations translate assignments into tests of their autonomy and even create situations where they struggle over control with supervisors. Both realistic and unconscious expectations ask whether the organization offers opportunities to use personal knowledge to make independent judgments.

3. Initiative versus Guilt

The child's ability to walk confidently not only reflects his physical maturation, but also symbolizes his emotional autonomy, and it presents the possibility of taking initiative to accomplish specific tasks. The world becomes a domain the child can consider attacking for his own purposes. Confronting society, however, the child encounters other interested parties and must establish terms for peaceful coexistence. In particular, the child's sexual development brings him into rivalry with the parent of the same sex for the affection of the other parent. The Oedipal complex brings the child into decisive conflict with his parents over acceptable expressions of both sexuality and aggression.[12] The outcome determines whether a young person can freely initiate plans or whether he holds back for fear of retribution.

During this period, earlier images of parents as omnicompetent are supplemented by new images of parents as both powerful and moral. If a boy, for example, contemplates a project to overthrow his father and gain his mother, the father's power foreordains the outcome: outside the child's imagination, defeat is certain. But even success at such an Oedipal project would be bittersweet. If the boy fantasizes defeating his father, he experiences losing someone whom, indeed, he loves. Moreover, unconscious hopes for success are certainly balanced by anticipations that his father will strike back, successfully. How, under these circumstances, can a child ever learn to exercise initiative safely and effectively?

As in earlier stages, parents' collaboration is necessary for development. Tacitly, unconsciously, parents and child make a deal. If he will relinquish specifically sexual initiatives toward them, they will permit him other initiatives. Moreover, they will not physically watch over him, constantly telling him what to do and avoid, if he will make their regulations his own moral rules. He must substitute new mental representations of them for their physical presence. Fear of physical retribution for transgressions will be superseded by a new emotion, guilt, wherein the child feels as if parents "inside" him morally condemn any violations. Thus the child develops a "superego," or conscience.[13] In return for renouncing sexual and aggressive challenges to his parents' power, he gains membership in their moral community.

When adult workers say they want to be able to take *initiative* in an organization, they repeat not only the language, but also some of the wishes, of the child. They enter a setting where others are hierarchically in place, and they want to be able to plan and implement projects with, but if necessary against, those others. Most commonly, workers speak of wanting *authority*, which usually means the ability to tell others what to do. When people say they must have authority equal to their responsibility, they want an instrumental solution to a common bureaucratic problem,[14] but they are also tacitly pleading for moral order in the work world. Sometimes workers use the word *power* to describe the same expectation, being able—with impunity—to get others to help execute projects. Some related wishes refer not to contemporary relationships with coworkers, but to the future: people say they want opportunities for *advancement*. Unless an organization is expanding or turnover is significant, advancement means displacing higher-ups. In general, workers' expectations that an organization give them opportunities to satisfy their ambition encompasses all these wishes: to take unimpeded initiatives on behalf of reasonable projects and personal interests.[15]

Adults may enjoy successful initiatives for two reasons. First, they succeed at projects that mean something to them. In addition, insofar as they unconsciously associate contemporary actions with the earlier testing of parents' authority, success may also bring the pleasure that might have come from defeating a parent. This unconscious reward may add an incentive to act authoritatively at work. However, if people have not really settled the earlier dilemma, they may either create initiatives simply for testing their power against imagined parental proxies, or they may hold back from acting for fear of imagined reprisal or guilt. All these expectations of opportunities for initiative express the general concern that power in organizations be morally regulated.

4. Industry versus Inferiority

At last the stage is set for the challenges of industry, described earlier. A sense of industry depends on basic trust in the world, an ability to act autonomously, and confidence that one can take initiatives with impunity. Moreover, one consequence of the resolution of the family conflict over initiative is that the child can turn outward, to the larger world, to continue developing. School is the place and time where young people attempt to master culturally valued work methods in the company of others. They will now learn to win recognition by producing things. Success in developing a sense of industry means that young persons have the confidence that they have physical skills or mental methods that enable them to shape the world according to their designs.

Most adults enter work organizations with expectations related to a sense of industry. They know implicitly that the social requirements of work rest on this psychological accomplishment. After all, work, stripped of everything else, is the exercise of technique, the execution of method. Even if people have done similar work elsewhere, each job is somehow different. Each job is at least a momentary test of one's abilities: Does one really have what it takes? People go into organizations with the central expectation that they can work *competently*.

Workers express this wish in a variety of ways. They may ask for the opportunity to *learn* specific *skills* or the tools of a particular trade. Professionals say that they expect the chance to *solve problems*. Especially when people begin working, they want to show themselves, at least as much as any boss, that they can do a job, because working lies at the core of adult identity. However they put it, people want an organization that permits them to learn and successfully exercise socially recognized *work abilities*. For those who enter an organization with a secure sense of industry, success at work is doubly rewarding: not only is a job well done, but they can feel reassured of their adult competence. These possibilities may motivate others who lack this sense of industry to try harder. However, feelings of inferiority can also cripple them from grappling directly enough with work problems to master them. Instead, they may end up continually blaming their failures on "the equipment" or other people.

5. Identity versus Identity Confusion

Rapid new bodily growth makes adolescence a period of seemingly unending movement: not only physical, but also social, political, and ideological. Nearly constant change stimulates young persons to seek an identity; some coherent set of habits, motives, and interests that they can regard as who they are and will remain even as the world fluctuates. Moreover, they want the assurance that their image of themselves is shared and endorsed by others.

The discovery of an identity is not a deduction from past biographical facts so much as an experiment. "Of the many new ways of thinking and acting available to me, which can I securely choose with others' support?" Adolescents consider different social affiliations, to see who may accept them in ways they can regard as their own. In addition, they examine ideologies that may define their place in the larger society and give it an overarching meaning. Thus a search for personal identity involves questions about fidelity: Which groups and which worldviews is it safe to have faith in? If adolescents fail to find answers matching the complexity of their past, they will confront adulthood confused about their identity and unable to make realistic choices.

Eventually, most adolescents decide how they will approach the basic adulthood tasks of loving and working.[16] They make choices about sexual identity, and they begin to think about occupations. A challenge in establishing an identity is to connect the techniques associated with the prior sense of industry to realistic vocational decisions. Whatever income and status future work brings, it will also identify who one is.

These concerns clearly form part of adults' expectations of work organizations. Not only do people want to do work (expressing their sense of industry), but they want to be workers (expressing their identity). Being a worker entails a social role: people "put themselves into" their work, colleagues provide appropriate assistance or appreciation, and family or other members of society treat the activity as important. This is what people have in mind when they say they want to *practice* their *profession*. Furthermore, when they say they want a workplace that enables them to advance and grow in their profession, they assume that their *work identity* continues to develop with new experience and skills.

Finding a work identity in an organization means taking a work role and making it one's own. A cohesive personal identity provides both the motivation and the resources for this project. Workers whose identity is confused may be able to satisfy job requirements but will have difficulty developing and sustaining solid relations with coworkers.

6. Intimacy versus Isolation

With a secure identity, a young adult is prepared to consider intimate relations with others. The rewards of closeness are attachment and caring. However, someone whose identity is weak may fear being overwhelmed by others. People must reveal their wants and weaknesses, in the hope of being nurtured but with the risk of being rebuffed or rejected. Moreover, along with the satisfactions of being cared for come obligations of caring for others.[17] Joining another requires both the strength to take these chances and the will to abide by commitments to others, even when they demand sacrifice. Failure of nerve leads to isolation.

The most important new intimacies are sexual relationships, but close friendships hold out many of the same benefits, along with associated risks. Community and work organizations, involving many people, also provide opportunities for closeness. One may feel close to the organization as a whole or to some of its members. In either case, affiliating with the organization similarly requires a secure identity and a willingness to modulate it in embracing collective aims. As more and more work requires personal contact—between collaborators or with clients—some closeness with others on the job is often unavoidable.

Many degrees of *organizational affiliation* at work are possible. One common expression of a wish for intimacy at work is the desire for *supporttive colleagues*, people to work closely with or people to share ideas with. Sometimes people want personal relations with coworkers without thinking of these friendships as part of the organjzation. They expect to feel close to peers without feeling close to the organization. People may speak more broadly of attachment at work with the hope that the organization will provide a *community* or be like a family. They look for both close individual relations and an organizational setting that feels intimate and supportive. They want people to look after one another, to care about personal problems even when they have nothing to do with work. They know they can do a job, and they want more than its formal rewards. They work at least eight hours a day at something they take seriously, and they want to be among others who care as they do. They will share their wishes and ambitions, and strengths and weaknesses with others, and they are ready to think of others' accomplishments and problems as in part their own. Beyond this, workers may talk of *identifying with management or an organizational mission*. They want to think of their efforts as serving the organization and equate organizational interests and welfare with their own. In this case, organizational affiliation involves feelings of intimacy beyond or instead of close social relationships.

Anything more than superficial involvement in an organization requires a secure identity and a willingness to compromise with a collectivity. Those who are comfortable with closeness are more likely to succeed at work affiliation. Each collaborative act will give them pleasure beyond any satisfaction at seeing a job well done. Those not prepared for intimacy may remain so isolated that they cannot be effective at jobs requiring social interaction, or they may exploit work relationships for practice at intimacy more appropriate elsewhere.

7. Generativity versus Stagnation

Maturity stimulates two further changes. As bodily growth slows, adults recognize that future development must involve changes outside themselves. At the same time, the emotional maturity that permits intimacy with a partner now makes it possible not simply to procreate, but to rear children. Adults may see themselves as parents and expand their intimate relations to include children. Hints of mortality encourage people to redefine themselves from "the younger generation" into an older generation and to look for continuity in their posterity. Not only do they extend the circle of their love, but they seek to teach their offspring what they know and can do. Selfishly, they want their children to resemble them, but they do so with the confidence that their own lives have acquired value worth passing on.

Adulthood is a time of general *creativity*. This can be a period of peak activity at work, where people "generate" products and programs to match their children at home. They may decide to "give it their best shot" at work, to change an organization in ways that will affect their successors, to make or compose something that others will keep and appreciate. Along the way, after they have done their best and liked it, they may find junior workers to mentor. They can raise these "children" to succeed them at work.[18] Adults who cannot extend the sphere of their intimacy to include people or things that will succeed them, become isolated in time. They get a feeling of stagnation, a sense that their impact declines with their bodily condition.

Older workers in particular join organizations with these expectations; others acquire them as they mature in their organizations. People may speak of a desire to *supervise* after having worked alongside others. Being an administrator has many meanings. For some it is a way to be a boss and to tell others what to do for a change; for some it is an avenue for promotion and salary increase. Still others choose administration because they want the opportunity to use their experience to guide colleagues in doing better work. Those who do not acquire formal authority may speak of a wish to *mentor* others, to offer younger workers career advice and to initiate them into the organization.

Any of these possibilities enriches work's meanings and satisfactions and strengthens ties to an organization. However, someone whose "work is his whole life" may place excessive demands on an organization. For example, an administrator may try to manage without appreciating what followers expect from leaders or may expect employees to provide the love and continuity that only children can give. In either case, subordinates may act only out of fear and destroy anything an administrator wants to pass on.

8. Integrity versus Despair

In the end, people want to make sense of it all. Passing their most generative period, contemplating death, they look for reassurance that their lives had meaning. They look beyond present circumstances to the past, searching for continuities with those who went before and seeking signs that those who follow might similarly draw comfort from connection with them. If they are successful, they will find fellowship with the ordering ways of other times and will come to some terms with their own mortality. Otherwise, they approach death with despair.

Few people face work organizations with demands that they provide an ultimate meaning. One reason is that organizational retirement policies often separate people from work at the time when life's meaning becomes a growing concern. Indeed, an unwilling removal from work may itself be a cause of despair. A second reason is that other institutions, such as religion and philosophy, make more direct offers of wisdom and integrity than the workplace.

A few individuals find positions as *advisors* or participants in future planning that enable them to settle personal and organizational accounts at the same time. Others who stay at work and expect the organization to help *make sense of life* may become less and less tolerant of bureaucratic procedures and increasingly alienated from their activities.

DEVELOPMENTAL ISSUES IN WORK ORGANIZATIONS

Adult work activities and psychological developmental challenges are reciprocally related. On the one hand, success at work depends on completion of certain developmental tasks. At a minimum, work requires a sense of industry. Fitting into an organization calls for a secure personal identity. Working closely with colleagues depends on comfort with intimacy. Thus someone who has not satisfied the requirements of these stages has limited chances of work success.

At the same time, work is part of a person's life, and work activities provide material with which people can confront and resolve developmental challenges. Apprenticeship is an example of a deliberate organizational practice to help establish a sense of industry on the job. Interactions with supervisors and peers help solidify personal identity, as well as learn to work closely with colleagues.

The discussion of Erikson's framework suggests that some developmental stages—and their corresponding organizational expectations—are more important to, or more compatible with, organizational membership than others. An expectation that a work organization provide the chance to develop or use work ability, tied to a sense of industry (4),[19] is necessary for entry. An interest in work identity, related to a sense of personal identity (5), improves a fit. A wish for organizational affiliation, linked to a sense of intimacy (6), creates still more possible connections. These three expectations may be called *work* expectations.

In contrast, when workers are concerned about any of the three stages and expectations preceding industry, they are unlikely to develop the interest in work ability normally necessary for membership. This may occur either when an individual's sense of identity is focused on one of these stages or when organizational conditions make the individual insecure about achievements in one of them. Thus concerns about initiative and power (3), autonomy (2), or basic trust and recognition (1) may conflict with entering a work organization and may be called *prework* expectations.

The final two developmental stages and their work expectations go beyond what is essential for membership, often are unrelated to it, and may even lead away from it. Accordingly, interests in generativity and mentoring (7) or integrity and making sense (8) may be considered *postwork* expectations.

Thus Erikson's framework considerably extends our understanding of the attachments between workers and organizations. People are attracted to work, as to other activities, for reinforcement of past developmental successes and for assistance with current challenges. These developmental expectations add to the pleasures of work—and ties to the organization that provides it. When work disappoints current developmental hopes or overthrows a past accomplishment, people may withdraw from it, try to re-do earlier developmental tasks through it, or take revenge on it—and the organization. In short, whatever people consciously do at work, such as carrying out specific operations and earning a paycheck, unconsciously they continually measure the organization for its supply of developmental supports. They may find special satisfactions in work without being quite aware of the causes; they may also grow disaffected without knowing the full reasons.

The themes of the developmental stages and work expectations associated with them are summarized in figure 1.

THE EXAMPLES REINTERPRETED DEVELOPMENTALLY

This framework may be illustrated by reexamining the four vignettes in the first chapter. In each case, the perspective brings to light an unconscious developmental logic in the worker's actions and attitude toward organizational membership. The new interpretation shows each person actively using the organization to support developmental interests. In this view, behavior that may have seemed senseless earlier looks meaningful for the workers involved.

Figure 1. Work Expectations Associated with Developmental Stages

Developmental Stage	Work Expectations
Prework Expectations	
1. Basic trust vs. basic mistrust	Recognition, responsibility, reciprocity, credibility, supervision, and pay
2. Autonomy vs. shame and doubt	Autonomy, independence, and control
3. Initiative vs. guilt	Power, initiative, authority, and advancement
Work Expectations	
4. Industry vs. inferiority	Competence, work ability, learning skills, solving problems
5. Identity vs. identity confusion	Work identity and practicing a profession
6. Intimacy vs. isolation	Organizational affiliation; identification with organization, management, and/or organizational mission; supportive colleagues; and community
Postwork Expectations	
7. Generativity vs. stagnation	Mentoring, supervising, and creating
8. Integrity vs. despair	Making sense and advising

Charles Latham: First Establishing a Professional Identity

Latham wanted to become a planner but felt treated like "a bastard child" as a social planner in a physical planning agency. Veteran staff members presented themselves as "a club you had to graduate into." As years passed, club members did not legitimate the bastard child, but the child did not clearly try to graduate into the club. To the contrary, he spent more and more time with people in other agencies, doing work that was not only foreign, but also invisible, to the planners who could legitimate him. And yet this route outward eventually led him to the center of the organization. "Dramatically" and "immediately" he became "a member of the club."

One can see in the earlier account of Latham's career an ambivalence about becoming a member of a collectivity. He wants to join the planning department but does not want to accept the organization's priorities or traditional professional norms and methods. He concentrates on deviant activities which, at best, can give him a peripheral role in the agency. Even when he moves to the center of the organization, he takes a role that allows him to retain divided loyalties. And yet eventually others come to accept him, and he feels like a member of the organization. His deviance is more than simply rebellion or withdrawal. Erikson's framework helps understand why Latham found entering the organization so difficult and how his move outward may involve a partly conscious, partly unconscious plan to become an organizational member after satisfying developmental prerequisites.

Latham had studied planning in graduate school. He had taken courses in planning methods and, as anyone taking a first job, was concerned about testing the usefulness of what he had learned. He wanted to know whether he could plan competently. In Erikson's terms, he wanted to build up a sense of industry in social planning, and avoid feeling inferior to other practitioners (4). Once he could consolidate his planning skills, he wanted, as he says, to establish a professional identity as a planner (5). This would mean he could think confidently of himself as a planning practitioner, no longer a student, and others would consider him someone to be included in planning projects. Thus the planning department was an appropriate place to work on these related developmental tasks. As many others in the agency before him, he could learn work skills, articulate a work identity, and become socially and emotionally part of the organization. After all, as he realized from his internship, members of the department thought of themselves as a close and caring family, and they were open to new members.

Although Latham's ambivalence about joining the organization may have several roots, some of his conflict may have arisen at this point. Developmentally, someone must have a secure work identity (5) before feeling that closeness to coworkers and affiliation with an organization (6) are possible. Otherwise, one simply feels overwhelmed, without a secure foundation for relations with others. Thus when Latham said he wanted to become a member of the planning agency and become a competent social planner, he was describing several accomplishments that had to follow a specific developmental sequence. In particular, he could not become a psychological member of the planning department if he were unsure who he was professionally. Although in many cases a new professional may proceed through these three developmental stages relatively easily, Latham faced a realistic conflict in his department. He liked the emotional closeness of the staff enough to want to be part of it (6), and yet this predominantly physical planning agency offered limited opportunities for establishing himself as a social planner (5).

If he were ever to feel close to coworkers and identify with the organization, somehow he needed to establish a professional identity first. Turning outside makes sense in this context. Consciously, he described this move as necessary for becoming a social planner. Unconsciously, he seems to have recognized that he had to succeed as a professional on his own terms before he could join the department he wanted to belong to. Thus, moving into a network of social agencies may be seen as part of an unconscious plan to develop in a normal sequence. His apparent ambivalence about membership in the planning department at least partly expresses this developmental need.

Once he had received the validation of other professionals and elected officials, he was able to join an organization, such as the planning department. The fact that he eventually became part of the agency through a community planner role reveals more of his developmental plan. This role makes sense as his compromise with the organization: he took a position as a mainstream physical planner in return for others' acceptance. Developmentally, once he convinced himself that he had a professional identity (even if as a social planner elsewhere), he was psychologically free to take a wide range of planning positions. In addition, the community planner role makes sense as the department's compromise with Latham: in exchange for his moving into the professional mainstream, coworkers would let him have a role that allowed him time and loyalty outside the agency. It is as if unconsciously both he and they recognized that he had established a professional identity but had to practice at the next developmental task, collegiality and affiliation. Perhaps he and they felt he had special concerns about emotional attachment and autonomy. The role enabled him to deal with ambivalence about making a commitment to organizational peers.

This interpretation suggests that Latham's mixed reactions to organizational membership involved in part a conflict between more or less conscious wishes to become an active participant in a work organization, and more or less unconscious needs to establish the developmental prerequisites first.[20] One reason why ambivalence about membership stands out in his story is that we generally consider joining an organization a simple matter. Any problems apparently involve willful resistance. Latham shows some of the psychological complexity of the seemingly simple social task of entering an organization. Although his hesitation might be interpreted as unconscious willfulness, his intentions were directed planfully toward growth, rather than against membership *per se*.

Because of his developmental focus on professional identity when he entered the organization, affiliation would inevitably become an issue for him. Still, he was interested in becoming involved in the organization, and the staff "club" did encourage closeness among workers. Hence, once he satisfied the developmental requirements, feeling like a member, though by no means certain, was likely. Significantly, even after he left community planning, neither he nor his colleagues doubted he belonged.

Barry Landsdowne: Hesitating to Be Himself

Barry Landsdowne is no longer a special assistant to the boss. Not only has he lost his position of importance, but he has also lost his sense of himself. He feels embarrassed still being around the agency, but he isn't certain what else to do. He could retire early, and he has thought of going into teaching, but he is disturbed to find himself unsure about whether he knows anything worth teaching. Erikson's framework suggests Landsdowne's wish to be a special assistant and his current bewilderment are related and shows how an individual's character may limit his organizational opportunities.

Even though he is in his fifties, Landsdowne feels confused about who he is, what he considers important, and what kind of work he should do (5).[21] More disturbing yet, he does not discern any special competence (4) on the basis of which he could forge a new work identity. Indeed, earlier he was not much more specific about his expertise. He says he enjoys "problem solving," but he has generally thought of his abilities in terms of personal relationships: rather than being able to *do* particular things, he has been able to *assist* others in doing various things. When he worked closely with his friend the secretary, he seemed competent; only when he lost this relationship did he question what he could do.

This uncertainty could be related to other issues with which he has had difficulties. In order to have a sense of industry (4), one must unhesitatingly take initiatives and exercise authority (3). Landsdowne notes that he has never been "comfortable in an authoritarian mode." Although it is unclear how carefully he chose these words, being authoritarian is different from being authoritative. One can be an expert, as Landsdowne says he likes, without being a despot. Still, he says, others treated him warily, and he responded in kind, by holding back his opinions and simply making suggestions. This might be politic for an outsider establishing new relations with career staff members, but his repeated references to his discomfort with authority and reassurances that he wasn't tyrannical strike oddly for the special assistant to the director of a large agency. Such a conflict about exercising authority—wishing to be an expert but not wanting to offend anyone—is consistent with Landsdowne's lack of ambition to become a boss himself.

This ambivalence, in turn, seems related to a prior uncertainty. Taking initiative (3) depends on having confidence in one's autonomy (2). Landsdowne's current doubts about his abilities may reflect earlier doubts about his ability to act independently. Although his past must be a matter for speculation, the record of his career is that he chose not to become a boss and remained an assistant, carrying out another's wishes.

Someone who doubts his ability to act autonomously, perhaps who feels ashamed by how little he can do on his own, may unconsciously take one of two courses. He may continue to practice autonomy, trying to arrange situations where he can gain confidence in his ability to control things (2). Alternatively, he may fall back on prior security, getting recognition from trustworthy persons in power (1). Landsdowne appears to have chosen the latter course, playing the faithful advisor to an appreciative boss. The satisfactions of being a special assistant are clearly related to the accomplishments of this first developmental stage.[22]

Doubts about one's autonomy may influence one's life in two directions. First, they inhibit moving ahead, not only to taking initiative, but also to subsequent work in developing a sense of industry and a stable identity. Landsdowne did exercise some authority (3), had some acknowledged expertise (4), and developed a particular organizational role (5). But in each of these areas doubts or fears held him back. At the same time, self-doubt may focus one's life on earlier accomplishments in getting recognition and reciprocity from others. Landsdowne repeatedly sought, and usually found, credibility as a special assistant.

This interpretation suggests that Landsdowne's preference for the role of special assistant and his uncertainty about his identity are related, as reactions to doubt about his autonomy. Although the continual turnover at the top of his agency and his own aging make questions about his identity especially prominent now, they are probably lifelong questions, never substantially settled. When circumstances permitted him to succeed as a special assistant, his role provided some answers. Moreover—it is important to add—he performed a vital service for his boss and the agency. However, because his primary developmental concerns involved prework expectations, when conditions, inevitably, changed, he was likely to encounter uncertainty about not only his attachment to the organization (6), but also his role and identity (5) and his competence (4). Thus his developmental position suits him well for one type of role, but limits his ability to choose others.

David Ryan: Seeking Initiative to Pass on a Heritage

Ryan believed his agency's apparent promise that it would reward his competence, and yet, as he moved higher, he found more constraints on what he could do. Although he continues to succeed in bureaucratic terms, he is failing in his own: he cannot use his abilities to create something to pass on to others. Now he prepares to quit for a private business where he can make more of himself. Erikson's framework helps understand Ryan's feeling that the agency has betrayed him.

Ryan started out in the organization as an ambitious young man who would learn what it took to get ahead. He got his break when a senior manager recognized his computer expertise and became "a minor mentor." During the next few years he himself rose into the managerial ranks. Developmentally, his growing computer competence (4) helped him establish a work identity (5). Recognition and promotions gave him "a good feeling of belonging" (6). Then he confronted two changes.

First, he moved from technical positions into administration. By his reports, he made the transition smoothly, secure enough in his identity to switch organizational roles. But he found the new roles required different competence. Specifically, managerial effectiveness demanded more initiative and aggressiveness toward others. He says that, though he has no problems asserting himself, agency mores and organized polit-ical interests limit what he can accomplish on his own.

This role change introduces a familiar theme. Advancement to man-agement throws technicians into situations where their accustomed skills are useless and, after being effective, they become incompetent. This perverse "reward" for success smacks of perfidy. Ryan's career supports his contention that he had the requisite managerial skills, that he could go head to head with others when necessary. However, unlike the techni-cal arena, where he could analyze and analyze until he found a solution, in the political arena there were limits to how much he could accom-plish, no matter how much he organized and strategized. In this situa-tion, Ryan, who was first a technician, expresses a common complaint that technically designed policies often violate sound judgment. In addi-tion, as a politician, he complains that he cannot win all the time.

Ryan undergoes a personal change as well. After becoming a mem-ber of the organization, he develops new interests in the next "stage in my life": he wants to own and run something and collect and distribute the rewards in his own way. Thus, even if he had stayed in technical work, he might have become discontented and felt less a part of the organization. He would need a formal or informal role change to satisfy new work expectations.

Ryan's sense of betrayal and disenchantment has two developmental bases. First, the organization, after supporting his development for years, seemed to say finally that there were limits to how much development it would permit. After making him competent (4), finding him a work identity (5), giving him a sense of belonging (6), and thus enabling him to think about developing a heritage (7), it denied him a ready legacy. It built him up and then let him down.

In addition, the politics he encountered when he became a manager challenged even earlier developmental accomplishments, causing him to regress from his more advanced interests, and calling into question his recent achievements. Ryan's resentment of "the political people" reveals an unconscious basis to many complaints about politics. He says that the agency is the one domain in his life where he has difficulty taking initiative (3). Although the reasons involve external obstacles more than internal threats of guilt, still, organizational conditions challenge his prior success at exercising power.[23] As a result, he has less confidence that he can carry out other activities dependent on this earlier development. Although he continues to advance, he has difficulty feeling that the skills the organization rewards represent real competence (4). Consequently, he loses faith in the work identity he has built up (5), and he has trouble identifying with a department that has given him positions with limited discretion (6). Finally, while he thinks of passing on his accomplishments, he concludes that he has nothing in the organization that he could transmit to others (7).

Ryan illustrates the psychological costs of promotion from success in technical work to frustration in management. Politics imposes real constraints on personal ambitions, but it also unconsciously pulls workers back from previous developmental accomplishments.[24] A common immediate consequence is loss of confidence in one's competence. All that follows from that—confusion about one's work identity, disaffection with an organization, and a sense of stagnation—represent the unconscious meanings of becoming deskilled.

Mary Beecham: Trying to Create an Identity at Work

Mary Beecham laments that bureaucracies "give you a feeling that if you died tomorrow, nothing would change in the world." Her only conclusion is, "Take not thyself too damn seriously!" She feels that bureaucratic work is not meaningful, and that the most one can expect from an organization is a salary, benefits such as health insurance, and possible friendships. Her early confrontation with death has led her to demand meaning somewhere in life. Erikson's framework suggests that for her this normally ultimate concern is closely tied to not only what she suffered, but also what she missed as a result, earlier in life. She demands that the organization help her develop, even if her aims are not directly related to work.

When heart disease set in, Beecham was at the age when children normally experiment with the world to forge a sense of industry (4). Instead, she was bedridden, able to manipulate the world only in her head. Moreover, if she was going to die, there was little sense in developing life skills. Any identity she gained was negative, as a sick person who was not going to live. Adolescents elaborate identities in social interaction with peers, trying out, rejecting, and accepting various relationships. Instead, her only contacts were with immediate family members and doctors. Under these conditions it would be nearly impossible for her to develop any independent identity. Her years of illness were a moratorium. Only when she was surgically reprieved could she continue with life concerns. She unconsciously began to pick up where she had left off more than a decade earlier.

In college she chose a highly abstract field of study. Perhaps it reflected her cerebral, asocial experiences. Perhaps it safely skirted threatening emotional issues. At any rate, she says she liked it because it led toward single correct answers. Thus, chronologically past normal adolescence, she was beginning to form a sense of industry (4). She took her first job without having given much thought to her life's work. Yet, obviously intelligent, she advanced in the bureaucracy, unconsciously using her first positions to consolidate her abstract interests into a practical competence. Eventually she became an administrator.

One must speculate about her subsequent political difficulties. In part, she was the victim of well-organized interests that would have troubled anyone in her place. However, it is noteworthy that, although others saw her as an adult with college degrees, she probably still had not settled the question of her personal identity (5). If she were unconsciously to use the social relations of her job to negotiate such an identity, she might look for honesty, cooperation, and acceptance. These expectations would have been a poor guide in a highly political bureaucratic position. She clearly describes her defeats as devastating. Although she does not say so in so many words, she seems to have experienced her political beating as almost a recapitulation of her illness.

In her present position she is much more cautious and expects less. She says she knows not to take herself too seriously. She enjoys a few friendships with other workers. In saying she cannot take herself too seriously, she may unconsciously mean that she is not sure she has a self to take seriously—that she has not yet secured an identity. In the friendships she may be turning once more to the work of adolescence— experimenting with relationships, to learn a little more about whom she can safely be with others.

Thus her complaints about the senselessness of bureaucracy may have two meanings. One is an early concern, stimulated by her years of confronting death, with finding integrity in the face of despair (8). But the other appears to be finding a self that could experience integrity (5). She does her current work well despite puzzled detachment from it. It reinforces her feeling of competence (4).

Although identity is a "work" expectation, Beecham's present quest for identity does not include work. She came to the agency with the unconscious expectation that it help her develop work ability, and after early success she looked for a work identity as well. However, she was so traumatized that, as she resumes her identity project, she does not consider the agency or work part of it. For now, she does not use the organization to grow into it, but, instead, to grow apart from it. If she succeeds in securing an identity, she might once more begin to take herself—and then a work organization—seriously. At least for the time being, she is someone concentrating on personal development, using the job as a means to a private end.

ORGANIZATIONAL CAREERS
AND THE UNCONSCIOUS WORLD OF WORK

Erikson's psychoanalytic framework makes two contributions to comprehending what people want from work organizations and how they experience membership in them. First, it reveals a developmental course that orders people's lives and in the service of which they try to use work organizations. Second, it shows that these private programs are both conscious and unconscious. The cases illustrate the psychological complexity of the process through which individuals assess and decide whether to join organizations. Consciously and unconsciously, people choose to identify with organizations when they feel that their developmental needs are compatible with organizational demands and resources.

This psychoanalytic perspective provides explanations for sociological findings that organizational careers follow typical sequences of challenges and concerns. Schein (1978), for example, conceptualizes careers as the course through which individuals reconcile their changing needs to those of organizations. Organizations require efforts that will lead to productivity. Individuals' expectations, Schein observes, are shaped by stages of personal development through which they move and that lead them to focus on certain tasks at work and elsewhere. In constructing a model of developmental issues, Schein draws on Erikson and others.

Kram and Isabella (1985) studied organizational careers and find four typical stages, each characterized by different focal concerns and peer relationships. In the Establishment stage, paramount concerns are establishing competence (4) and professional identity (5). In the Advancement stage, people begin to feel equal to coworkers (6) as they think about moving ahead. People in the Middle Career stage focus on learning to develop subordinates and on managing fears of their own obsolescence, both matters of generativity (7). The Late Career stage focuses on understanding and making sense of work (8). This sequence of concerns clearly follows Erikson's developmental stages. In addition, the study implies that an organization can foster career development only if it enables workers to act effectively at this succession of tasks.

Dalton, Thompson, and Price (1977) similarly observe four typical stages in professional careers. Stage I, being an apprentice, is concerned with taking initiative (3), acquiring and refining work ability (4), and developing a work identity (5). Stage II, being a colleague, involves developing close relations with coworkers (6). Stage III is being a mentor (7). Stage IV involves being a sponsor shaping organizational direction (8).

Many of the professionals and managers Kram and Isabella talked to had moved beyond the beginning career stage. Nearly half were in Stage II, and another quarter were in Stage III. Although the authors designate the third stage as mentoring, most whom they located there had simply advanced to managerial or supervisory positions and were executing the responsibilities of these positions. Relatively few had become mentors working closely and individually with junior workers. Kram and Isabella do not mention Erikson, but his developmental framework can explain the sequence of concerns they discover. In addition, the distribution of people highlights the centrality to career success of the "work" expectations of work ability, work identity, and organizational affiliation.

This book examines how the beginnings of organizational careers— the first encounters between worker and organization—affect the subsequent unfolding of careers. We advance this inquiry by looking next at the tasks involved in becoming a member of a work organization.

Part Two
Initiation into Organizational Roles

Organizational Demands of the New Worker: Sociological and Anthropological Accounts

Joining an organization is an everyday event that seems quite simple. Staff members recruit applicants for available positions and select from the prospects. Personnel officers have the newcomers complete appropriate paperwork, and then they are members of the organization.

This superficial view says nothing about the experience of organizational entry—for either the newcomers or the veterans. For instance, the examples in chapters 1 and 2 show that someone may not feel like a member until some time after he has formally become part of an organization. Neither may coworkers regard him as a colleague until later. As the four cases suggest, subjective membership depends on the individual's (conscious and unconscious) perceptions that the organization has satisfied certain demands. Implicitly, entry requires negotiation over whether the organization can meet individual expectations. Veterans in an organization also have interests, which shape their requirements of newcomers, and they negotiate actively with newcomers for these interests.

In general, both newcomers and veterans have interests in not changing. Although joining an organization means change for an individual, and although recruiting a new member means change for veterans, nevertheless, both parties imagine they can undergo this transition without really altering who they are. In addition, the two sides have specific interests they seek to protect in the entry process. The earlier cases offer individual examples: to maintain autonomy, to stay close to someone in power, to accumulate a heritage, and to find meaning in work. For their part, veterans want to preserve specific production practices and social relationships. Formal orientation programs are an expression of organizational wishes to make the new member adjust to the organization as a condition for entry. In addition, veterans and newcomers resist change in a variety of informal ways.

The following two chapters examine these interests and negotiations in organizational entry. This chapter looks at veterans' perceptions of newcomers: what they want from them, what they fear about them, and how they attempt to initiate them into the organizational fold. Sociological studies of organizational entry, research on group development, and anthropological accounts of traditional rites of passage reinforce one another in showing veterans respond to their concerns about new members by tacitly organizing a three-stage initiation ritual to convert outsiders into insiders. Chapter 4 turns to the newcomers' concerns. Psychoanalytic studies of childhood suggest that individuals unconsciously anticipate such an initiation but expect to control the outcome themselves. Psychoanalytic research on play and planning shows how newcomers unconsciously initiate themselves into organizations. Together, these chapters portray organizational entry as a complex, deep, protracted, and largely unconscious negotiation between two highly interested parties.

ORGANIZATIONAL SOCIALIZATION

Many observers see the process of organizational entry as not simply an aggregation of isolated events, but as the enactment of related stages in an at least tacitly organized socialization.

One group of studies conceptualizes this process with a focus on managerial concerns. They interpret the events of entry with an emphasis on organizational expectations of new workers. Typically, Wanous (1980; and Wanous, Reichers, and Malik 1984) synthesizes a number of models of organizational socialization to identify four stages of socialization: (1) confronting and accepting organizational reality, (2) achieving role clarity, (3) locating oneself in the organizational context, and (4) detecting signposts of successful socialization.

Wanous' formulation makes four assumptions common in the sociological literature and in managers' thinking about newcomers. First, socialization is a process of learning, in which new members develop progressively more realistic views of their organizations. Second, although this learning has its frustrations, socialization is basically devoid of conflict. The main source of difficulty is new members' unrealistic expectations, and recruiters themselves may be accountable for imparting distorted images of their organizations. At the least, veterans do not deliberately set out to create problems for the initiates.

Third, the neophyte is pretty much a *tabula rasa*. Although family, friends, and cultural values shape occupational decisions, once someone considers entering a particular organization, recruiters and other organizational representatives have dominant influence over his thinking. At the least, organizational membership tends to be a large part of the new member's identity and is relatively isolated from such other identities as family member or citizen.

Fourth, most stage models (e.g., Buchanan 1974; Porter, Lawler, and Hackman 1975; and Feldman 1976) also assume that socialization is a conscious process. Learning is cognitive and overt. Conscious aims do not conflict with unconscious wishes or assumptions. And whatever emotions attach to other social relationships do not impinge on organizational performance.

Schein (1978), while sharing some of these assumptions, has added more realistic considerations from his research. He regards new recruits as fully formed personalities who confront organizations in efforts to satisfy various occupational and personal needs, which may conflict with organizational expectations. Hence, when new members enter organizations, they may not simply acquire more and more realistic information about the organizations, but may be pressed to change in fundamental intellectual or emotional ways. Organizational socialization requires some resolution of this conflict. Schein observes initiation follows three stages in accomplishing this change: (1) entry (including recruitment and selection), (2) socialization (on the job), and (3) mutual acceptance.[1]

Graen (1976), studying what happens once employment begins, offers a particularly sophisticated view of entry. He conceptualizes stages of initiation in terms of what veterans must do to convert newcomers with conflicting aims. As a result, he finds that what Schein calls "socialization" really involves the first two tasks of a three-stage process. Graen draws on Lewin's (1951) model of how individuals change. First, individuals approach new situations with old ideas and will not be prepared to change until some of those ideas are "unfrozen." Once this has happened, change is possible. Finally, change is consolidated when new ideas are "refrozen" in connection with other ideas. In looking at new employees, Graen finds stages corresponding to such a learning process, which he calls (1) *initial confrontation*, (2) *working through*, and (3) *integrating*.

The first stage features what Hughes (1958) has called "reality shock." New members encounter differences between their expectations and supervisors' requirements. To make their demands clear, supervisors often deliberately create "upending experiences" (Schein 1978) to shake recruits out of past assumptions and confidence. They may give a battery of tests that no one can pass perfectly. They may give difficult or impossible assignments. In a variety of ways, they emphasize that company procedures are unique and that prior skills cannot simply be transferred into a new setting.

For example, Schein's interviewees complain about "working with people you can't control" and "having to check with everyone all the time." One summarizes the initial confrontation with exasperation:

I thought I could sell people with logic and was amazed at the hidden agendas people have, irrational objections; really bright

people will come up with stupid excuses . . . they have their own
little empires to worry about. (1978:94-95)

Initiates learn that the organization is unlikely to change and that they
must be willing to adjust if they want to become members.

    Once the new worker is prepared to accept the authority of veteran
workers, the second stage begins. In repeated confrontations, both sides
test one another and negotiate how work will proceed. By this time, the
newcomer has a fair understanding of technical task requirements but
must work out role relationships. Formal role definitions provide some
structure, but many important relationships are ambiguous and must be
agreed on. The new worker must figure out who is really important for
getting work done and what superiors really expect and reward. He
must identify a reference group within the organization, colleagues who
share professional, economic, or political interests and can be depended
on for support.

    Schein's interviewees are struck at this stage by how much of their
work is undefined and must be settled informally. "Things are much
more disorganized at _____ than I expected." "I got no guidance from
my boss; had to define my own job." "Your job is what you make of it."
One summarizes the ambiguities:

> I had the problem of never having a problem which was clearly
> definable, hence had a hard time getting feedback, hence needed
> some direction on which problems are useful, which ones can be
> helpful to the company.

Another describes the solution he discovered:

> The projects are not integrated; hence I have little control over
> the people from whom I have to get work out. Hence I have
> become political to get my work done. (1978:97)

    The final stage begins when veterans decide they like the ways new
members work. Now veterans offer signs of acceptance. Supervisors
may issue favorable evaluations at the end of a formal probation period.
The new workers may get salary increases. Coworkers may show they
take the newcomers seriously by consulting them on problems. Veterans
may also show their endorsement by offering advice and practical support
on projects. Acceptance may be marked by formal signs of physical or
social inclusion, such as the designation of a private office or allocation
of specific privileges. Induction may be announced at a meeting or,
occasionally, marked by a special event such as a party.

Organizational Demands

An observer would be struck by the seriousness with which
treat newcomers. They may, indeed, be successful in initiatin
workers, but they begin by inflicting unquestionably humiliating e
iences on them. What accounts for the intensity, even cruelty, of t
initiation process? Studies of group development and traditional rites
of passage help understand the stakes in the conflict between veterans
and newcomers.

GROUP DEVELOPMENT

Interestingly, the stages in organizational socialization resemble stages
in group development. Tuckman (1965), for example, reviewed studies
of therapy groups, human relations training groups, natural groups, and
laboratory groups and found four typical stages, the first three of which
correspond to the three stages of organizational socialization. (1) People
initially come together for some purpose (Tuckman calls this stage *forming*)
(2) When they realize they will stay together, they actively promote their
own interests in a struggle over collective aims (*storming*). (3) As they
resolve these conflicts, they come to agreements on what they will do
and how they will do it (*norming*) (4) Finally, they work (*performing*).[2]

Correspondences between these stages and those of organizational
socialization become clearer with the recognition of the main difference
between the two processes. In the former, many veterans initiate one or
a few newcomers, whereas in the latter there are no veterans, and everyone
is a newcomer. No one in a new group has the security or power of
veterans in an ongoing organization, and everyone is more or less equal.

With this difference, the forming stage in group development parallels
the initial confrontation stage in organizational socialization: people
meet each other for the first time and find that things cannot proceed as
they have in the past. The storming stage is similar to the working
through: people struggle in an effort to convert others to their point of
view. The norming stage matches the integrating stage: people accept
one another on some agreeable terms. Finally, work in a group is like
work in an organization after socialization.

The similarity in structure between these two processes is related to
a similarity in aim: creating a cohesive collective actor from two or
more independent individuals. The psychological reasons for the structure
of group development shed light on why organizational socialization
proceeds as it does. Members of a new group typically go through the
first three stages before they get down to work because working in
groups arouses a conflict in them. On the one hand, doing work gives a
satisfying sense of competence and efficacy. However, joining with others
in order to accomplish work requires submerging oneself in a collectivity,

om and specialness to create a disciplined
ple feel anxious or angry about making
hey don't know the other people involved.
flict between wanting to do work and
tonomy. The first three stages of group
members' unconscious plan to deal with this conflict
get down to work. In particular, the storming stage involves
unting other individuals' differences, getting to know whether they
are sufficiently trustworthy to throw one's lot in with, and accepting the
necessity of hashing out some compromises with them.[3]

In short, group members unconsciously decide to proceed through certain steps in order to manage their anxiety about the uncertainties of forming a group with others. In this activity, every individual simultaneously feels like an applicant to someone else's group and the proprietor of a group considering whether to accept others.[4] The former experience is like that of an organizational newcomer, whereas the latter is like that of organizational veterans.

Thus study of the feelings underlying group development suggests one reason why organizational socialization follows the three-stage structure is to help veterans deal with their anxiety about admitting strangers to their organization. It also suggests that human beings react in certain typical ways to the entry of newcomers in a variety of social settings. Anthropological accounts of rites of passage add to the evidence of the generality of the treatment of new members and shed more light on the threats newcomers present to ongoing organizations.

RITES OF PASSAGE

Van Gennep's (1960 [1908]) classic study of rites of passage finds that these rituals have a structure that serves their purpose: managing the transition of someone from one role and status to another. The prior role is regarded as unacceptable or no longer acceptable, and the new role is preferable. The ritual accomplishes several ends. For both the initiate and the collectivity it regulates the uncertainties and anxieties of the transition. For the individual it provides a normally desired new status in a social unit. For the collectivity it neutralizes any threatening aspects of the initiate and makes the initiate benign.

Rites of passage provide socially meaningful answers to two questions. If someone is to move from a prior identity to a new one as part of a collective body, when does that person cease to hold the first identity, and when does he acquire the second? This question is crucial insofar as the prior identity is dangerous or "out of place" in the collectivity. For example, a society may allow adolescents unrestrained nonincestuous sexual activity with one another but expect that married adults be monogamous. The challenge to a marital ritual is to transform someone who was previously free to have sexual relations with many similar others to a member of the society of married people who no longer consider acting in that way and are sexually faithful to one partner. Hence, there is also a practical question: How can this change be managed so the initiate does not confront the collectivity with any harmful beliefs or actions and accepts a new identity?

Van Gennep discovered that a wide range of societies, both traditional and modern, accomplish this passage by creating a ritual that includes a period when the initiate is neither any longer what he has been, nor yet what he will become. This special time preserves the society by standing between it and any malignant forces in the initiate's past. For this reason, van Gennep found, rites of passage normally consist of three stages: (1) a stage in which members of the collectivity strip the initiate of a prior identity (which van Gennep called *separation*); (2) the crucial stage when the initiate, removed from the past identity, is prepared for a new one (*transition*); and (3) a stage in which the initiate acquires the new identity and is assimilated into the collectivity (*incorporation*).

Turner (1969) has studied the transitional stage in rituals in traditional societies to understand how it "works" in transforming identities. He concludes that, sociologically and psychologically, this stage represents a condition of "communitas," where people confront one another as whole persons, outside of partial social roles. People interact as individuals, rather than members or representatives of institutions. This stage contrasts with the prior and subsequent ones, where individuals act in roles as part of an articulated social structure. The immediacy of relations makes the encounter so forceful as to induce initiates to change.

A rite of passage begins with separation of the initiate from any previous social identity. This removal includes ridicule of past roles, ideas, and ways of acting, (e.g., as child, apprentice, or unmarried person) and may include physical assault. Such a stripping denies the initiate any further use of the powers or privileges associated with the previous role (e.g., the child's claims to help from adults or the adolescent's sexual freedom). Now the neophyte has no social connections other than the links to the initiators, and the transition may begin.

The initiate confronts all other members of the collectivity without cover or protection of the social structure. No longer do people meet as players in circumscribed roles, but as whole persons whose actions represent the entire community. Liberation from the constraints of social roles, interaction in deeply personal relations, and awareness that the actions celebrate the community as a whole, bring tremendous emotional power to the encounter.

In this condition the neophyte is assumed to possess nothing and is regarded as a *tabula rasa*. He is expected to approach others humbly and passively, to obey them as instructors, and to accept arbitrary punishment without complaint. Members of the community teach the initiate two lessons. The first is a cognitive and emotional lesson: the neophyte must understand that communitas is superior to any type of separation, whether acting on the authority of a social role or following biological urges at others' expense. This lesson prepares the neophyte for learning specific skills and knowledge required for a new social role (e.g., worker or sexually mature adult). Together, these two lessons make the ritual effective. Not only does the neophyte learn actions necessary for a new role, but he also learns that the role exists only on the experienced authority of the community to which he belongs.

Once the initiate has learned these lessons, he may enter the new role in the final ritual stage. Now the neophyte joins the collectivity in the dress and activities of the role (e.g., hunter, husband, or woman). Even though the role makes only partial claims on its new occupant, the memory of the transitional stage enforces those claims.

Initiation Ritual as Rebirth

The key to an effective initiation ritual—one that admits a new member without harm from any of that person's past—is first stripping the neophyte of his past identity and then exposing him to the unmediated power of the community.

Róheim (1942) reinforces this view with a psychoanalytic interpretation of the transition ritual as a rebirth. He observes that traditional societies often use words and actions to identify the removal of the neophyte from his secure social position as a recapitulation of the first trauma in life: expulsion from the mother's body. The effect is to enhance the initiate's anxiety during the ritual separation and to make him especially receptive to the terms of the collectivity in his search for a substitute object of affection and loyalty. Many societies organize the transitional stage as a rebirth, in which the initiate symbolically repeats the original birth trauma, as if now born again into a new status in the final stage of the ritual.

The symbolized separation from the mother arouses anxiety that motivates the initiate to consider the society as a new body with which to identify. At the same time, the metaphorical rebirth offers a means of dealing with the anxiety, because, by invoking the neophyte's own birth trauma, it reminds him that, in fact, he overcame that trauma and, by implication, should succeed this time as well.

In addition, the ceremony provides a substitute for ties to the mother. In puberty rites, when the initiate is prepared to reenter society, he is often given a representation of the father. The likeness portrays the father's phallic power but also stands for the moral code he follows as a man in society. The initiate's acceptance of the object, Róheim suggests, symbolizes his internalization of an image of the father as his superego, or conscience. The social ceremony explicitly enacts the unconscious bargain that concludes contemporary Oedipal struggles: taking the representation of his father, the youth symbolically absorbs the community's ethical code and is now equipped to act responsibly in his new role as a man.

Thus, Róheim argues that participants in traditional rites of passage experience the rituals as a rebirth from an earlier identity to a new one.

Erikson's perspective similarly suggests that rites of passage may be experienced as rebirth. Actions in the first stage regress the initiate to an earlier psychological and social condition by stripping him of certain developmental accomplishments. The second stage focuses the neophyte's attention once more on the earliest developmental task of infancy. And the final stage leads the initiate back through the stages of development stripped away earlier, this time in terms carefully controlled by the collectivity.

Which developmental accomplishments are taken away in the separation stage depends on (a) the initiators' intentions, (b) the initiate's biography (e.g., a girl becoming a woman and an adult becoming a shaman have different achievements they could lose), and (c) the social and psychological meanings of the biography (e.g., in different cultures these achievements involve different degrees of maturity or integration into mainstream social activities).

In general, the separation stage explicitly takes away three developmental accomplishments: affiliation with a community (6), such as that of apprentices or members of a foreign country; an identity or social role (5), such as that of pregnant mother or student; and competence (4), such as the skills of schoolboys or the hunting techniques of another society. Normally, when someone finds past competence no longer serves, he is thrown back to a concern with initiative and guilt (3). And yet the frustrating lesson of the separation is that any past moral code defining the terms of guilt is no longer accepted. This is the first of three developmental accomplishments tacitly thrown down. The humiliations of this stage show that even autonomy cannot be taken for granted (2). Ultimately, the separation moves the neophyte back still further, to reencounter the earliest psychosocial test of the infant.

Thus the challenge of the transition stage is to get recognition from the initiators (1) by taking the ritual activities seriously and by responding in good faith. Someone who does not deeply engage the ritual tests, whatever his actual performance, cannot expect reciprocity. Success demonstrates autonomy in terms of newly defined norms. At that emotional moment the initiation focuses on the activity Róheim considers central: moving the neophyte through the conflicts of the Oedipal complex, channeling aggression into newly sanctioned outlets (3). The initiate who passes this test then is prepared to learn new skills (4) to undergird the new identity.

The incorporation stage introduces the individual to a new role (5), such as adult male or mother. In addition, as the collective character of the ritual emphasizes, this role goes with affiliation with a new community (6), such as the society as a whole or a work group within it.

Thus, in terms of unconscious relations with groups in the society, an initiation ritual gives the neophyte an experience of returning to the first tests of the infant and then advancing with the initiators' guidance. At least unconsciously, veterans plan rituals in this way so as to manage the dangers represented by new members. Veterans render newcomers harmless by compelling them to surrender the life accomplishments that make them dangerous and to develop once again within the limits of the new society.

Rites of Passage and Organizational Socialization

Cross-cultural generalizations must be tentative.[5] Traditional societies and modern Western societies differ in their complexity and in the inclusiveness of roles. A member of a contemporary society is likely to hold more roles, before or after a ritual, than a member of a traditional society. In addition, the modern role occupant is likely to feel less encompassing loyalty to either an individual role or a group or society. Both differences suggest that the power of modern collectivities to enact transition rituals is at least not uniformly as great as that of traditional collectivities.[6] For example, contemporary initiators may not be able to create as intense an experience of communitas as their traditional counterparts.

In addition, as suggested earlier, the meanings and experiences of social roles and actions differ among historical and cultural settings. Not simply is the period of youth, which is of so much concern to Erikson, a product of the modern industrial economy, but its contours vary from country to country (1963 and 1965). Even contemporary childhood, with all its national variations, follows patterns of relatively recent heritage (Ariès 1962). Hence, a ritual that makes a young person a member of a modern bureaucratic work organization is both similar to, and different from, an earlier ritual that initiated another young person into a medieval guild.

With these cautions, it is useful to analyze the parallels between traditional rites of passage and modern organizational socialization.[7] They consist of similar series of three stages. In each case, the first stage (Graen's initial confrontation or van Gennep's separation) strips the newcomer of past roles, connections, and security. The second stage (working through or transition) puts the neophyte in direct confrontation with veterans, to recognize their authority and to take instruction from them. The final stage (integrating or incorporation) settles the transformed individual in a new identity and society.

These structural similarities offer evidence, first, that organizational socialization touches something deep and widespread in the individual's experience of social life. Entry into a collectivity is not a simple or casual matter. Societies create elaborate rituals in order to protect themselves when admitting new members.

Second, the sociological and psychological order of traditional rites of passage suggests that the sequence of the three stages in organizational socialization is not accidental. They are arranged so as to transform a newcomer by inducing his symbolic rebirth.

Hence, third, stripping new workers of prior roles, knowledge, or confidence in their initial confrontation with organizations is not incidental or optional, but central to the initiation. The ritual's purpose is to change someone with potentially dangerous outside loyalties into a docile supplicant for membership.

For example, new workers must be discouraged from believing they can have prestige outside the organization unrelated to their performance inside. They must also cease to assume that the ways they previously did things will suffice in this new situation. Only when they accept their economic and emotional dependence on their new coworkers will they be receptive to the lessons their colleagues want to teach them.[8]

The initial confrontation stimulates these developments in two ways. Socially, it leaves workers unable to trade their past connections for authority in the organization and forces them to establish relationships in the organization. Psychologically, by taking away past sources of self-esteem and identity, the initial confrontation makes newcomers anxious: they feel cut off; they doubt their worth; they feel alone. In this condition, they want relationships with new colleagues for reassurance.

Fourth, the working through stage in socialization is inevitably powerful emotionally. Separated from past social and psychological anchors, newcomers regard unstructured, uncontrolled negotiation of new relationships with organizational veterans as a promising but frightening experience. No matter how brief it may be, it leaves strong memories of the potential power of the work force, even after the newcomer has settled into a structured role. These memories add to other incentives to accept the role.

The physical violence of many traditional rites of passage is absent from contemporary organizational socialization. And yet the violence remains emotionally. Taking a new identity requires giving up an old one, watching the old one perish. Rebirth must follow a death. From the veterans' perspective, the potential risks in the entry of a new member may seem so high, the symbolic murder of a past identity may seem necessary.

One other difference between traditional and modern Western societies is that members of the former often say and show explicitly what remains tacit or unconscious among members of the latter. Thus it is clear that initiation is a rebirth in New Guinea, for example, but it is less clear what modern organizational veterans and new workers think about their negotiations over membership. Nevertheless, the burden of evidence from traditional rites of passage, as well as group development, suggests that these meanings are among those that motivate veterans who "socialize" their future colleagues.

The correspondences among stages in organizational socialization, group development, and rites of passage are summarized in figure 2.

Figure 2. Correspondences Among Stage Models

Learning (Lewin)	Organizational Socialization (Graen)	Group Development (Tuckman)	Rites of Passage (van Gennep)
I. Unfreezing	I. Initial confrontation	I. Forming	I. Separation
II. Change	II. Working through	II. Storming	II. Transition
III. Refreezing	III. Integrating (Working)	III. Norming	III. Incorporation
		IV. Performing	

PROBLEMS IN ORGANIZATIONAL INITIATION

When an initiate in a traditional society does not satisfy ritual requirements and become an adult member of the society, the normal explanation is that the individual failed in some way. Collective expectations are assumed to be legitimate, and there is little suspicion that the ritual itself was faulty. Traditionally, modern managers have taken a similar perspective on personnel matters. These assumptions underlie probation periods.

More tolerantly, a recruit's failure to make it with an organization may be interpreted as a problem of "fit." Some individuals have more of the ability, experience, or personality that an organization requires than do others. At the same time, certain organizational initiations are more congruent with some persons' aims, expectations, or abilities than with others'.[9] Nevertheless, most managers who accept this view assume the basic correctness of their organization's goals and efficacy of its orientation program.

Alternatively, organizational entry may fail because conditions that made traditional initiations work do not prevail in modern society. Although contemporary sociologists increasingly talk of "organizational culture," no work organization is bound as tightly by any set of norms as are traditional societies. Workers hold many, conflicting identities and loyalties. There are few real "company men." Indeed, it is management's recognition of the diminishing power of appeals to organizational loyalty that has led to hurried efforts to examine—and invent—"organizational culture."[10] Organizational values and practices are increasingly questionable and questioned. As a consequence, modern organizations cannot summon the magic—or feeling—with which traditional societies empowered their rituals. In short, faulty organizational rituals may be another reason why recruits do not become members.

Employee turnover is a sign of the breakdown of organizational socialization. Most turnover takes place during the first months of a job (Porter and Steers, 1973; Mobley, Griffeth, Hand, and Meglino 1979; and Muchinsky and Tuttle 1979). Mowday, Porter, and Steers (1982) find that how employees see the fit between their expectations and organizational conditions on the first day of work influences whether they stay or leave. Kotter (1973) describes job leavers' unhappiness in terms of a failed initiation. They feel they joined their organizations to use their skills for individual accomplishments in interesting and meaningful work but, instead, were asked to give up prior skills (a demand of initial confrontation) in order to work in groups (a condition of working through) and to assume loyalty to the organization (the result of integrating). Other studies elaborate.

Leavers are more likely than those who stay to feel they could not use their skills for achievement and recognition (Ross and Zander, 1957; Dunnette, Arvey, and Banas 1973; and Porter and Steers 1973). Leavers are more likely to feel that they did not get responsibility commensurate with their ability (Waters and Roach 1971 and 1973; Taylor and Weiss 1972; and Mobley, Griffeth, Hand, and Meglino 1979). Finally, leavers are more likely to complain that they did not get significant autonomy or control over their work (Guest 1955; Ross and Zander 1957; Schein 1968 and 1978; Waters and Roach 1971 and 1973; Taylor and Weiss 1972; and Mobley, Griffeth, Hand, and Meglino 1979).

The early beginnings of turnover point to problems starting with the first stage of organizational socialization. Leavers' complaints that their expectations were disappointed indicate that the initial confrontation failed to eliminate their former identities—that these newcomers refused to give up who they had been. Complaints about lack of responsibility show that these new recruits wanted their old identity acknowledged, while the organization would recognize only a new one. Complaints about lack of authority express their concern that veterans simply tried to overpower them in the initial confrontation. Complaints that work is not meaningful indicate that these workers continue to interpret work differently than others in the organization.

These newcomers would provide a cynical view of organizational socialization. Veterans may attempt to strip recruits of prior identities and confidence, but the old members do not offer meaningful compensation. The unstructured negotiation of roles and rules in the middle stage arouses anxiety without providing an anchor. There is no true communitas, no open confrontation of persons as members of a collectivity, no emotionally rich experience in which both initiate and initiators endure something powerful together. Instead, the old members contemptuously set up obstacles for the newcomer without endowing the obstacles or their passage with meaning. During this time, the new member may learn job skills but never comes to feel that the organization has emotional priority over self-interests. Hence, when the old members eventually recognize the initiate in a formal role, the acceptance feels more like a coerced condition than a mutual choice.

These are not arbitrary accusations. They fit together in developmental terms. Leavers sense that socialization efforts stripped them of the security their identity previously offered without providing a replacement. The initiation induced a regression to earlier developmental concerns without supplying a means for new advancement.

Leavers' primary complaint is that the organizations deprived them of the sense of competence that their skills previously gave them. They could no longer achieve what they were capable of. Thus they experienced entry as an attack on their work ability (4). Throughout this period they could not get other workers to go along with them (3). Nor could they even act autonomously or control their own work (2). Fundamentally, they could not get others to recognize them or give them responsibility commensurate with what they could do (1). Each complaint describes how organizational conditions upset an earlier developmental accomplishment. Each of these prework challenges draws a newcomer's attention away from work. In addition, each makes it harder to maintain or establish an identity as a worker (5), much less identify with the organization (6).

Tacitly, the job leavers recognize what organizational entry demands. In their own language, they report that organizational conditions threatened the survival of their personal identities. They indicate that when initiation is half successful in this way, it does not succeed at all.

Instead, they are left anxious and angry, and they leave, in search of a place that will accept their competence and identity.

Certainly some job leavers are poorly skilled, temperamentally unsuited to organizational work, or deliberate job-hoppers. But too many make the same complaints to attribute the departure of all to personal unsuitability. They raise questions about not only the efficacy, but also the benignity, of contemporary organizational initiation activities. Even some who succeed in entering organizations may suffer injuries described by early leavers.

IMPLICATIONS FOR ORGANIZATIONAL ENTRY

Organizational veterans tacitly expect newcomers to pass through a three-stage initiation ritual, giving up their prior identity to get a work role. Yet modern organizations cannot always make the ritual work. Their activities, to use an anthropological term, do not seem sacred.

Whatever the policies of particular organizations, all operate in a fragmented, differentiated society. The four workers described earlier, for example, have many, often conflicting social affiliations. As a result, they have not only the social and economic freedom to negotiate relations with work organizations—something that varies with political economic structure, state of the economy, and class position—but they have the psychological freedom to do so, as well—something distinctively modern.

What is new is their conviction that they have a right to individual psychological contracts with the organization. Whether they can negotiate salary or benefit conditions with their organizations—something especially difficult in civil service bureaucracies—unconsciously they assume that they are entitled to their own terms on a wide range of developmental resources. And they have made many complicated demands, which organizations cannot easily satisfy.

As a result of these changes, many workers feel that organizational socialization is not a process of progressive incorporation into a collective body, but one in which two parties negotiate unmistakably, even if often unequally. Managers who worry about "corporate culture" recognize this, and workers who leave new jobs before getting settled in show this.

Thus there are two models of organizational entry in conflict. Studies of organizational socialization show that veterans, responding to deep human concerns about admitting new members to their work society, design three-stage initiations. Often these efforts succeed in transforming new workers. Even if they fail at that, they may still secure veterans against the dangers of newcomers. However, studies of job leavers, as well as the four case examples, show that many workers bring complex, often unconscious demands to organizations and are willing to join only if they can negotiate personally satisfying terms. They do not believe in organizations enough to give up everything on faith, but will warily exchange one item at a time, in their own order. The people in the four examples and the job leavers show what workers will do if they do not find organizations responsive.

Leaving is immediately a problem of organizational entry. It is also a problem of organizational commitment. Porter, Crampon, and Smith (1976) say that workers' commitment on their first day on a job is a good predictor of whether they stay or leave. Furthermore, clearly, if workers leave, they never become committed to an organization. Thus whether people become members of organizations has a great deal to do with whether people can commit themselves to places of work. Some obstacles to commitment and entry, such as the differentiation of modern society, lie beyond organizational policy. However, the outcomes have a lot to do with what workers want and how organizations respond.

The next chapter, completing the conceptual introduction, looks at new workers' expectations of organizational entry and their reactions to veterans' demands.

The New Worker Responds:
A Psychoanalytic View

Traditionally, we think of work as an activity in which people make or transform things. Coworkers are not so much collaborators as simply others who do more or less the same thing nearby. While friendliness adds to the pleasures of tasks that may themselves be tedious, personal relations are not integral to the work. The Hawthorne studies showed this view to be an illusion: even if work involves mechanical operations on inert materials, workers' social relationships affect both their happiness and organizational productivity (Roethlisberger and Dickson 1939).

The Hawthorne studies themselves were an indication of emerging new types of work: managerial and professional work that consisted of ordering and transforming relations among people. More and more service work consists of "producing" services or managing others who do so. No longer is there a clear separation between the content and the context of work. "Getting work done" involves collaborative social relations that contain aspects of friendships and authority relations. Thus, as the sociological studies in the last chapter show, anyone beginning work must learn both how to accomplish certain tasks and how to get along with a multitude of organizational colleagues.

A psychoanalytic view of these tasks of organizational entry sheds light on the unconscious aims, calculations, and fears that accompany overt, conscious intentions to "get in" and "get on with" work. We will first look briefly at psychoanalytic thinking about the general meaning of work. Then we will look at psychoanalytic thinking about the issues raised in joining a complex organization and undergoing an initiation like that described in the last chapter.

WORK

Psychoanalytic Thinking about Work

Psychoanalytic thinking about work is based on assumptions about the composition and dynamics of the human mind. At birth it is considered to be only id—libido, or sexual instinct. The mind is not conscious, and it directs the body toward actions that will avoid tension and bring physical pleasure. As some of these efforts meet with frustration from the external world, some libido goes into the creation of an ego, which serves as an increasingly conscious reality-oriented guide to action. It looks for actions that successfully compromise between libidinal impulses and external constraints, satisfying the organism's drives but also ensuring its survival. Later on, as chapter 2 described in different terms, as a result of Oedipal conflicts, some libidinal energy goes to make up the superego, or conscience, which serves as a partly conscious moral guide to action. The superego normally urges actions in conflict with libidinal aims, and both may be thwarted by external reality. The ego has the challenge of selecting compromise ideas and actions that satisfy all.[1]

In this traditional view, work activities are considered part of a repertoire of ways in which the ego directs the organism to act in the world it encounters. Metapsychologically, in terms of the premises of psychology, it is nothing special. Hendrick (1943a and 1943b) was one of the first psychoanalytic writers to think about work as a distinct human activity, something not derivative from other drives. He regarded working as an autonomous human interest, governed by its own "instinct to master," as independent and powerful as the sexual instinct. He took the deviant position that the ego may have an interest (and energy) independent of the libido. Consistent with Hendrick's view, White (1963) postulated that work expresses independent "effectance" energies in the ego striving for competence. Nevertheless, both acknowledged that, despite their claims for the autonomy of work interests, they resemble other ego activities that are the traditionally conceptualized compromises with the id, superego, and outer world. Metapsychologically, Hendrick and White's positions are unconvincing, but what is important is their clinical observations that work is a strong motivation in adult activity and development.

Erikson (1963 and 1968), as noted earlier, regards work as one in a series of challenges to the ego in organizing relations with the social world so as to permit development. Although he differs with Hendrick and White in not asserting independence for a "work instinct," he agrees with them on the importance of work in individual growth. A combination of developing biological potentials and social expectations lead older children to try to develop a "sense of industry" and to avoid feelings of "inferiority."

In describing the requirements for work and a sense of industry, Erikson employs traditional psychoanalytic language to say that the individual must "sublimate," or find socially acceptable expressions of, the drives that impelled earlier development. A central lesson of the Oedipal conflict is that future success requires modulating sexual activity and aggression so as not to offend others and bring harm on oneself. Although adulthood permits relatively free expression of sexuality and aggression in certain situations, many others, including work, require that these wishes be expressed indirectly, if at all.

When Erikson treats work as an expression of both libido and aggression, he recognizes the coequal status of aggression with libido as a basic human impulse. Traditional psychoanalysts acknowledge only libido as a biological instinct and regard aggression as a creation of the ego (itself a derivative of the id) to attack or defend in situations of frustration. More recent analysts, some citing Freud's later thinking, some citing ethological evidence, argue that aggression and libido are both biological drives, that human activity is the product of two independent instincts. The resolution of this metapsychological conflict does not affect Erikson's analysis. Even if aggression is not innately human, by early childhood it becomes a well-learned, well-practiced impulse and way of acting.[2]

The challenge of work is to learn to compromise how one might want to act with what is considered effective, pleasant, safe, and appropriate for getting a job done. This compromise is "intrapsychic," in the mind, for two reasons. The first is that people are not conscious of everything they want, such as sexual relatedness or aggressive conquest. The dangers in the untrammeled expression of these aims lead people to repress them, to keep them from consciousness. These dangers are the second reason why compromise takes place in the mind rather than out in the world. By consciously and unconsciously figuring out how it is safe to think and act before acting, people can be safer and more effective in relations with others.

As Erikson suggests, work requires two related compromises. The first, discussed earlier in chapter 2, involves the individual's ego identity and related developmental needs, which a specific organization may or may not satisfy. Persons with "work" expectations are more likely to come to terms with organizations—and compromise less—than others with prework expectations. Nevertheless, as the examples showed, even individuals with "work" expectations may have to give in on what they do or when they do it.

At the same time, different stages in the development of personal identity require different expressions of libido and aggression in social relations. Achieving autonomy, for example, involves aggressively estabblishing personal bourdaries; in contrast, intimacy involves sexually and affectionately collapsing boundaries and joining with another. The metapsychological status of libido and aggression—whether only the former or both are biological instincts—is unimportant here. What matters is that infants, children, and adults experience themselves as *wishing* to act sexually and aggressively toward others.[3] Thus, when Erikson speaks of the need to sublimate libido and aggression, he means that people must learn to moderate these wishes in order to get along in specific social situations.

Psychoanalysts characterize efforts at such moderation as intrapsychic compromise among id, ego, and superego interests. Traditional analysts would argue that this process involves literal vectorlike compromises among energized mental agents. Later analysts would identify the id, ego, and superego with wishes to act in particular ways—to reduce tension and to find pleasure, to get along with reality, and to act ethically, respectively.[4] Efforts to compromise among wishes feel like intrapsychic negotiations because people experience sexuality and aggression differently than the ego. The latter feels part of oneself, who one is. In contrast, the former seem "id-like"; they seem alien and impersonal, and people tend to disavow them.[5]

Sublimation

Here it is helpful to look more closely at what people consciously and unconsciously do when they try to "sublimate" aggressive and sexual wishes to conform to work requirements. Acting aggressively means acting against the resistance of an object or another person. *In extremis*, aggression,[6] in attacking physical objects or people, may harm or destroy them. The normal social consequence of acting aggressively is to separate oneself from others, by destroying them or by driving them away. In this way, aggressive action, unlike libidinal action, may be self-defeating, in that it must cease if it totally does away with its object.[7] People who are targets of aggression are likely to resist, because they do not want to be harmed or at least because they do not want to be changed. Their likely reaction—reprisal—is the central danger of aggression.

Sublimation represents a compromise with violent expressions of aggressive wishes and aims to avoid risks of retaliation.[8] People may be able to satisfy aggressive wishes in certain indirect but socially sanctioned ways. At work, for example, supervisors may control or guide subordinates, making them do certain things but not destroying them and possibly helping them. Or, professionals may direct their attack against intellectual problems, which not only are defenseless, but whose solutions may please many people.[9]

Acting libidinally, in contrast, means acting so as to merge with an object—approaching, preserving, and enjoying it. Nevertheless, a sexual advance, because it aims to change another's activities and boundaries, is partly aggressive. People respond to unwelcome advances the same ways they respond to other attacks—with resistance and perhaps with retaliation. Even if the object resists without being punitive, the refusal frustrates and may humiliate the initiator and may lead him to intensify the advance or to attack the recalcitrant object. Any of these possibilities contains the general dangers of aggression and adds to the risks of sexuality.

Sublimation represents a compromise with dangerous expressions of libidinal wishes. People may act on sexual wishes in certain indirect but socially approved ways. For example, where sexual relations with coworkers are unacceptable, someone may find related pleasure in intimate friendship, collegiality, and cooperation. The results may be both emotionally enjoyable and economically rewarding.

Thus when libidinal or aggressive wishes threaten to bring the individual into dangerous conflict with other actors, sublimation is a response. But it is more than expediency. As indicated earlier, the Oedipal conflict ends when the child takes his parents' moral standards as his own, in the form of a superego, or conscience. Youths and, later, adults experience the superego as ideas that express ethical admonitions. Thus, specific social relations may not only be safe or dangerous; they may also seem moral or immoral. Sublimation denotes efforts of the ego to inhibit aggressive or sexual wishes that seem dangerous or immoral and to plan alternatives that offer satisfaction to original anticipations but involve more neutral or acceptable objects. While following one's conscience may disappoint certain aims, it brings the loving feelings of going along with the ethics of caring parents.

Sublimation involves an addition of caring libidinal actions to what would have been only destructive, dangerous aggressive actions. Klein (1975b [1932]) and Sharpe (1930 and 1935) suggest that this combination of impulses gives individuals benefits beyond safety and moral security. These psychoanalysts believe that aggression, hate, and destructive fantasies are common in human thought and action. They argue that human beings unconsciously recognize their unconscious impulses and, in response, seek reassurance that they have not really harmed other persons whom they may think of aggressively but also love. Even if hostile wishes never result in action and real retaliation, their fantasied success leads to punishing guilt feelings. Hence, reparation, Klein and Sharpe believe, is a primary creative motive in human development.

Accordingly, they call attention to the importance of sublimation in defending against guilt by symbolically repairing any imagined aggressive damage to others. Thus, a combination of libidinal and aggressive wishes in sublimation offers a valuable compromise reward. The aggressive component may in an attenuated way continue to express the original aim and bring symbolically related rewards, while the libidinal component reaffirms the intactness of a loved or feared external object, so that neither retaliation nor guilt results. Klein and Sharpe may overestimate the extent of aggression in human thought and action, but their observations about the reparative function of sublimation are important.

The Challenges of Sublimation at Work

Work requires acting on an object aggressively enough to change it in desired ways, but lovingly enough to preserve it from destruction. When work was primarily agricultural, people approached their tasks with considerable anxiety about harming "Mother Nature" by extracting too much from the ground (Róheim 1971 [1943a]). Craft and industrial work, in contrast, because they shape inanimate materials, involve fewer overt risks of guilt about destruction. However, service work, because much of it involves controlling relations among people, most directly presents dangers of being overly aggressive. The surgeon's worries about killing a patient on the operating table are only the most explicit of a range of concerns shared by all whose work requires them to develop specific relations with other persons.

Working in an organization complicates these challenges by introducing a multitude of superiors, peers, and subordinates with whom workers must get along. To do so, a worker must care about them sufficiently, and get them to care sufficiently about him, to permit him to act appropriately aggressively to accomplish tasks without fear of reprisal or guilt.[10] In addition, an organization offers relationships that may become satisfying in themselves. Overtly, colleagues offer friendship or even romance. Unconsciously, coworkers may become characters in dramas reenacted from childhood experiences. In these instances, relations with coworkers present opportunities for expressing combinations of affection and aggression not directly related to getting work done. In any case, joining an organization raises the question of how much affection one wants in relations with coworkers and what will be the cost of obtaining this affection. Must one agree not to act as aggressively as work requires or one wants?

Entering a work organization requires a newcomer to compromise in expressing aggression and libido toward veterans. This effort is complicated by the fact that many wishes are unconscious, shaped in particular by earlier Oedipal experiences and now transferred to organizational relationships that at least superficially resemble past family relationships.

For example, in the case of aggression, a boy feels intense anger toward his father for holding the mother's sexual affection. Yet the boy must find ways of expressing his anger without provoking reprisal from the powerful father and without causing the cataclysmic destruction of the father, whom he loves and needs. In the unconsciously negotiated Oedipal bargain, the two establish a more or less peaceful relationship as the boy chooses to identify with the father, to seek to become like him, rather than to continue to try to replace him. In so doing, the boy internalizes the father's norms in the superego. The "force" of his conscience comes from a diversion of some aggressive wishes away from his father and, through moral rules, toward himself. In return, the parents accept the boy as a member of their ethical world. At the same time, the boy also sublimates aggressive wishes into efforts to establish a sense of industry, whereby he will direct his aggression toward objects of work, rather than toward his father.

This challenge continues throughout work life. A man must channel his aggression toward work materials, rather than unconscious substitutes for his father or the mother whom he failed to win away from the father. Otherwise, involuntary father- or mother-substitutes are likely to strike back. Hence, aggression must be monitored and tempered by appropriate caring for others.

Thus, organizational entry requires at least minimal caring for new colleagues. Insofar as joining involves developing amicable relations, it inherently satisfies some libidinal wishes. Work that involves social relations also offers satisfaction. With libido, as with aggression, a new worker faces the challenge of expressing related impulses appropriately.

With sexuality, just as aggression, the roots of adult wishes are formed much earlier. An infant has his first love affair with the nurturant mother. As he psychologically and physically separates from the mother, the child creates "internal" images of her that substitute for her when she is gone and that may continue to be objects of affection. Subsequently, the child's most intense romance is with the Oedipal parent. Libidinal resolution of the Oedipal conflict requires the child to accept his secondary status in the parents' affections and to begin to care more specifically for peers. Thus, first experiments include what Sullivan (1953) calls relations with "chums" and usually continue with heterosexual relations in adolescence. Adult romantic success entails finding an acceptable substitute for the original Oedipal object. Regardless of whether adults marry, they may continue to think of others as potential romantic objects, or as substitutes for the Oedipal parent.

The challenge at work is to feel and act affectionately enough toward others to develop successful working relations but to limit one's libidinal aims so as not to disrupt relations among people who must collaborate. An office romance, for example, arouses jealousies among those who are excluded, and it is nearly impossible to redefine a failed romantic relationship as "only" collegial.[11] In this context, keeping the aggressive task requirements in mind helps order one's efforts.

ENTERING AN ORGANIZATION:
PERSONAL IDENTITY AND SELF-INITIATION

Becoming a member of a work organization requires two unconscious negotiations. Generally, a worker must try to get the greatest support for the development of his identity consistent with what organizational veterans demand and offer. As part of this process, the worker must sublimate aggressive and libidinal wishes sufficiently to be effective but accepted by colleagues.

Compromises are worked out in concrete relations with coworkers. Chapter 3 described veterans' demands of new workers and ritual efforts to get them to make concessions. This chapter examines newcomers' efforts to anticipate and to control these negotiations, in order to *initiate themselves* on favorable terms. This section looks at how concerns about identity development shape self-initiation, and the next looks at sublimation's requirements for self-initiation.

Organizational veterans submit new workers to a three-stage ritual, in which they attempt to strip neophytes of their prior identity and to impose a new one. Job leavers provide examples of those who do not accept these terms and leave because they cannot negotiate any other. How do newcomers negotiate with organizations?

At least unconsciously, new workers recognize veterans' intentions to alter their identity. In response, they unconsciously plan a self-initiation to secure their identity while accommodating the veterans. In designing this self-initiation, new workers draw on the earliest model in human experience for managing an identity transition: the steps of separation and individuation through which the infant develops an identity distinct from the mother. This psychological process consists of four stages, which parallel in structure and aims the three social stages of organizational initiation. What differs, as the following discussion shows, is newcomers' intentions to determine the outcome of the transition. Thus, negotiations over entry consist of competing unconscious efforts to establish and control multistage initiation rituals.

The Model of Separation and Individuation

Adulthood initiation into formal organizations is a complex phenomenon that different people experience differently. As a transition, however, it recapitulates a universal life experience, beginning with birth itself. Erikson's developmental framework emphasizes the centrality of transitions to growth, in which progress requires passing from success at one task to uncertainty at another. In the first transition, the infant, after having assured himself that the world is basically trustworthy, must struggle to establish his autonomy in it. Unconsciously, experiences in this transition form a model for anticipating and managing subsequent tests in developing a personal identity. Hence, when adults enter a work organization and confront challenges to their work ability, work identity, and organizational affiliation, they unconsciously draw on what they learned earlier.

For infants, transition, which involves leaving a relationship (even though as a step toward entering another), arouses anxiety about being abandoned, losing a parent's love, and, consequently, being annihilated.[12] In the first transition an infant can have no memory of past success or confidence of any in the present. When adults encounter transitions, they unconsciously remember the first infantile transition and experience anxiety associated with that situation.[13] Thus, adults unconsciously assess the risks of organizational entry in the context of these earlier experiences. In addition, they attempt to manage contemporary transitions and their anticipated anxiety in ways that succeeded earlier.[14]

Mahler, Pine, and Bergman (1975) have studied the infant's first transitional experience, which they characterize as a process of separation and individuation. Beginning in the first year, the infant, impelled by biological and social developments, attempts to separate from a close symbiotic relationship with the mother and to establish an individual identity. This change amounts to a rebirth, in which the infant goes from being an ambiguous part of a one-person entity (infant-mother) to establishing a two-person relationship (infant and mother). The infant's psychic, cognitive, and physical immaturity means that he carries out the project at the time of his greatest vulnerability. Hence the episode, which extends over approximately two years, strongly affects all subsequent ideas about relationships, changes in them, dangers in transitions, and the possibilities of new relationships.

Success requires that the infant move from considering himself one with the mother to recognizing the mother as a separate object, or person, and substituting "internal" objects—images or ideas—for the mother and the lost relationship with her. This process goes through four stages.

First, the infant must cognitively, emotionally, and physically begin to *differentiate* himself from the mother. This beginning separation arouses tremendous anxiety, for the infant gives up what he has experienced as the foundation of existence with nothing definite to replace it. For example, when the infant experiences himself as one with the mother, feeding is a certainty; once the infant sees the mother as separate, nurturance becomes a question for which the new relationship may or may not provide a satisfactory answer.

Hence the next phase, which may overlap the first, involves the infant *practicing* being on his own. He experiments with distinguishing his body from the mother's and with establishing a specific bond with this separate person. From these tests the infant begins to develop an autonomous ego, with which he begins to regulate his relations with others so as to preserve himself in the social world.[15]

Following this, a third phase entails *rapprochement* between the individuating infant and the mother. This is a period of resolving a basic ambivalence: the infant wants to become still more an individual but fears to lose his previous identity with the mother. He vacillates between being separate and the same, being distant and close. Gradually, the infant begins to find security in new ways of relating to the mother, even while hesitating to give up the earlier accustomed safety. *Hi* succeeds *bye-bye* as the infant's most important word. Recognition of others makes this the beginning of true social interaction. The infant's ambivalence reaches its peak in a "rapprochement crisis," out of which comes an individual solution regarding the relationship with the mother.

In a final phase, the developing child *consolidates* his individuality. This means elaborating social relations and ideas about them to be more consistent and realistic. Doing this requires at least unconsciously reconciling conflicting perceptions and impulses. For example, the child comes to find that other persons are neither completely good nor completely bad, not totally lovable or totally hateful. Just as the child sees himself differentiated from the mother, he can find that individuals have many aspects within them.[16]

An infant can succeed at these tasks if two conditions prevail. First, he must design his own solutions to the problems of how to separate from the mother and how to relate as a separate individual to her. The alternative, individuality designed and enforced by a parent, is self-contradictory. However, the infant can differentiate and individuate itself only with the mother's responsive support. She encourages separation without imposing it and is available to accept the infant's tests without being hurt by them or going away. Paradoxically, while assisting the infant in separating, she must let him regard his particular course as his own choice.[17]

Implications for Organizational Entry

From unconscious memories of success at this first transition, an adult draws inferences regarding the encounter with a work organization, which also demands an identity change. He assumes that the episode will proceed through ordered stages. In addition, he expects the contemporary transition to allow him to experiment with new and old identities before taking a new role.

These conclusions are evident in studies of other adulthood role transitions, where people follow a model resembling the infantile separation and individuation stages. Ebaugh (1988), for example, describes the process of role exit, whereby people voluntarily leave accustomed roles to assume new ones defined primarily in terms of the absence of the former role. She has studied, among others, ex-nuns, retirees, ex-cons, widows, alumni, transsexuals, and ex-doctors. Role exiting is a social and psychological process analogous to becoming an organizational member—willingly giving up a previous role and accepting a new one. In the end, the new work role is not considered simply the absence or opposite of the earlier one, although the first stage of initiation emphasizes the negation of the prior role as a condition for entry.

Ebaugh observes that people leaving roles go through four stages in taking a new role. These stages correspond to those of separation and individuation. (1) "First doubts" about keeping a role are analogous to the differentiation phase. (2) "Seeking alternatives," experimenting with new ways of acting, is similar to practicing. (3) "The turning point," the moment when someone decides leaving is right, corresponds to the rapprochement phase and its crisis. (4) "Creating the ex-role," by putting elements of new behavior, dress, and speech into a coherent role, is like the consolidation phase. These stages follow a logic of change: people do not give up security until they have somewhere else to go.

Cooper and Gustafson (1981) have studied how organizational members attempt to create roles that fit their personal plans, or work intentions. They find that relations among workers follow an unconscious process similar to the separation and individuation that Mahler, Pine, and Bergman described. Individuals begin by tentatively differentiating their plan from those of others, next practicing ways of carrying it out, then experimenting with large and small behavioral innovations before coming to rapprochement with others on a role, and, finally, consolidating it.

They observe that, just as infants play with alternative mental images and social relations with the mother, adult workers play with alternative conceptions and realities of roles and relations with colleagues. The following excerpt from a consultation with a mental health organization illustrates this process:

> From a *planning* point of view [i.e., the perspective that individuals unconsciously seek to implement plans in their social relations], what happened next was quite fascinating. Planning hypotheses would predict that individuals really could not tolerate prolonged states without some developmentally progressive steps being taken. But since the work situation had so thoroughly deteriorated, individuals began to reorient themselves within their work roles to

seek other avenues for their individual development. During this period, for instance, one individual decided to pursue further mental-health training, another quit the job to follow a private-practice career, yet another willingly took on service responsibilities in other parts of the mental-health system that had a future, and another individual considered a complete career change. Absenteeism and illness increased. Whenever possible, individual plans were pursued in the job context: if, for whatever reason, individuals could not manage to incorporate their individual plans in the job, new careers were pursued—in fact or fantasy. (Cooper and Gustafson 1981:717)

Here, too, there is a simple logic of change: as people try to create satisfying roles, they make use of whatever materials are available. They search on the job first and look elsewhere if necessary.

These studies show how adults changing social roles unconsciously follow a model derived from the first transition of infancy. Significantly, the phases of the infant's separation and individuation parallel the stages of organizational initiation. (1) The differentiation phase is analogous to the initial confrontation (the separation stage of rites of passage), in separating the individual from old attachments. (2) Practicing and rapprochement match the working through (the transitional stage), where the individual tries out new ways of acting, to see which may feel right, be effective, and meet with others' approval. (3) Consolidation is like integrating (the incorporation stage) and what follows: everyone agrees on the individual's new ways of being and acting. Figure 3 summarizes these correspondences.

Figure 3. Correspondences Between Self-initiation and Social Initiation Stages

Self-initiation	Social Initiation	
Separation-Individuation	Organizational Socialization	Rite of Passage
I. Differentiation	I. Initial confrontation	I. Separation
II. Practicing	II. Working through	II. Transition
III. Rapprochement		
IV. Consolidation	III. Integrating	III. Incorporation

These similarities suggest a hypothesis about the unconscious meaning of veterans' actions in social initiations. They may tacitly organize initiations in three stages because the order repeats (their unconscious memories of) the mother's action in helping the infant separate and differentiate itself earlier.

At the least, the parallelism between newcomers' plans for self-initiation and veterans' plans for initiating them reinforces the order of events in organizational socialization. The crucial source of conflict, as job leavers' complaints register, is that each party wants the initiation to promote its interests. Veterans expect new workers to change identities while taking on a new role. New workers expect to retain and consolidate their identities, changing only in ways that advance their personal development.

In addition, new workers' unconscious memories of the mother's role in infancy encourages them to expect supervisors to act in specific ways during organizational entry. Generally, they expect veterans to allow them to have sufficient control over their roles that accepting a role feels like a free choice. They do not want veterans to impose predesigned roles on them, and they expect veterans to respond supportively as they attempt to test and negotiate working relationships. If these expectations are not met, new workers will react in ways related to how they might have responded in infancy.

Unconsciously, they will think of themselves partly as infants unable to control or establish appropriate social roles. Feeling such impotence in adulthood is likely not only to puzzle them but also to enrage them — why can't they do the (seemingly) simplest things?[18] Superimposition of this unconscious anger on realistic frustration at the requirements of socialization compounds the intellectual and emotional complexity of joining a work organization. Furthermore, insofar as newcomers act on these unconscious assumptions, they will be ineffective in satisfying veterans' expectations of adult workers.

This understanding of the infantile separation and individuation process teaches two lessons about organizational initiation. First, new workers attempt to initiate themselves in ways that advance their personal identity while avoiding annihilation by the organization. The structure of newcomers' self-initiation parallels and reinforces the stages of organizational socialization, but the aims are diametrically opposed: to persevere, and not be dominated. Second, although veterans appear to be the more powerful negotiating partner in organizational entry, new workers' unconscious expectations present a potent "take-it-or-leave-it" position. If veterans simply compel a new worker to take an organizational role, the newcomer may unconsciously react with impotence, anxiety, and anger that make him incapable of being effective in the role. An organizational victory by force is illusory.

Both lessons suggest that many of the "socialization failures" reported in the sociological and managerial literature on organizational entry are not accidental, nor are they the result of any simple "mismatch" between an individual and an organization. Instead, they reflect the outcome of a complex, largely unconscious, always self-interested negotiation between an organization that wants to preserve its integrity and individuals who want to preserve theirs.

ENTERING AN ORGANIZATION: SUBLIMATION AND SELF-INITIATION

A newcomer entering an organization must not only reach terms on how his identity may develop, but, as part of this, must also compromise on ways of acting aggressively and libidinally. Young persons first develop sublimations during latency, between the Oedipal conflict and adolescence,[19] and their choices set patterns for the rest of their lives. For example, they may unconsciously direct aggressive wishes into becoming surgeons, or they may transform erotic wishes into a generalized solicitude for others. In addition, new situations throughout people's lives challenge the direction or the expression of their original sublimations and raise questions about whether the old solutions will be acceptable under new conditions. Thus, people normally attempt to sublimate aggressive or libidinal wishes when they encounter situations where their accustomed expressions of these wishes are impossible or imprudent.

Entering a work organization presents significant challenges in this respect. Membership entails making compromises between the aggressiveness required to do tasks; the libidinality needed to get along with colleagues; the everyday conditions under which people collaborate and get work done; and personal moral norms about aggressiveness, libidinality, and work relations. Thus an entrant must find ways of acting aggressively and caringly that both fit in the organization and do not violate his conscience.

Sublimation is an internal, intrapsychic, negotiation through which someone unconsciously looks for such compromises. This negotiation follows three stages.

(1) It is set into motion when the individual experiences a conflict between libidinal or aggressive wishes (or both) and moral norms expressed by the superego. In particular, the individual confronts a guilty "reproach" from the superego: how could he want to act so aggressively, for example, when he must know that doing so would harm others?

(2) The individual still seeks some way of expressing the forbidden wishes. He may begin by promoting the original wishes more aggressively, but he will probably find the superego unrelenting. Eventually, the reality-oriented ego tries to mediate the conflict between the aggressive or libidinal wishes and the superego, to find ideas or actions that will satisfy these wishes in the outer world without offending the moral strictures of the conscience.

(3) When a compromise is found, sublimation is successful. The original wishes may be less biologically driven and more cognitively mediated, less directly aimed toward somatic satisfactions and more adapted to socially defined objects, less urgent—and yet still unconsciously related to the original aims. The individual may express his original wishes to attack or love, for example, in socially acceptable ways and, therefore, without fear of punishment or guilt.[20] In short, the individual succeeds in taking active control of a situation where before he was passively constrained.

The stages of the mental process of sublimation are analogous to those of the social process of organizational initiation. (1) The conflict between aggressive or libidinal wishes and moral norms is similar to the initial confrontation, where veterans refuse to let a newcomer continue to pursue old aims. (2) The search for compromise among the wishes, reality, and conscience corresponds to the open testing and negotiations of the working through. (3) The selection of a compromise matches integrating: acceptance and enactment of a new role.

There are good reasons for these similarities. Sublimation is the newcomer's private, mental, largely unconscious response to veterans' public, social, largely visible challenge. As part of their terms for entry, they are asking a new worker not simply to change identity in some general way, but also to renounce some specific ways of acting aggressively or libidinally. Two examples below will illustrate how sublimation issues shape initiations. Thus, the three-stage unconscious sublimation process, set in motion by the initial confrontation, is a realistic response to veterans' demands. A newcomer then attempts to work through this process to find a successful sublimation. The major test is the second stage of socialization and sublimation, where each side tries to dominate or deceive the other.

In addition, the stages of sublimation resemble those of separation and individuation. (1) The conflict between wishes and moral norms is like the infant's conclusion that it can no longer be one with the mother and must begin to differentiate itself. (2) The search for compromise corresponds to practicing and rapprochement. (3) The selection of a compromise is like consolidation.

The two processes, originating in different periods of life in response to different crises, are structurally similar because they share a developmental logic. When old ways of being no longer suffice or succeed, individuals experiment with new ideas about themselves and others, new actions, and new relationships until they find ways of continuing to be themselves in a changed world. The activities of separation and individuation are a negotiation over personal identity, while those of sublimation are a negotiation over libidinal and aggressive wishes. The structure of these negotiations matches that of organizational socialization. Not only does a newcomer's unconscious method of resolving issues of identity and libidinal or aggressive wishes reinforce the structure of social-ization activities set forth by veterans, but these two unconscious processes realistically fit the negotiations of the transitional, working through, stage of initiation. Where veterans overtly try to convert new workers, the newcomers look for ways around the veterans.

Figure 4. Correspondences Between Stages of Sublimation, Organizational Socialization, and Separation and Individuation

Sublimation	Organizational Socialization	Separation and Individuation
I. Conflict between wishes, reality, and conscience	I. Initial confrontation	I. Differentiation
II. Search for compromise	II. Working through	II. Practicing
		III. Rapprochement
III. Sublimation	III. Integrating	IV. Consolidation

A worker's original sublimation experiences affect him at organiza-tional entry in two ways. First, they provide a model of a successful three-stage process for resolving differences with others whom he loves or needs but who are powerful and potentially dangerous. At the same time, the experiences shape assumptions about those others, such as organizational veterans. For example, if early sublimation efforts were successful, newcomers may expect that supervisors and other members of the organizational "family" want to reach a compromise that enables the newcomers to become part of the organizational moral community. Moreover, they will expect veterans to give the caring help in finding compromises that they experienced earlier in their own families.

Two examples from other cultures illustrate how veterans' and neo-phytes' concerns about aggression and libido can influence and appear in initiation activities. Poole (1982) describes an initiation ceremony among the Bimin-Kuskusmin, in New Guinea, and tells how the older men teach the younger to express their aggression in acceptable adult ways. In the early phases of the ceremony the men subject the youths to considera-ble physical and emotional abuse. The young men react with growing anxiety and then anger. These activities, Poole says, are intended to elicit aggression that later phases can formally direct into approved social roles. "Eventually, after later initiations [ritual phases], the boys' trauma of ritual violence is ideally converted into the adult aggressive behaviors of warriors, husbands, and ultimately [ritual] initiators" (Poole 1982:150).

Schieffelin (1982), reports on the *bau a* of the Kaluli, also of New Guinea. He describes a collective self-initiation, in which young men demonstrate their sublimation of aggressive and libidinal wishes. In a first stage, the men introduce the initiates to the *bau a* hunting lodge. In a second stage, the youths perform actions that reveal their ambivalence regarding how aggressively or sexually they may act. During the ensuing drama the youths show that aggression leads to hunting, and that sexuality leads to marriage with a stone goddess, symbolic of their own later marital partners. In these ways, they demonstrate their sublimation of dangerous wishes and do the transitional work of initiation themselves. In a final ritual stage they return to the world of adult men with offers of an alliance.

These examples show initiation ceremonies that have been designed to help entrants sublimate aggressive and libidinal wishes. The second example shows neophytes who understand this requirement and organize their own initiation to manage the transition on their own terms.[21] Recognizing the inevitable, they turn their passive plight into an active ceremony. Although New Guinea manhood rituals and modern organizational socializations are different in many ways, they share initiatory purposes and structure. The examples are helpful because New Guineans' explicit aims in their initiations suggest some of the unconscious meanings of organizational socialization for contemporary workers.

In any society negotiations over aggression and libido depend on both the range of available social roles and initiates' developmental demands. This examination of sublimation offers two lessons about organizational socialization. First, when new workers experience organizational socialization as a demand for sublimation of aggressive or libidinal wishes, they unconsciously plan a self-initiation that follows the stages of earlier sublimatory successes. This effort reinforces the order of veterans' initiation efforts, but it also gives newcomers special expectations about the outcome of the initiation: they want to be able to find compromises that satisfy not only the veterans, as representatives of organizational reality and morality, but also themselves, as human beings wishing to act aggressively and libidinally toward other people in the world.

The second lesson is that successful initiation depends on veterans giving newcomers the opportunity to find their own ways of expressing these wishes in organizational roles. If veterans think of themselves as only the crudest voices of organizational "reality" or "morality," they will fail to provide the caring that encourages an entrant to seek a compromise in good faith. The result will be a "socialization failure" that may vindicate the organization but lose a potentially productive worker.

PLAY IN SELF-TREATMENT AND SELF-INITIATION

The common themes in the preceding discussions of personal identity and sublimation are injury and self-treatment. Workers approach organizations aiming to advance their personal identity and to express libidinal and aggressive wishes in certain ways, and they experience the demands and constraints of socialization as injuries. In response, they prepare self-initiations to treat themselves for these injuries and to gain entry.

In order to understand the injury that organizational newcomers experience, it is helpful to examine the psychoanalytic concept of "trauma." Freud (1977 [1920]) established its original meaning as an experience in which the ego, as the mental link to reality, is overwhelmed and unable to act. He thought of infantile and early childhood relations with parents as the locus for trauma and argued that a situation could be traumatic as a result of either an overpowering external event or an irresistibly strong libidinal impulse. However, after observing the emotional toll of World War I on returning soldiers, he acknowledged that many situations, including some in adulthood, could be traumatic. His enlargement of the concept encouraged subsequent expansion to include a variety of upsetting experiences.[22]

Regardless of whether trauma is narrowly or broadly conceived, it is not inherent in any specific objectively measured event, but refers to an individual's experience, or interpretation, of an event. Similar situations may affect different persons differently, depending on such things as their developmental position, their ability to cope with the situation, others' responses to the situation, and related past experiences. Trauma may block further development or stimulate growth. For example, although Erikson does not speak of trauma, each of his developmental stages presents traumatic experiences to a growing person, who finds that accustomed abilities are ineffective and that he must give up secure ways of acting in order to learn to meet new challenges. The tests of each new stage confront a personal identity traumatically, and yet the conditions of each stage also stimulate the growing individual to render the experience benign and developmental.

Thus, a collision between a new worker's organizational expectations and veterans' demands and offerings may mean different things to different individuals. For some, as examples in the following chapters illustrate, the conflict may be as traumatic as anything Freud had in mind, and they may not recover from their initial confrontation to take an effective work role. Others, as examples also show, may feel injured by early disappointments with an organization but still manage to assess their situation realistically and get all or some of what they originally wanted. The term *injury* will be used for this range of initial experiences, some of which may be traumatic. *Trauma* will be reserved for overwhelming experiences.

People may respond to injury in two ways. The first is *repression*, where they push thoughts of the experience from consciousness and attempt to act as if it had never occurred.[23] At best, repression is a partially successful defense against an injurious experience. On the one hand, superficially, someone succeeds in "forgetting" what took place. Still, unconsciously, this person remembers the injury, associates it with a variety of other thoughts, and then attempts to avoid thinking about those related matters or acting in any way that evokes them. As a result, this person will narrow his mental and social world by tacitly ruling these dangerous areas "off limits."

Play

Alternatively, people may attempt to confront and learn from an injury through *play*. The structure and aim of play are repetition: play repeats a passively suffered injurious experience in a symbolic way that permits active mastery of it (Waelder 1933; Peller 1954; Klein 1976; and Freud 1977 [1920]). "Making passive into active"—this "reversal of voice" (Klein 1976)—offers the opportunity to contain and compensate for the anxiety suffered in social relations.[24] Play is an *intention*, an attempt to master something injurious. Whether it has the joyful quality conventionally associated with "play" depends on its success. Play that succeeds is pleasurable because it brings relief from the remembered injury by mastering it.[25]

Originally, infants play to deal with the anxiety of separation from the mother. Winnicott (1953) characterizes the prototypical play object (e.g., a blanket or teddy bear) as a "transitional object." The object has two important characteristics. First, substantively, for the infant it is a symbol of the relationship with the mother.[26] Thus, in manipulating the physical object an infant unconsciously can try out different relations with the mother, experimenting with a transition from symbiosis to separateness.[27] By holding it, picking it up, and putting it aside, the infant attempts to make sense of, gain control over, and become more comfortable with the disturbing physical and emotional separation from the mother.

Second, although the object is the infant's first possession, it has an ambiguous ontological status and location. To the infant the object seems neither fully separate nor wholly part of himself. The object itself is in transition between the original state where infant and mother both seem one and a world where they are separate. When the infant manipulates the object, the infant is in transition. Playing with an object that is not part of himself, not part of the mother, somehow part of their relationship lets the infant (with the mother's collusion) avoid answering the question whether they are one or two until he can develop a secure separate identity in relation to her.

Thus, the substance and the function of the transitional object are linked to one another and to the problem the infant is trying to solve. Playing with a transitional object enables him to manage the emotional dangers of moving apart from the mother by creating images of her that can substitute for her in "internal," mental, relationships when she is physically absent.

Later in life, children and adults engage in play for similar reasons. Only the content of play, the nature of transitional objects, changes, to fit the growing complexity of the inner world and the external environment (Peller 1954; and Erikson 1977). For example, instead of playing with teddy bears, adults usually play with abstract ideas or interpersonal relationships. Some of these activities are more conscious than the infant's play, but many are similarly unconscious, and all involve efforts to manage and control something troubling.

Three aspects of play are important in considering how organizational members may playfully respond to the injury of initiation. First, the forms and purposes of play are similar to those of rituals. Both are concerned with enabling someone to move from an unacceptable (e.g., obsolete, dangerous, or injured) status into a desirable one. Both deal with the problem of removing a person from an old role and enabling that person to enter a new one. In rituals the transitional stage makes this change possible by permitting an individual stripped of prior ties to negotiate new relationships with a collectivity.

In play the transitional object performs a similar function by allowing experimentation with relationships. An individual may act simultaneously as if old relations both have been severed and continue and as if new relations are being established and yet are not necessary. At the moment the player can securely enact new relations with others, the transitional object and play are no longer necessary. Thus play can be considered an individually designed ritual.[28]

Important implications of this connection rest on a second characteristic of play: it is intentional, planful (even if usually unconscious), problem solving. This deliberateness of play is inherent in its conception as repetition (Waelder 1933; Peller 1954; Klein 1976; and Freud 1977 [1920]). The problem-solving intentions of play are evident in a variety of settings. In psychoanalysis, patients unconsciously play with their analysts to resolve traumatic problems (Winnicott 1971; and Weiss, Sampson, and the Mount Zion Psychotherapy Group 1986). In group therapy, people play with one another to plan actions that help individuals solve unconscious problems (Gustafson and Cooper 1979).[29] In organizations, members unconsciously play to solve individual or collective problems, ranging from how individuals can securely become members to how organizations can improve productivity (Cooper and Gustafson 1981; and Hirschhorn and Krantz 1982).

Thus organizational recruits, at least unconsciously anticipating changes demanded in entry, unconsciously play with expected dangers by designing their own initiations. These rituals, dealing with the anxiety of losing old connections to gain new ones, follow the pattern of the first play activities, in separation and individuation, just described. The playful actions of the self-initiation can be seen as a response to the steps of the organizational socialization.

In the *initial confrontation* (I),[30] veterans show the new worker that accepting an organizational role will require giving up a comfortable familiar identity. Thus the role is a source of injury. As such, it becomes both a reason and the material for compensatory and reparative play. Literally, the new worker engages in "role play." Accordingly, in the *differentiation* stage of the playful self-initiation, the newcomer begins to think about the organizational role in ambiguous ways. He may imagine taking a new role, but one that lets him join the organization without endangering his old identity.

In the *working through* (II), veterans insist that the new worker actively follow them in trying out the responsibilities, authority, and accountability of an organizational role. In response, the newcomer creates a transitional object, in the *practicing* stage of the self-initiation. This transitional object is highly abstract—the organizational role itself. The newcomer imagines—mentally picks up, manipulates, examines, and puts down—a variety of roles that might permit him to join the organization without losing connection to his past identity. He tries out pieces of these roles in reality, to see how coworkers react. At this point, the new worker thinks about a role that permits him both to take on an organizational role and yet not really be contained in the role.[31]

Practicing leads to efforts at *rapprochement*, in which the new member tries to settle on and in a real role that is comfortable enough to him and acceptable to new colleagues. He revises his mental images of an organizational role while he adjusts his social relationships, to see how closely he can make the real organizational role fit his transitional role. When the newcomer is satisfied the two are close enough, he will relinquish the transitional role. In other words, when a new member feels he can depend on others to accept his individuality, he will embrace a relationship with them and let go of at least some past connections.

In *integrating* (III), veterans endorse the new worker's arrival in an organizational role. In the *consolidation* of the self-initiation, the new member establishes personal signs or symbols of being settled in place. The correspondence between stages of organizational initiation and self-initiation, again, are summarized in figure 3.

This is how successful self-initiatory play takes place. At any point, a newcomer may feel insecure and refuse to go ahead. For example, he may be unable to imagine a transitional role that helps move from an identity outside the organization to membership inside. In such a case, the organizational socialization becomes a source of still further injury. In turn, the new member may attempt to play to repair or compensate for this injury. This play will follow the structure just described, although the content will be more complex.

Self-initiatory play, as the examples in the first two chapters indicate, may go on for years, manifesting itself in much of what observers call "informal" roles and activities.[32] The specific content of play depends on several factors, including the new worker's personality, the actual socialization circumstances, and relations among veterans.

Here a third characteristic of play—its developmental variability— is important.

Play as a Developmental Activity

Play takes different forms and involves different themes at different stages of development. The infant's use of a teddy bear and the adult's hypothetical ideas about an organizational role are both examples of play with transitional objects, but they differ obviously in substance and meaning.

In identifying different types of play with different developmental stages, Erikson (1977) emphasizes the intentionality of play. He accepts the traditional psychoanalytic view that play is an effort to repeat and overcome past injuries, but he adds that people want to work through injuries in ways enabling them to resolve current developmental dilemmas. Thus as people confront new challenges, their play changes.

Infants play, as already noted, to develop a sense of basic trust in a world in which they are separate from the mother (1). Adult workers experience related concerns for getting supervisors' recognition, acquiring responsibility, and working out reciprocal role relations. An initial confrontation with an organization may threaten workers' security in these matters either because they have never come to feel basic trust in the world (and it is a general issue for them), because the initiation specifically puts the trustworthiness of the world in question, or both. In any of these cases, their play will focus on challenging supervisors and other veterans to recognize them and to assign significant responsibility.

Young children play to secure their autonomy from shame and doubt (2), and adult organizational counterparts are establishing autonomy and authority. If organizational initiations leave new members without guarantees of authority, they will play to get it. For example, they may subvert supervisors' assignments or challenge their evaluations in order to assert their independence.

Older children play to resolve the conflict between initiative and guilt (3). Their play involves contrived dramas, in which a coherent plot goes through conflicting turns before finding an acceptable resolution. Adult workers may look similarly for ways of taking initiative without being punished. New members who feel the organization denies them this possibility may devise roles in "dramas" to create space for guilt-free actions.

Latency age children play to establish a sense of industry (4). Their play centers on organized games, through which participants discover successful methods of following rules to goals. Adult workers may share concerns about learning and using effective techniques. Those who feel their organizations deny them the opportunity to work competently may invent side-games in which they can use their skills.

Adolescents play to establish a distinct identity by experimenting with meaning (5). Adult workers who feel the organization does not give them a meaningful work role may challenge veterans to prove that their procedures make sense. For example, new workers may push supervisors to clarify ambiguous roles and show what they "really" mean.

Late adolescents play to develop intimacy by experimenting with different affiliations (6). Adult workers who feel initiation does not really connect them with supportive colleagues may play to establish intimacy. For example, new members may create or volunteer for groups with the primary aim of socializing.

Adults normally play to enact generational relations with others (7) and to establish the integrity of their lives (8). Organizational expressions of these aims include mentoring newcomers and advising others how to do things. If organizations do not give senior workers formal opportunities to do these things, they may create informal possibilities through play, for example, by adopting new members or by advising others on how to organize their careers.

Outcomes of Self-initiation Efforts

As workers approaching organizations play to initiate themselves, three types of encounter are possible. First, the newcomer may readily fit and respond to organizational demands, and veterans successfully initiate him. In this event, self-initiation activities are congruent with, and reinforce, the organizational socialization.

Second, a new worker may hold expectations that conflict with those of the organization, but he may successfully initiate himself into the organization. The new member may change sufficiently to satisfy veterans' initiation requirements but may also get them to change their expectations. In this common negotiation, the two parties gradually reconcile their role demands.

Third, the worker and the organization may want incompatible things, and neither can successfully work out entry. Self-initiation is impossible, and the newcomer may either become a socially and emotionally marginal employee or leave.

These encounters may lead to three different statuses and relationships with an organization. Newcomers who fail to negotiate satisfaction of their developmental work needs but do not leave are, simply, *employees*.

Those who succeed in finding responses to their developmental needs in work organizations, who easily or with effort initiate themselves, can be considered *members*. We may speak of their actions in terms of "joining," "entering," or "becoming part of" an organization, or just "becoming members."

Some of those who negotiate entry do so around the expectation of organizational affiliation, a wish for intimacy. They not only feel part of the organization, but they belong to the organization in the ambiguous sense that each is part of, and has claims on, the other. They feel close to coworkers and identify with organizational management or purposes. They are emotionally attached not just to individuals but to the collectivity. If these people have no unsatisfied work expectations, they are *members with intimacy*. We may speak of their relationship with the organization as "affiliation," "intimacy," "attachment," "identification," "belonging," or "feeling part of" it.

Members without intimacy have greater ties to the organization than do employees, but both identify with personal aims or outside groups more than with the workplace. If employees or members develop interests in affiliation and successfully negotiate satisfaction of these and expectations, they may become members with intimacy.

A PATH TO HAPPINESS
AND THE NATURAL HUMAN AVERSION TO WORK

Freud (1962 [1930]) believed that work has manifest benefits for both society and the individual. It contributes to economic production, and, by focusing energy on concrete, cooperative tasks, it binds individuals to a social order. When Freud wrote of work, he used the language of biological drives, and he praised its advantages in terms of sublimation:

No other technique for the conduct of life attaches the individual so firmly to reality as laying emphasis on work: for his work at least gives him a secure place in a portion of reality, in the human community. The possibility it offers of displacing a large amount of libidinal components, whether narcissistic, aggressive or even erotic, on to professional work and on to the human relations connected with it lends it a value by no means second to what it enjoys as something indispensable to the preservation and justification of existence in society. Professional activity is a source of special satisfaction if it is a freely chosen one—if, that is to say, by means of sublimation, it makes possible the use of existing inclinations, of persisting or constitutionally reinforced instinctual impulses. (1962 [1930]:27n)

"And yet," Freud immediately continues,

as a path to happiness, work is not highly prized by men. They do not strive after it as they do after other possibilities of satisfaction. The great majority of people only work under the stress of necessity, and this natural human aversion to work raises most difficult social problems. (1962 [1930]:27n)

When Freud characterizes work as "a path to happiness," he refers to work's best possibilities: putting oneself into making things that others appreciate. When he speaks of a "natural human aversion to work," he acknowledges that joining an organization, for work as for anything else, is always a compromise of something essential. Some people successfully, even uneventfully, become members of work organizations. Perhaps they are especially fortunate in finding places that accommodate them. Perhaps they can compromise without feeling they give up anything vital. Perhaps, the keen observer might find, they achieve peace with their organization by battling it symbolically elsewhere. Even when entry is successful, and especially when it is not, it is clearly a more complex and uncertain drama than the sociological models imply.

As psychoanalysis shows, organizational socialization is not the conflict-free learning process those models depict. An adult is hardly a *tabula rasa*, and few of the salient meanings of organizational membership are conscious. Although the term "socialization" connotes a gradual, benign induction of new members, in fact, adult workers normally regard themselves as already socialized, and they treat organizational entry as a subject for negotiation.

Moreover—and this is an important psychoanalytic contribution—workers (largely) unconsciously plan to initiate themselves into organizations. In the process, they try to use organizations to promote their personal development. The conflict in organizational entry comes from newcomers' sense that organizations' conditions for membership are not consistent with their growth. Workers know these things and will tell them to anyone who cares to listen.

The next two sections of the book relate workers' stories of their encounters with organizations. Part 3 describes people who, by and large, end up finding work a path to happiness. Part 4 looks at people who have difficulty overcoming an aversion to work in their organizations.

Part Three
Trying to Grow at Work

Becoming a Member:
Looking for Work Ability, Work Identity,
and Organizational Affiliation

A recent survey of American workers found that they want the following things in work: interesting activity; appropriate help and equipment; proper information; enough authority to get the job done; opportunity to develop special abilities; job security; and seeing the results of their work efforts (U.S. Department of Health, Education, and Welfare 1973). These responses are typical of such surveys (compare, e.g., Yankelovich and Immerwahr 1983). These common desires are the "work" expectations[1] of work ability (4) and work identity (5).

These preferences are not surprising. To the contrary, they seem obvious, common sense. Yet it is important to analyze why they are so widespread and why they seem to be so inherently reasonable. Part of the explanation is that, by definition, work involves work ability, doing a job. Managers and workers expect it. The connection is tautological.

However, a "work identity" is not so simply a part of working. More than having a job title, it means thinking of oneself as a particular type of worker, being regarded by others as a worker—these are complex psychological demands for special social relationships. To someone whose work is "only a job"—using his work ability without feeling invested in the effort or its products—such expectations certainly seem extra. A work identity is not intrinsic to a job in an organization. Rather, this expectation involves personal needs that extend beyond work—specifically, developmental needs.

Both work ability and work identity seem "naturally" related to work in part because they express developmental concerns that are prominent when people take their first jobs. At one of the few times in people's lives when they think explicitly about what they want from work and perhaps make deliberate job choices, securing a sense of industry and consolidating an identity are important aims. As a result, even after people have succeeded at these tasks and move on to seek other rewards from the workplace, they still most easily associate it with work ability and work identity.

Another reason why workers commonly voice these expectations is because they are unconsciously linked to another interest: becoming a member of an organization, affiliating with it, becoming close to coworkers (6). Developmentally, work ability and work identity must precede the intimacy of identifying with an organization and colleagues. At the time when people begin work and consider what they want from it, most think about joining an organization in only a formal way—getting a paycheck and benefits. They are not ready for closer attachments.

However, intimacy is part of normal development. People want organizations to help with work ability and work identity not just for any financial gains, but because they are part of a lifelong development effort. These two organizational expectations are stages in a strategy eventually to join an organization intimately—to become close to colleagues and to identify with collective actions and purposes.

The sociological literature supports this psychoanalytic view of organizational affiliation, which sociologists think of in terms of "organizational commitment." It involves identification with an organization, including "a strong belief in and acceptance of an organization's goals and values," "a willingness to exert considerable effort on behalf of the organization," and "a strong desire to maintain membership in the organization" (Mowday, Porter, and Steers 1982:27). Some writers use the term organizational citizenship to refer to expressions of this identification in relations with coworkers, such as altruism, conscientiousness, sportsmanship, courtesy, and "civic virtue" (Organ 1988). Significantly, Reichers (1985), reviewing sociological research, finds an implicit developmental relationship between organizational commitment and other work expectations. Consistent antecedents to commitment (6), he reports, are resolution of role conflict and ambiguity (establishment of a work identity) (5), and job challenge (using work abilities effectively and satisfyingly) (4). Thus, the Eriksonian perspective suggests that people will look for close organizational attachments after securing their competence and worker identities, and the sociological literature reinforces Erikson's observation that these aims are developmentally connected.

This chapter examines the experiences of people who bring each of the "work" expectations to their organization. These stories offer views of organizational initiation and self-initiation at their potential best. These are the situations where newcomers' developmentally based demands are most likely to fit with veterans' own demands and willingness to comply. Moreover, these expectations are most directly likely to lead toward organizational membership, including membership with intimacy.

The stories reveal a great deal about organizational entry. In particular, they suggest answers to two questions: What determines whether self-initiation is successful or unsuccessful? And what makes intimate membership easy or difficult?

The cases are specimens[2] of organizational experience. They illustrate the variety of encounters with organizations without any claim about the distribution of experiences. The examples have been selected with two aims: to show some of the expressions of each of the expectations, and to show different degrees of success in initiation and self-initiation. The cases are organized according to the dominant work expectation involved. A wide range of processes and outcomes are depicted in the cases as a whole, although those grouped under any one expectation include only some of these. Since the stories are meant to be specimens, the presentations emphasize different aspects of initiation or self-initiation prominent in particular cases.

WORK ABILITY: HAVING WHAT IT TAKES

A Straightforward, Successful Initiation: Mel Thomas

Sometimes organizational entry is relatively simple and free of conflict. For example, someone recruited into a position may have an accurate view of the job and be realistically wanted by staff members. If he has the repertoire of technical and interpersonal skills the position calls for, and if he and the veterans are generous and flexible in accommodating one another, joining up may be relatively uneventful. This harmony may be still more likely if the new person already has relations with new colleagues from past work — if, in some sense, the new position is a continuation of old work. Entry may also be smooth under these conditions when the newcomer enters in a relatively high position: he is considered as important as the position, and the authority of the position enables him to control many of the conditions of entry.[3]

Entry may also be straightforward when someone is starting out in the work world, when he has relatively few strong preferences, and when he is willing to accept veterans' conditions for joining.[4] Mel Thomas, for example, simply wanted to earn a living at something interesting and safe.

Since his graduation from high school three years earlier he had done clerical work in an industrial plant. One day, while walking through a production area, he was injured by falling metal, which convinced him that even office work was a threat to his life if he stayed with the company. He began to look for more technical work, and a friend suggested he take the county civil service examination. A few weeks later the planning department called and asked if he would like to be a drafting aide. He accepted, with little idea what the work involved. In developmental terms, he approached the organization with a desire to learn skills that would help him earn a living (4), and, after that, offer him a work role that would last him a long time (5), though he had few specific requirements in either regard.

He got involved in a variety of projects. To his pleasant surprise, some of his research was used in planning. In addition, shortly after he arrived, the county executive asked his research group to take on some special assignments. Gratifyingly, the work was not simply safe, but it was diverse and exciting. Thomas started to think about advanced, specialized training, and he enrolled in college at night. He took a variety of urban planning courses, as well as computer classes. He was developing a sense of competence in the computer field (4).

Thinking back on his history in the organization, Thomas believes coworkers not only helped him learn new skills, but readily accepted him socially. He describes no abrupt initial confrontation (I) or tense transition (II). "Just over a period of time you [got] that feeling of acceptance" (III). In particular, he contrasts the "family-type" atmosphere of the agency with the anxious competitiveness of the manufacturing firm he had worked with earlier.

> From day one, it was like you were not a stranger. You were not shunned at any level, whether you had a degree or not. Other places I worked, it took months before people came up and talked with you.

His account of subsequent experiences is consistent with this view. Developmentally, confidence in his abilities turned his attention to creating a work role for himself, but also, socially, colleagues accepted him more and more as he broadened his skills. He was promoted several times. In addition, his new training coincided with the beginning of automation in the agency, and many people valued what he could do for them. As computerized information systems replaced index cards, notebooks, and file folders, the data management division became more useful to planners. They, in turn, were pleased to find they could now get information that not only improved their work, but that also increased their prestige outside the department. Thomas had developed a prominent role (5).

Perhaps oversimplifying, nevertheless, he draws a simple lesson from his advancement, when asked what advice he would give others starting out in the organization today.

> If you feel weak in skills such as speaking, presentation, or writing, try to improve yourself that way, because it is a very critical part of the department. And just take each day as a challenge. Each day is a different challenge. That is the thing that keeps me going each day.

Eventually, he says, he and others in his division became "the back-bone of the department, as far as data is concerned." This acceptance encouraged him to continue in college at night until he got a degree. As the "backbone" metaphor conveys, he saw himself, finally, as integral to the organization. He no longer simply socialized with others in the agency, but he identified himself with them collectively as professional colleagues. Now he is one of those who "familiarize [newcomers] with the depart-ment and restaurants." Today, after two decades in the organization, he feels closely committed to it and says, "I am a very loyal soldier in the workplace." He adds, "I have decided that my career will be with this department until I retire" (6).

Thomas' story of his easy entry illustrates a general lesson about organizational initiations. His developmentally based expectations of the organization were congruent with organizational needs, and both emotionally and socially he continually became more a part of the organization. His entry was facilitated by his weakly defined "work" expectations, as well as by veterans' open incorporation of newcomers. In addition, in contrast with others discussed later, he had no conflicts about prework issues that interfered with joining. Nevertheless, although his membership proceeded in an orderly manner, it was not instantaneous. Beyond being friendly, veterans needed to see that he had a useful organizational role before they considered him a member, and he had to feel he had an identity as a planner before he became attached to the department. Thus Thomas offers an example of organizational member-ship with intimacy.

Playing as a Means of Self-initiation: Charles Latham

When a newcomer's expectations conflict with what an organization can offer and when he cannot readily go along with veterans' initiation conditions, he may try to initiate himself, to find a compromise permitting him to become a member of the organization. Charles Latham's story, presented earlier, offers a counterpoint to Thomas'. Though both started out with interests in developing work abilities, Latham had firmer ideas about what he wanted to learn, and he describes his coworkers as less open to newcomers. As a result, he designed a self-initiation, in which he played with aspects of the veterans' initiation that bothered him. His relations with other staff members went through three stages.

He approached the department with an interest in becoming compe-tent in social planning (4), a deviant field. When he initially confronted the veterans (I), he felt they were aloof, considering themselves "a club that you had to graduate into," and regarding his field as "a bastard child."

The working through period (II) began with a six-year standoff. During this time of little progress in the relationship with the department,

Latham took steps to enable himself to reapproach veterans and negotiate entry. He became involved in social planning projects with people outside the agency as a way of playing with the injury of being "bastardized." He turned the passively experienced condition of being excluded as a deviant professional into an active one of deliberately looking for outside connections where he would be respected. He gained a position from which he could look down on, or out at, the rest of his department. At the same time, he succeeded in developing the competence he came for originally.

Relations with agency veterans were largely struggles over whether he could show them any ability they recognized as part of a planner's role (5). When, after a half dozen years, he took the community planner position, he made a compromise that allowed them to compromise as well. In tacit negotiations, he agreed to do mainstream physical planning, and they acknowledged his competence. He agreed to take on a central organizational role, and they included him in many of their projects (5).

These events might seem to complete the working through. After many years, Latham and the veterans each modified their demands, resolved their original conflicts, and accepted one another. And yet the actions that satisfied Latham's expectations of establishing work abilities and a work role also prepared him to expect close affiliation with the department (6). Just as his original demands were being worked through, he had a new demand, and the years of "aloofness" took on a new meaning. When he wanted legitimacy for his skills, the aloofness was a rebuff to his claims to competence. Now that he wanted close attachment, the aloofness represented a different injury, a bar to social affiliation.

However, once he and the veterans had worked through so much, they seem to have tacitly agreed to one more set of compromises, to complete his initiation on the expanded terms. A community planner is responsible for spanning boundaries between the agency and community members. Latham used the role to play in organizationally legitimate ways with the injury of years of shunning. He turned the passive experience of ostracism into active alliances with outsiders, with veterans' support. For their part in this tacit negotiation, other staff joined with him in reversing his sense of exclusion by making external activity central to doing his job. Working in this role thus enabled him to treat the injuries of a prolonged entry and to identify with professional colleagues who, in turn, accepted him (6).

The almost instantaneous transformation of Latham's relations with other staff members after he became a community planner signaled his integration into the organization (III). He emphasizes that mutual acceptance was not superficial. He became involved in deep, intimate relationships. "We have a fairly strong sense of family here. We do a lot together."

There are a number of people in the department who go out of their way to make it feel like a family. . . . People will walk the extra mile here. Rank is no consequence here, except maybe on the director's level.

Citing an example of uncommon closeness in the department, he stresses that, at last, he becomes part of it. Now he "can just walk into [my supervisor's] office, even when he is talking with people. When you can do that, you are talking on a family level."

Latham summarizes his personal development during the initiation in terms that echo Erikson:

I have changed a lot. I have matured a lot. . . . After becoming a community planner and being accepted, it was thrilling for me. I felt more competent and secure.

Latham's story shows the importance of a newcomer's self-initiation efforts in joining an organization. It illustrates the meaning of "playing" with a role: trying out alternative roles, using them to see which one offers relations with veterans that (a) support personal development, (b) repair injuries from the initial confrontation with the organization, and (c) prove useful to veterans' work. The length of the working through period in this case reflects the complexity and rigidity of Latham's expectations, as well as the extent of his hurt from the initial confrontation. Whether play is successful, as it eventually was here, depends on both the newcomer's resourcefulness and flexibility and veterans' willingness to accommodate some of the newcomer's demands.

Self-initiation Efforts that Never Succeed: Leonard Davis

Sometimes a newcomer has reasonable "work" expectations, and veterans are willing to accommodate him, but, nevertheless, self-initiation efforts fail. The injury of the initial confrontation may be so upsetting that the newcomer never succeeds in treating himself for it. Even though coworkers regard him as a member of the organization, he feels that entering the organization demands so much from him that he cannot be himself and be in the organization. Leonard Davis, for example, has worked in a federal agency for more than twenty years without ever feeling like a member of it. His story shows that even "work" expectations do not assure entry, and it introduces themes of disappointment explored more fully in the next section of the book.

Davis grew up in a large family in a small town. He was the fifth of nine children behind four brothers considerably older than the rest. He warmly recalls their relations.

The four older ones finally adopted one of the younger ones, and you were a special pet. It helped us to grow. Like my older brother adopted me, taught me to drive at an early age, taught me bad language, to play ball.

When he graduated from high school, he joined the Army and went to Officer Candidate School. After leaving the Army, he worked in various jobs for about ten years. Then he took a federal civil service examination and got a job in a federal agency. He advanced to a position in a regional office in a small city. For several years he did casework, helping clients get the agency's services, but gradually tired of day-to-day work with the public. In considering alternatives, he thought about training, which he had done in the Army. The logical place to find a promotion was the department's national headquarters, and he interviewed successfully for training work there. The office had a work force twice the size of his hometown's population.

Developmentally, Davis came to the national office to solidify expertise in training (4) as a means of improving his status and income. However, his initial confrontation with the organization (I) so overwhelmingly made him feel inadequate[5] that, despite others' acceptance, he never felt secure in his ability. As a result, he never felt confident about his identity as a trainer (5), nor did he feel comfortably part of the organization (6).

As soon as he arrived, he says,

I felt I had made a big mistake. There were too damn many people. I didn't feel my wife and I would adjust to a large city. I didn't feel my children would adjust to large schools. . . . I didn't feel at ease for probably a year. I would still get lost in the hallways after several months.

Not only was the organization large, but it was also foreign. He says entry was "a culture shock."

Until that time, I hadn't worked with people with varied backgrounds. . . . Below, people like myself, without college degrees, military. I worked with a woman who had worked on three different newspaper staffs. . . . A small Jew lady, she was open, upfront, used slang, knew writing. It was hard to get into the bureaucratic style of writing.

Most of all, he felt inadequate educationally. He had no college degree, and everyone else, it seemed, did and would do better than he ever could.

I felt handicapped by my lack of formal education at that time. I didn't have a degree. My credentials above high school were OCS and a few business school courses. So I was apprehensive, trying to expand beyond what my formal education allowed me to do. I was very apprehensive. . . . One employee, whom I later became friendly with . . . I was not here two weeks, when she told me I would never be promoted, because I didn't have all the degrees, the background. One coworker was a professor from Yale—no, Princeton. I got partial acceptance. "Most of what you have to offer is your military background. Let's see what you can do."

The section he worked in was small. Staff members knew each other well and were suspicious of him as an outsider. They seemed to fear he would deprive them of limited promotional opportunities. All this made him anxious about his job, conducting training classes for new employees. "Every new class that I taught, initially I was overly apprehensive. I was never confident about lesson plans." Thus the shock of Davis' initial confrontation was a product of both challenges from veterans and his own invidious comparison of himself to what he imagined others expected from him.

His encounter with the organization challenged several aspects of his identity. Whether others meant to affect him in these ways is less important than the reality of the "message" he heard. After being a significant person in a small town, he was no longer important. He did not speak an acceptable language. He was provincial. Centrally, he did not have the ability to do the job (4).

In response, he attempted to initiate himself, to work through (II) these questions about his competence, in two ways. One involved the formalities of his job; he worked on his performance as a trainer. He painstakingly prepared lesson plans. In the military, training consisted mainly of lecturing recruits; here he had to learn to be more interactive. Taking instruction from the former newspaperwoman, he self-consciously dropped his "slang" and improper language. He also took her advice on how to write memoranda, and she edited his material. These efforts paid off.

After a couple of years I was no longer apprehensive about my work. After eight months, I got into supervisory management training: first-line supervisors, one of the hardest jobs in management. I got pretty good reviews as a facilitator [teacher]. It helped more than the support I got from my peers.

These activities succeeded in satisfying coworkers' initiation terms. Indeed, over the years he was promoted several times, eventually into middle management.

However, these efforts did not complete his entry because they did not repair the injury to his identity sufficiently to enable him to take an organizational role with confidence. Here he tried a second set of actions, not overtly related to the job but directed to the trauma of his initial confrontation with the organization. Partly consciously, partly unconsciously, he attempted to play with what had injured him earlier: feeling insignificant and incompetent in a mammoth organization.

Repeatedly, he created situations in which he could be a significant part of a small organization, capably contributing to its welfare. Soon after arriving, he joined the Reserves, reinforcing a former, successful identity. He resumed training there and did well. He joined the community association in his new neighborhood. The area was a small town like his birthplace, although residents saw government workers as intruders. By working with the association, he simultaneously helped initiate himself into the locality and found a place where others considered him useful. He joined a church and over the next few years held a series of elective offices. Later, he helped organize a nonprofit philanthropic organization and served as a chairman of the board its first year.

Each of these settings was the counterpoint to the federal bureaucracy. Each was small, and he was usefully important and appreciated in each. These were places beyond the language and credential concerns of the workplace. These activities were efforts to compensate for deprivations of that organization and to treat the injurious loss of competence and self-assurance inflicted by it. On the one hand, these activities seem to concede that the work organization will never let him feel competent. On the other hand, their satisfactions undoubtedly helped him continue working there.

Accompanying these efforts to reinforce his sense of efficacy was one other overt self-initiatory activity, designed to certify him as competent. As soon as he arrived at the agency, he enrolled in night classes to get a bachelor's degree. After nearly a dozen years he graduated. The agency newsletter reported the event, and his coworkers held a celebration. Although no single event marked his integration into the organization (III), this episode could be considered to cap his initiation. Finally, more than a decade after he had arrived, this credential should have satisfied him, as well as his coworkers, that he had what it took to be a member.

And yet he minimizes the impact of the degree. After being inferior to other workers for so many years, he does not feel he really caught up with them. He continues his outside volunteer work, which he says is what really allows him to use his abilities. Significantly, he says the most pleasurable activity at work the last couple of years has been what might be seen as another type of play with his initiation injury:

he has trained four secretaries to do professional work. He has done for them what no one did for him: he gave them the gift of competence. He has unconsciously attempted to repair the injury of being deskilled by moving from his passively suffered trauma to actively teaching others who seem to be in his earlier situation. Still, he continues to feel like an outsider, and he is relieved to be approaching retirement.

Davis' story shows that veterans and a newcomer may not only have different criteria for entry, but also different perceptions of whether the newcomer has become a member. Here veterans believe they have successfully initiated the newcomer, while he continues to feel that he has failed to initiate himself. Despite his promotions, he has never managed to recover from the trauma to his sense of competence and to regain self-assurance. Subjectively, he is stuck in the middle stage of his self-initiation. He has never found a transitional role that could both satisfy veterans (as he sees them) and enable him to remain the small-town, slang-speaking Army man he likes.

His experience is analogous to—though it is not the same as—an infant's failure at separation and individuation. He feels as if he has been forced to *differentiate* himself from his old self and his rich small-town attachments. He has accepted some of the changes imposed on him, but for years he has *practiced* new ways of acting without ever integrating them into a cohesive identity permitting *rapprochement* with organizational veterans. At work, he is without a psychic anchor.

In this predicament, his outside activities with the Reserves, community, and church compensate for these deprivations. Developmentally, they enable him to be competent (4), have an important role (5), and be integral to these groups (6). He has successfully used these settings to create a transitional role for initiating himself into alternative "work organizations," where he can be competent and himself.

Davis' experiences show that even "work" expectations do not ensure organizational entry. His story illustrates typical reactions to disappointment, which will be discussed further in the next section of the book.

WORK IDENTITY: BEING A WORKER

Unconsciously Leaving an Organization, the Better to Initiate Oneself: Everett Parsons

Someone may take a job confident about his abilities but still uncertain about how to mold them into a professional identity. City planning, for example, includes skills in designing housing developments, interpreting zoning regulations, and calculating the economic impacts of new office buildings. However, being a city planner—taking the role of a planner—involves thinking about oneself exercising such skills in a particular way. In working with others, someone becomes formally and informally responsible for certain tasks, and these skills become a repertoire he draws on to carry out those tasks. Colleagues and clients come to assume they can depend on him to do these things well, and this belief leads to continuing requests for work. In the process, everyone, particularly the planner, comes to identify the planner with the performance of these skills. Among other things, the planner becomes emotionally invested in doing these things well, and his self-esteem turns on the results of these efforts with others.

Everett Parsons was a young city planner who was confident of his abilities (4) but unsure about his professional identity (5); he wanted his new organization to help him develop this identity. Encountering new colleagues who had no use for his skills, he had to devise a self-initiation. Although, like Latham, he eventually succeeded, unlike Latham, he turned to activities not directly related to his job in order to prepare himself to enter the organization. Some of his most important work was unconscious.

Parsons was one of the first three architects hired by a county planning department twenty years ago. The director recruited them together from a graduate urban design program with talk of innovative professional work. However, once Parsons arrived, he found it very difficult to become part of the department. Not only was he new, but the socially oriented staff had little understanding of what designers did. In accentuating his feelings of difference, he notes that the other two architects, at least, had the beneficial social connections of private schooling, whereas he had attended public schools.

He describes a painful initial confrontation with the organization (I), in which he was professionally isolated from the rest of the staff. The architects worked together on a project on low-cost housing technologies. Not only did the issues seem esoteric to more socially oriented colleagues, but the study was not connected to day-to-day activities of the department. The designers spoke their own language. In addition, they were set up in a location separate from the rest of the staff. In understatement, Duncan recounts,

> As to our relation to the organization, we were kind of looked upon as unique, in the sense that there had not been a group of people in this organization like this. It took time for us to fit in.

Describing his feelings of this period more vividly, he remembers,

I was nervous for the first two to three years, because we [architects] were involved in our own little study, but at the same time I didn't understand everyone's role here. I knew [only] their formal role. I was hesitant to ask questions, and I was hesitant to participate. I didn't want to seem naive.

Few staff members were interested in his work or asked him to help with theirs. He was particularly anxious about presenting his work to others because he anticipated that they would not consider it important.

Gradually, others began to negotiate a role with Parsons (II). They started asking him questions in areas where they thought he might be helpful. Parsons responded in two ways in working through relations with the veterans. Overtly, he made efforts to meet colleagues and persevered in presenting his ideas to them. In the process, he not only responded to the questions, but also encouraged them to let him participate in their work.

However, a crucial part of his effort in the three-year transition involved privately playing with his ideas and feelings about his role as a designer. He took up painting. He describes his personal change project in this way:

In the first three years, the job was very tense, and I was trying to find a way to escape from that. And I began to develop as a painter. So there is a definite linkage to my background. And for eight or nine years I poured heart and soul into that. Things came back into work, such as graphics, murals, signage. And there was a rebirth, and the director saw it. . . . I was energizing myself on my own.

Painting can be seen as an effort to play with and master the injury of his isolation and professional rejection. As such, it had two purposes. One, he notes, was to provide "escape" from the disappointments and pressures of the organization. But his observation that the painting produced new work assets makes clear that, consciously and unconsciously, it was also an effort to create some connection between his past identity and a work identity that would satisfy both veterans and himself.

Painting was a transitional activity, helping him manage and reduce the separateness he felt others imposed on him. It was a way of playing with those parts of his new role that were frustrating. For example, although his formal assignment involved the designing for which he was trained, staff members did not ask him to do design work for them. As a substitute, his painting gave him opportunities to design and portray things. Crucial to the efficacy of painting as a transitional activity was its "linkage" to both his identity as an artist and his formal design work. Gradually, his confidence in what he painted, as well as his growing graphic ability, began showing up in his work. His painting was a "rebirth," and a new Parsons appeared at work, acceptable to, and accepted by, the veterans, several years after he first arrived. He succeeded in finding an organizational identity (5) for the competence he valued (4).

The director's new attitude toward Parsons formalized his integration into the department (III). The director not only praised Parsons' growing ability, but initiated projects that could capitalize on it. He assigned Parsons more and more jobs requiring his skills. Other staff members also asked his assistance, and he felt secure holding his own with them. He saw his drawings used in actual construction, and his name was publicly associated with his work. Finally, the director changed his job title from "architect" to "urban designer."

Parsons shows how the play of self-initiation may take place outside an organization, even without conscious connection to the challenges of work. He describes his experience in a language of rebirth similar to that of the infant's separation and individuation. Through his efforts, he reaches *rapprochement* with coworkers, who permit him to *consolidate* a new organizational and professional identity. Taking a different path than Latham, he succeeds in finding membership with intimacy.

A Promotion and an Unsuccessful Self-reinitiation: Claudia Bender

People may succeed in becoming members, only to find later on that their wants have changed, that the organization has changed, or both. They no longer feel like members and must decide if they want to reinitiate themselves or if they want to move on. David Ryan matured in the organization and came to expect from it something it could not offer: the chance of passing on a heritage to his children. He decided he had outgrown the organization and began to plan his withdrawal.

Claudia Bender offers another, common example. She succeeded in settling into a technical position and then, after several years, was promoted into administration. The new position does not fit her needs as well as her old one, and her previous accommodations to the bureaucracy no longer serve her. She has lost the work identity she established earlier and has had to struggle to recreate one. Thus, after many years, she is once more like a new worker, injured by the organization, and trying to reinitiate herself. Paradoxically, the reward for past success has had the effect of emotionally expelling her from the organization.

A little over fifteen years ago, Bender decided she did not want to make a career of teaching junior high school science, and she enrolled in a graduate program in biology (4). When she got her master's degree, she applied for a number of civil service positions in search of a career that better fit her scientific interests (5). She took the first job offer she got, in a large state environmental agency. She adjusted pretty well to her work, doing independent research alongside other analysts. As far as others were concerned, they had successfully initiated her into a work role.

However, despite her success on the job, she found it difficult to feel committed to the role (5) or identify with the organization (6), because of certain aspects of the bureaucracy. First, its hierarchy was different from anything she had been used to.

> In the school system . . . your peers are your *peers*. Everyone was on the same level. When I came here, it took getting used to people working on different levels. People would ask [what my job title was], wanting to know what slot to put me in.

In addition, she was surprised at how childish so many people seemed.

> Having been in school or teaching school all the time, I was used to personalities, personal differences. But, at least with kids, I looked at it as a temporary thing. They would have time to grow up! Here, I am an optimist. Everyone is grown up. It came as a shock to me. Not everyone has grown up and matured. I have since grown myself. I was being childish expecting everyone to be an adult. I asked myself why, and I got back to this hierarchy thing.

Hierarchical structure and childish behavior each threatened the identity she brought into the organization. First, as part of a hierarchy, she would have to accept segmented relations with others. After initially responding personally to others, she found they expected her to adhere to a narrow impersonal role. When she reacted emotionally to others' appeals, she found they were often just using her to get ahead. In the hierarchy she would have to give up spontaneity for calculation.

The second cost of bureaucratic membership would be giving up her adulthood. She quickly concluded that childishness is a natural consequence of hierarchy. Subordinacy encourages people to think of themselves as children and to act immaturely. In particular, they do not take initiative and depend on others to do things they could do themselves. Not only does Bender find some of her colleagues burdensome, but, as someone with two college degrees and two children, she is unwilling to act childishly herself.

Even though she found her job satisfying and got along with others, she felt she could not sacrifice her identity as the hierarchy demanded. In this respect, the independent nature of research provided a reasonable compromise between organizational demands for work and her insistence on being herself.

In fact, she was so successful that she was offered the opportunity to become a supervisor. She took the position for its status and pay, although she quickly found the abilities that made her a good analyst did not make her a competent manager. In addition, the adjustments that had served her as a researcher no longer worked as an administrator. The essence of administration is contact with others, to manage, appease, and get things from them. The story she tells of her administrative work is one of deskilling and growing detachment from the organization.

To begin with, she observes that she does not like to exercise authority:

> I don't normally take any position of authority. I have no qualms about working in an organization. I belong to a public service organization. I don't mind working on committees, but I would not take a committee chair. Pretty much I just take an opposite role.

She acknowledges that this is a problem for her when she acts as a supervisor:

> It is sort of—I will not say natural. You are assigned the title, people come to you, and they expect certain things of you. You try to give people what they want. I see it as part of my job. Whereas when I am not here, I don't feel like I have to.

Thus her supervisorial role, as every role, requires her to act in ways that are not spontaneous; in particular, it requires her to be unnaturally authoritative. She is essentially entering the organization a second time, and this is her injury.

She tries to take the role in good faith, continuing with the compromises she worked out in her previous position. What makes this difficult is that, as a supervisor, she must interact with others in many segmented roles. Not accustomed to administrative work, instead of developing and implementing her own agenda, she finds herself responding to others' demands. She tries to find out how to get others what they want and yet discovers she cannot easily even do that.

> When I first started working here, I thought things were clear-cut, but the more I am here, the more I see there are exceptions made to the rules and regulations. It is kind of disappointing.... You convince yourself that you have done this and this and this, and then you see that you didn't have to. I will not say "disappointing"; I will say "confusing."

In addition, as an administrator, for better or for worse, she is an authority in the hierarchy, and others respond to her with all the childishness she dislikes. She tries to be sensitive to personnel problems without experiencing them as personal problems, but this approach goes against her grain. She seems to cope in an unsatisfying way.

> I have become a little hardened. I don't take things as personally as I used to. I figure as a supervisor you can't take things personally. Now I don't have to deal with anyone on a personal basis. I try not to act on a personal basis. I don't feel as hurt by people's actions as I used to. [Not acting personally means not] expressing your feelings about situations, for one. People can come to you with problems. If you remain objective about the problems, that is, holding back from getting really involved in the problem. . . . I just don't listen to people's problems any more. I say I'd prefer not knowing.

Developmentally, Bender's promotion has several costly consequences. First, it requires her to compromise her identity more than the research position did. Every day, on the line, she must act impersonally and calculatingly. She cannot identify with the supervisorial role (5) in the same way she could pretty much reconcile herself to the earlier one. Insofar as she has a tenuous work identity, she is still less likely to feel like a member of the organization (6).

In addition, the administrative position requires abilities she does not readily have. Being able to act impersonally and calculatingly, whether it is spontaneous or intentional, is part of the necessary competence. So, too, is the ability to conceptualize research tasks in terms of organizational mission, resources, and strategies. Thus the promotion that comes as a reward for her scientific competence leaves her feeling incompetent (4), further limiting the likelihood that she will identify with the role.

Being deskilled may itself have further developmental consequences. Someone who cannot successfully express a sense of industry (4) has two choices. The first is to work harder at becoming competent. In a case like Bender's, this may mean trying to master administration, or it could mean reconsidering technical work. If the latter is impossible (because, for example, it would mean a loss of income) and if the former is difficult, then Bender might turn back to her last successful developmental accomplishment. This could mean looking for ways to exercise power (3), a choice that would not be consistent with her personality. Or it might mean looking for ways to demonstrate her independence (2) or to get recognized (1).

Bender chooses to concentrate on improving her competence. She continues to work on administration, but she also nurtures a fantasy of returning to technical work. She says she wants to do administrative work for only a few more years and then return to the laboratory until her retirement. Whether she seriously intends to make the turn back or not, the thought serves as a playful way of treating the blow to her ability. By thinking of herself as only a temporary administrator, as *really* a scientific researcher—and by playing with different images of what she will do in the future—she can reconcile herself to her frustrating position. She can think of herself as competent (4) and might persuade herself that there is something about her consistent with a work identity (5) in the organization.[6]

Bender's story shows how changes at work, including such favorable ones as promotions, may cause injuries that detach members from organizations and require them to play and initiate themselves once again. In particular, her example illustrates what often happens when management promotes a technician who is not suited to administration. There is not simply a risk that supervision is poorly done. In addition, there are developmental reasons why inept supervisors will feel less loyal to the organization than before. On top of this, they may divert a lot of effort to demonstrating their power or independence or getting recognition.

Bender's experience goes with Davis' as an example of disappointed "work" expectations. In her first position she had membership without intimacy, and in her second she lost even the feeling of membership. Her theorizing about the effects of bureaucracy on people's behavior offers some insights into "the natural human aversion to work," to be more fully examined in the chapters of the next section.

ORGANIZATIONAL AFFILIATION: IDENTIFYING WITH OTHERS

Latham and Bender present contrasting views of organizational affiliation and the possibilities of intimacy with membership. Latham wanted and eventually found membership that brought him intimacy with coworkers and a strong identification with the organization. Bender, in contrast, thought of a nonintimate form of membership—a sort of good organizational citizenship—but failed to establish that.

Part of the explanation for their different expectations and experiences can be attributed to personal differences. Latham is more outgoing than Bender, more likely to engage others in discussion. In addition, though they both took their work seriously, their organizational careers were located differently in relation to their overall patterns of development. Latham came to his organization when he was young, just out of school, and single. His work on a sense of competence and a work identity were part of his general work on a sense of industry and a sense of identity. When he thought of organizational affiliation, it was as part of emerging general possibilities of intimacy. In an important sense, he had grown up in the agency, and it provided a ready arena for practicing intimacy.

Bender, in contrast, came to her organization somewhat older, with previous work experience and after she had married and had two children. She had already developed intimate relationships with family members, and work relations were emotionally secondary to those at home. Though affiliating with an organization could reinforce her general development, it was not essential to it.

Another part of the differences between their experiences pertains to the organizations they went to. Latham's agency is small, nonhierarchical, and informal; many staff members compare it to a family. Bender's department, in contrast, is large, bureaucratic, and rule bound; deep loyalty matters less than day-to-day competence and amicability. Thus the culture of one organization encourages intimate associations, whereas that of the other accepts good citizenship.

Clearly, organizational norms may shape workers' expectations, so that they come to expect what they can get. In addition, norms can reinforce personal orientations, such that workers may choose organizations that satisfy their expectations and let them remain pretty much who they are. Latham, for example, ultimately found a good match with his agency. Others, such as Bender, who are less comfortable with personal obligations to coworkers, may prefer impersonal organizations of limited liability.

Still, even with these variations, whether a worker expects and finds a close attachment to coworkers or an organization depends on the worker's developmental expectations and how the organization responds to them. Latham did not become an emotional member of his organization until he had negotiated ways of showing his work abilities and taking a work identity. Then he was prepared to experiment with intimacy, and he was fortunate to find colleagues who responded to that as a legitimate desire.

When Bender says she was disappointed with her coworkers, she, too, describes the effects of organizational norms on development and work expectations. Although she was not interested in deep loyalty to the organization as a whole, she had impulses to identify with others in her work groups. She initially reacted caringly to her coworkers, only to find many were manipulative or immature. She concluded that bureaucratic subordinacy infantilized people so as to make them unable to relate closely to coworkers. Her own experience shows this in a similar way: working conditions, particularly the obligations of administration, frustrated her development and diverted her from thinking about intimacy. Thus her story shows how organizational conditions may both disappoint and discourage interests in intimacy, a general problem examined in more depth in later chapters.

A final example shows organizational affiliation at its best. Sally Ransom tentatively returned to work after four years off with young children. She had no specific aspirations but also no problems in mastering the work. She quickly discovered that she wanted to become part of the inner circle, and she set out to develop in ways that would make this intimacy possible. Her story focuses on the emotional and strategic contexts of intimacy.

Choosing to Become an Intimate Part of the Organization: Sally Ransom

Ten years ago, when Ransom decided to go back to work, she took a federal civil service examination, got invited to a training course with an entitlement program, and accepted a job there. She received several promotions, and today she does special projects for the departmental secretary. In telling her story, she emphasizes that she decided early on that she wanted to have a career in the organization and then used the organization for her development.

When she began, she said, she "was not looking for anything in particular." She "was not looking for any great job," and she certainly had no special interest in this agency. Her first job involved collecting information about claims for agency benefits. She had to make complicated calculations to determine eligibility. She doubted that she would be good at the work or find pleasure in it. And yet she found she could do it; if anything, she was overqualified for what she did, and much of it was tedious.

Many of her coworkers were complacent, doing only as much as they had to to get paid.

> It was different from anything I had encountered. I had never been in a large organization where people just did average work. There was a lot of mediocrity. I really lived a sheltered life. It really shocked me. People just did what they had to to get by. That is really different from how I grew up. You do your best and work your hardest. I also saw people who were never going to get promoted and who said, Why bother? And that affected other people.

And yet, perhaps because she had deliberately chosen to return to work, she took her work seriously as a measure of herself. Once she had reassured herself that she had the ability to do her job (4), she began to think more about what she did in terms of establishing a work role (5) that others would recognize and that would help her move ahead to more interesting work. She started to volunteer for activities that she might enjoy or that might catch others' attention. In contrast with her coworkers, her ambitions grew.

By the third year—when I started out [in Grade 5], I thought I would get Grade 10. But as I got closer to that 10, I got antsy and thought I would move on. I had never thought of being a manager.

She passed probation without question, received two promotions, was given her own trainee three grades higher than herself, and increasingly took initiatives, even in doing a lot of boring work, "because it was good for my career." A few years and three promotions later, she moved from casework with the entitlement program into departmental budgetary analysis. It was as if she had to reinitiate herself by reestablishing her abilities and role.

I had to learn new things. I took that opportunity—I called it "creative authority"—to be a little freer with my own personal judgments if I couldn't find a specific answer. I would document what I had done and why I did it. It was a period of real growth. I got to be an expert on a lot of areas. [Nobody liked to work in one particular area,] so I decided that was something I could be an expert in.... Some accepted me right away, and some were suspicious. But they were not really a threat to me, because they didn't work that hard. I surprised myself. I started out as a very shy person. I wanted my own niche. And I discovered that I really wanted the limelight.... Then I discovered when I was working on special projects for the secretary that I really liked it a lot. And I was meeting a lot of neat people. And they remembered who I was. So I started volunteering for a lot of positions, which gave me a lot of exposure. So I really had to work my tail off. I was working weekends, New Year's Day, took work home at night. It seemed to be worth it. I got a lot of personal satisfaction.

Having reassured herself and others that she could competently carry out a succession of roles, she began to expect more from the organization: her own niche, the limelight, and, finally, closeness to the secretary (6). This meant becoming an insider, working closely with top managers who made policy. Emotionally and intellectually, it entailed sharing decision makers' sense of stewardship for the agency.

Her campaign to move up and in may be considered still one more self-initiation. She wanted something additional from the organization and had to negotiate with new people to try to get it. The tests of this period would involve not her technical skills but her ability to work closely with the people she wanted to join. Would they feel comfortable with her? She started by signaling others that she was interested in being involved in some of the secretary's projects.

Her eventual success depended not just on her developmental readiness, but on her past experience. Throughout her life she has been interested in creating or joining groups. When growing up, she belonged to the 4-H Club, church, and singing groups. She and her husband maintain church ties and participate in vocal groups. She was raising three children. Thus, thinking of organizational affiliation was an extension of past relationships.

However, even though she has kept and developed intimate relationships in adulthood, she thought about close connections at work only after she had established a work identity. Her training course gave her a foretaste of future possibilities. Students attended class away from departmental headquarters. "And they were all new too. And we formed a bond. When we got to the headquarters building, we knew each other." This positive experience encouraged her to think that closeness at work was possible, but only developmental readiness in the organization led her to pursue it.

Shortly after she reached Grade 12, she was invited into the department's management development program, and soon afterward she was asked to join a work group advising the secretary on automating data processing. Still once more referring to self-discovery, she describes this as a spur to further development.

> I discovered I could do a lot of molding, send the project in the direction I thought it should go. That is when I first started learning about the politics of the organization. [I began to] see the rest of the agency, find out what was going on nationwide.

Originally assigned to back up another group member, she eventually replaced him and found her own recognition and further chances for advancement.

These organizational opportunities, coming in response to her previous development, stimulated her to grow further. Her view of both the organization and her relationship with it changed.

> In the beginning I didn't know that much about the organization, the structure of it. Even as I began moving up, the organization was that thing out there. I had to overcome it to get where I want to go. Now I feel I am part of the organization, using it for my benefit.... There are a lot of opportunities that come out of the organization.

After eight years, she felt deeply part of the organization. Moreover, the connection was realistic. She identified herself with the secretary and other managers of the departmental mission, but she recognized the organization as something separate from which she could get acknowledgment and power.

Symbolic of her affiliation with the organization is her changed approach to data analysis. In her early positions she had worked on a lot of tedious calculations, to find the correct answers for complex entitlement problems. Now, in her higher position as policy analyst, she realizes,

> There are a lot of things we can do with numbers. Depending on the politics of the organization, we can make people look how we want them to look—good, not so good, or average. We have a lot of power as a result of this. I like to manipulate the data as many ways as possible to see what conclusions we can come to, and go for it.

Two things have changed. She sees herself as a master of numbers, rather than their servant. And, crucially, she identifies a "we" as part of whom she analyzes the data.

Even in the large bureaucracy where Ransom works, intimate feelings of membership are possible. She identifies the organization with a specific working group, in her case, those around the secretary. Her wish for organizational affiliation grows out of her success in establishing a competent work identity. While each of her promotions has challenged her, each time she found ways of succeeding. Moreover, her past group memberships and intimate family relations have helped give her the emotional strength and security to experiment with attachments at work. In the end, she not only identifies with the organization, but she also identifies with the work.

LESSONS ABOUT ORGANIZATIONAL MEMBERSHIP AND INITIATION

Many of these people come to feel that they are members of their organizations and have intimate attachments to coworkers or organizational purposes. They satisfy deep personal needs regarding work. Furthermore, although they do not say so, they probably please their managers, since someone committed to an organization is likely to work productively for it. Their stories offer four lessons about conditions for successful organizational initiation.

First, unconscious developmental interests in work ability, work identity, and organizational affiliation are important both for motivating organizational entry and for satisfying veterans' expectations of newcomers. Superficially, this observation is hardly novel. After all, people take jobs they think they can do or learn, and organizations value competence and interests in acquiring it. People who identify with their formal role are likely to want to stay in an organization and be accepted. People who want to be part of an organization may work especially hard at developing relations with coworkers.

These observations also have a deeper meaning. If interests in gaining competence, identifying with a formal role, and belonging to an organization represent developmental accomplishments and if they have developmental prerequisites, they are not merely matters of conscious choice. Nor can organizations command, coerce, or induce compliance with competence, role, or other membership expectations when a new worker lacks the unconscious readiness.

Second, consistently, organizational initiation is likely to be successful when veterans' expectations of a new member are congruent with the newcomer's developmental agenda. Latham provides a clear example. Even though he was initially unable to take a formal role, much less embrace an organization, he was able gradually to enter and increasingly to identify with an organization as he found opportunities to resolve successive developmental dilemmas. Crucially, the organization gave him opportunities that served veterans' needs as well as his.

Third, organizational initiation is likely to be successful when it permits a newcomer's self-initiation. Veterans' demands on a new member should not traumatize the worker. In addition, the newcomer should be able to devise a personally satisfying compromise with organizational terms. Without both conditions, a new worker may be accepted by veterans without feeling like a member. In short, self-initiation requires that the newcomer be able to play with organizational expectations—to imagine them differently and to renegotiate them—so as to treat and compensate himself for any initial injury. Parsons provides a good example of a newcomer who manages both an overt organizational initiation and an unconscious self-initiation. He succeeds in coming to feel like a member because he can play with the initial organizational injury in a way that permits him to identify with a formal role. Still, the effort took three years.

Fourth, "work" expectations do not ensure successful entry or membership. A newcomer's "work" expectation may rest on weakly established personal development and be vulnerable to serious injury in the initial confrontation with the organization. For example, Davis was sufficiently insecure about his competence, and the demands of the big new organization were sufficiently great, that he never recovered a sense of work ability from which he could move ahead and initiate him-self into the organization. On the other hand, a worker may be developmentally secure but lack the abilities an assignment demands. Bender encountered this problem after her promotion. Another possibility is that a worker with developmental prerequisites for membership and reasonable "work" expectations, nevertheless, presents expectations that do not fit an organization.

In any of these cases, veterans' responses are crucial. They influence whether and how much a newcomer feels injured in the initial confrontation, as well as whether the newcomer can negotiate compromise terms for membership in a working through period. Because organizational entry is a transaction, both newcomer and veterans share responsibility for the outcome.

The next chapter looks at people with postwork expectations of their organizations. They also use the workplace to develop, but what they want from work may be more important to them than it is to their employers. They are as likely to grow through and out of organizations as they are to grow into them.

Growing In and Out of the Organization: Mentoring and Making Sense

Mentoring and making sense of life are postwork expectations. Some organizations want applicants for certain positions to have one of these interests, especially mentoring. However, more often, veterans do not expect them and pay little attention to their manifestations. When deciding whether to accept someone as a member, veterans are normally much more concerned about how the person performs and gets along with others.

For the individual, mentoring and sensemaking are late developmental concerns. People entering organizations at an early age may not give them much thought, either in relation to work or otherwise. If they emerge later on, they will require a new self-initiation in order to retain membership. Interests in mentoring and sensemaking can be compatible with feeling like a member, but they may also lead someone to consider the workplace of diminishing importance in personal development.

Significantly, generative and sensemaking concerns apply to much more of life than work. In this respect, they have a symmetry with the pre-work expectations. The first three developmental stages involve the infant and young child's efforts to situate himself in the universe by replacing global relationships with particular ones. In this project he moves from an all-encompassing symbiotic relationship with the mother to separation from her and, eventually, to individual relations with many persons. Pre-work organizational expectations share some of those cosmic concerns.

The next three developmental stages, corresponding to the "work" expectations, involve much more specific relationships with various individuals and explicitly relate to work. The sense of industry and identity in particular require developing work skills and roles.

The final two developmental stages mirror the first three in returning to universal relationships. The question of generativity is which few individuals one may depend on to pass one's virtues on to posterity. Thus, the issue of parenthood matches the earlier issue of childhood.

The question of integrity, like that of basic trust, is global and nearly impersonal. Last in life one asks, now with a larger vocabulary, though perhaps no more words, how one is related to the cosmos. As these developmental tasks move toward the universal, they necessarily draw away from the particulars of work.

The following examples of postwork expectations show their variable role in organizational entry. Neither type ensures membership by itself, only in the context of a particular organization. They contrast with the "work" interests, which are necessary for initiation, and prework concerns, which, if dominant, are inimical to it. Crucially, when applicants expect to mentor or make sense of things but veterans are indifferent to these matters, it is less accurate to speak of veterans initiating newcomers than of new members initiating or reinitiating themselves. Consistently, the presentations focus on ways in which these workers play with roles to make themselves comfortable in their organizations. For some, these late developmental expectations recontextualize early organizational or even life experiences as injuries and focus play on treating or compensating for those injuries.

MENTORING: CARING FOR ANOTHER

Generativity is a broad wish to create representations of oneself for posterity. At work, it may be expressed in desires to produce a distinctive product, to shape an organization, or to mentor a protégé. The ways those who develop this interest satisfy it depend in part on the opportunities they have. Few have both the power and the vision to make over an organization or to establish a program in their image. Even creating a personal product is not a simple matter, as more and more workers, particularly professionals and managers, "produce" ephemeral services. When work consists of having ideas and designing personal relationships, when a dominant activity is talking with other people, and when the most tangible product is often a memorandum, workers do not readily know what a distinctive product would be. Ryan levels this complaint at the public agency he works in, though it is not clear that his service station has any more lasting products, other than the profits he can keep.

Thus professionals and managers especially may direct their interests in generativity into the possible expressions of mentoring, raising a successor who will carry on their aims and ideas. Mentoring may be the most accessible way to satisfy generative interests, and a protégé is a visible personal creation.

Mentoring involves a special relationship between two persons. The senior must want to teach another and must find someone seeking personal direction. The mentor must be drawn to the junior sufficiently to want to guide him in identifying and pursuing his ambitions. Part of this attraction may be sexual, but the mentor must express this affinity in terms of caring, rather than sexual desire.[1] At the same time, the mentor must not see the younger person's aims or abilities as a challenge to be resisted or resented.

Essential to treating a protégé this way is making peace with organizational constraints. Mentors need to have worked out their ambitions in terms of available organizational roles and relationships, directing their aggression toward their work and their libido into collaboration. If they have failed in these matters, they may treat potential mentees as sexual objects or turn their frustration aggressively against them. A mentor must be able to maintain earlier success in sublimating sexual and aggressive wishes so as to express them, first, in moving out to seek and establishing a mentoring relationship and, following that, in continuing to advise, guide, and influence the younger person.

Mentoring interests are radically different from any preceding them. As postwork aims, they are not essential to organizational initiation. More important, they express a wish to become an initiator oneself. How is an initiator initiated? The complexities of this process begin with the fact that mentoring (7), unlike the "work" interests of organizational affiliation (6), work identity (5), and work ability (4), involves two, rather than many, people. Mentoring is a private relationship. This is why libidinal sublimation is especially important in mentoring. Anything less would provoke primitive feelings of exclusion and jealousy.

In an important way, mentoring in an organization is a contradiction. On the one hand, organizational growth depends on the grooming of future creative and administrative leadership. In this respect, mentoring serves the organization. However, when an organizational member takes a mentor, he joins a new unit, a two-person group, which must work differently from the large organization and stand free of it. When the two are faithful to one another, they stand alone, separate from and possibly against the organization, which demands loyalty from its members. Why should management encourage mentoring if it is potentially seditious?[2]

Mentoring is subversive psychologically as well as politically. Entering the mentoring relationship, as entering the organization or any group, requires regression. In addition, the nature of the relationship encourages temporary—and possibly years long—regression in the service of the individual's ego interests of realizing personal ambitions. Levinson, Darrow, Klein, Levinson, and McKee (1978) observe the relationship progresses like the childhood separation and individuation process. The mentor serves as a parent who provides a stable but manipulable environment for the younger one to establish an identity. With this support, the protégé can temporarily regress to childlike cognitive and emotional conditions of differentiation, anxiety, experimentation, expectation, and, hopefully, independence. Thus there will be times when the mentee cannot give the organization his most sophisticated intellectual abilities.

In short, the mentor is not simply an initiator, but a subversive one. How does someone with interests in mentoring negotiate initiation to an organization on these terms? First, in most cases, because these interests arise after someone has been an organizational member for a time, they call for a reinitiation. Crucially, the opposite negotiating number is different than with previous work-related aims. In those situations, an individual negotiated generally with veterans as a group. Although demonstrating competence might require showing specific accomplishments to a small number of individuals, and although establishing a work identity in a formal role might involve convincing a few coworkers, it was clear that these examiners represented the entire body of veterans. Becoming a mentor, in contrast, is negotiated with a single other individual who has no authority to represent a collegium. Indeed, the mentee has low status and hardly could speak for others. In addition, their relationship remains more or less invisible to the rest, unless the mentor has a prominent position or unless the two flaunt their intimacy in a way that denigrates others or interferes with normal collaboration.

People who want to mentor someone express this wish in a variety of ways. Because of the special relationship between a senior and a junior, few people explicitly approach an organization expecting to mentor someone, although an interest in becoming a supervisor may express this desire. Certain work, such as training, involves teaching and provides opportunities for mentoring relations. More people, however, develop an interest in inducting newcomers as they mature in an organization. Some may even leave an organization if they cannot satisfy wishes to pass something on to a successor. Their departure, such as the one Ryan plans, may be considered a failed self-reinitiation.

The following examples show people who have already settled questions about their competence, work identity, and organizational affiliation. As they develop interests in mentoring, they associate them with different past experiences and use different contemporary opportunities to express them.

Playing with the Role as Transitional Object: Jean Wilson

Jean Wilson changed organizations to gain supervisory responsibilities. During nine years as an environmental planner in a county planning department, she did most of her work alone. The job gave her considerable autonomy but little support or collegiality. Most of her professional contacts involved interagency committees, rather than other staff members in her own department. She felt that she had developed considerable expertise in her field but that there were limits to what she could accomplish as a one-person division. She wanted to direct others in a larger effort, and she wanted to teach others what she had learned.

During this time she became acquainted with the environmental staffs at several other local planning departments, and when one of them advertised for a chief of environmental planning, she applied, successfully. Discussing her expectations and first impressions of the new organization, she notes that she had been working with it for several years already and was not really a newcomer.

Although it didn't seem to take long for others to accept her, she says, "There was a question mark in every mind, and they look at you every time they go by, like they do a double-take." People are concerned about

> everything, so they know how to relate, to know if you are going to step on their toes. With subordinates there is a touch of fear and trepidation, not knowing who their new boss is. With peers there is just curiosity. With subordinates: How is this going to affect me? How quiet should I be?

Choosing her own metaphor for entry negotiations, she describes using the role as a transitional object, to remain herself and yet gain membership in the agency:

> There is an envelope in which you can fit. But that envelope is pretty big. It is created by the person before you. You notice it when you step outside: "Arthur never told us that." "But I'm me."

The "envelope" contains the roles she can acceptably take with others with whom she must work. They give her certain expectations, and then she can try to promote others of her own. Socially, the envelope holds the communitas in which newcomer and veterans confront one another in the transitional stage of a rite of passage. To feel like a member of the organization, at some point she must conclude that there is a place within the envelope where she can be herself.

Her envelope included a lot of pieces left by her predecessor. He was a landscape architect, and he conceptualized environmental issues largely in terms of design. He had been the agency's voice on the environment for many years, and the ways in which he interpreted problems had molded others' thinking. In contrast, she was trained as an environmental planner with more specific interests in biological issues. Thus, one question was whether she could persuade staff members and people in other agencies to redefine environmental planning.

In working through these issues, she had to deal with something else her predecessor left in her envelope — relationships with the "power players" who made decisions about development and thereby affected the local environment. Because he took part in meetings with top elected officials, agency heads, and developers, she did so from the start. Thus, she had to negotiate the boundaries of environmental issues in a high-pressure political setting. She succeeded. She concluded that she had passed, that she had crafted a workable space in the envelope, when she heard that the "power people" had approvingly told others what she said in these meetings. As a result, her boss, peers, and subordinates could be reassured that she could fill the formal environmental planning role and, in turn, accepted her as an organizational member.

Once she felt part of the organization (6), she could move on to the more complicated initiatory task of becoming a supervisor to her own staff (7). Although she exercised the formal authority of the role from the start, this transition would mean becoming more than simply a boss who had to be obeyed, but someone who was respected and followed because she was admirable. The process was one of persuading her subordinates to accept her as a legitimate leader. In an important way, their thinking about her mirrored her development. Until they were convinced she was and would remain a part of the organization, they could not be concerned with considering her a teaching supervisor.

Taking the supervisory role, including its mentoring aspects, required a negotiation with her subordinates, who wanted more than her substantive expertise. She also had to show them that she recognized their ways of working and needs for support. Crucial to developing these relationships, she says, was her success with the agency director and the "power people." Her supervisees wanted her to prove she valued their efforts by demonstrating that she knew enough about the bureaucracy to get them important assignments and get their work a hearing. At the same time, getting a response from above made them feel she was herself powerful, someone worth following. In short, these were their tests of her, and in order to teach them, she had to convince them that she could be a model of what they themselves would like to be.

Describing what she has learned about her staff, as well as how she responds individually to them, she says,

> Some people are happy to work like crazy. Some people with kids have to be places. Every pianist can play a piano, but every piano is different. Some people like a lot of supervision. Some resent supervision. For example, I have one person who is very self-motivated, who is in a lesser position than some who are not self-motivated. So here I am giving task-by-task [supervision] to a person who is of a

higher level than someone to whom I can give a general concept. I also supervise someone who is equal to me in civil service level. It has not been a problem, but it has the potential to be a problem. . . . I have the virtue of more thorough knowledge of the subject matter, but he also has been in the bureaucracy longer. So he knows all the tricks about how to use the bureaucracy, with boards, et cetera. It is a whole new structure for me, but once you have been put in an organization, it doesn't take that much precedence.

She says she concluded that she had succeeded in initiating herself with her supervisees when they began to include her in their regular social activities.

Wilson's interests in teaching are consistent with and legitimated by her organizational role. The formal role requires her to manage subordinates to produce work she can present authoritatively to her boss and to the "power players." Although teaching may be instrumental to getting good work from her staff, it is invisible and "extra." Crucially, she can negotiate mentoring relationships with her staff only insofar as she seems authoritative, someone they would like to be like. Thus her opportunities for the informal teaching she values depend on her success at the formal relationships. But her success at teaching or mentoring depends on developing informal relationships with subordinates. She must discover which of her staff would allow her to instruct them, as well as which would resist, and accordingly modulate her expressions of authority and intimacy.

Mentoring as Gratitude for Earlier Help: Ralph Yarrow

First months or even years, as a number of workers have said, may be upending. People may feel uncertain about what they know, whether anyone wants what they can do, or whether they have a place at all. With time, newcomers may work through relations with veterans, recapturing or establishing their sense of competence, work identity, and attachment to the organization. Nevertheless, these accomplishments may not heal the pain of the initial isolation.

However, when people stay in an organization, move up in it, and increasingly identify with some part of it (6), they acquire the seniority, the opportunity, and, crucially, the developmental wish to introduce others into the organization (7). Orienting or mentoring a newcomer makes it possible to give another what one did not get oneself. Unconsciously, taking care of a junior worker allows someone to play with the injury of not having been properly cared for when he first arrived. The passive injury of having been left to float may be turned into actively providing an anchor for someone else whose situation one identifies with. Unconsciously, helping another like oneself allows one, finally, to treat one's own initial injuries. Ralph Yarrow takes pleasure in mentoring others because doing so, he says, allows him to give them some of the support that relieved his own pain after three or four years of floundering.

Yarrow grew up in a small town in Virginia. When the Korean War heated up, he was drafted. When the war was over, he returned home and went to college on the G.I. Bill. When he graduated, he took a job as a highway inspector. A friend of his wife suggested he try to get a federal job. He took a civil service examination and got expressions of interest from the Department of Health, Education, and Welfare (HEW) and two military agencies. Uncertain how dependable military employment would be, he interviewed with HEW, passed, went to a training course in another state, and began a series of positions as field representative in regional offices. After a half dozen years, about twenty years ago, he decided he wanted a promotion that would require moving to national headquarters. About this time, welfare reform created a major new federal program, and he moved to Washington as an operations analyst.

Just as his background resembled Davis', his initial confrontation (I) with the national office left him similarly overwhelmed.

> The first thing that strikes you is how large this thing is, and you wonder if you can ever understand how this thing works, if you will ever understand it. If you are working with any program, the first thing that strikes you is that you are doing only a part of it. There is no one group in here that handles all aspects of these projects. There is no one that writes the policy and does the systems work. You begin to wonder, Who will I go to for this and that? Will I ever learn how this whole place works? . . . Coming into a systems or operations area, it was very strange to me.

It made him feel helpless.

> At my age I didn't feel like a new kid. But I felt like a dumb one, not very smart. Nothing you had done in the past, my prior experiences didn't help me here. . . . It just takes you a number of years to find out how do I get something done. . . . Just becoming familiar with the bureaucracy. All bureaucracy is the same. It took me a good three to four years at a minimum.

The organization was huge, complicated, and confusing, and none of his past knowledge or ability worked in this new situation.

In the beginning, he says, describing the working through period (II) which may or may not lead to a transition into the organization,

There is a period of adjustment. They are looking at you, and you are looking at them. They are trying to assess your skills and weaknesses, and you are doing the same. There are people who come in who cannot adjust. They couldn't adjust to working in this complex with twenty thousand people. [The veterans] were basically evaluating me in terms of whether or not I had the mind-set to do this work: i.e., do you have a logical, rational mind? There are a lot of people who can't work technically that are particular to the organization I am in, which does systems analysis. It is a matter of looking for someone who could think logically and act logically. [At the same time,] I was checking these people out. I don't think I checked the people so much. Their level of knowledge. I was looking at the job. I was spending quite a bit of time thinking. Do I want to do this type of work? It is difficult to pick up and move. I was basically looking at this organization and the particular job I had been placed in. In my case the answer was yes.

During this period the agency provided training that was supposed to help new employees, but the teaching was abstract and disconnected from the personal relationships necessary for getting work done:

You go to various and sundry formal classroom training programs. That gives you a basic understanding of data processing and how operations around here work. After you come out of classes, you discover that you still don't know any darn thing.

"So what they generally do," what really helps, he explains,

is assign you to another person, what we now call a mentor. A non-supervisor who they will put a new trainee with till he can assimilate things on his own. You are constantly being reeducated. As you move into the management line, your emphasis begins to change. They teach you various and sundry management skills—not being so technically oriented, and how to work with people.

His mentor inducted him into the culture of the federal bureaucracy. He taught Yarrow how to write, and he advised him on formulating strategies. Crucially, the mentor had faith in Yarrow, supported him in his efforts to take initiatives, and provided him with a personal anchor in a large impersonal organization. Yarrow gratefully describes this help, referring in two different ways to feeling "protected."

You are more or less dependent on your mentor to guide you along. If you are asked to write a systems proposal, they will check it very carefully before it goes into final form. You begin to realize that [what] you are writing affects people's [welfare] checks. You are somewhat protected [by your anonymity] around here. You are not out on your own as you are in a small concern. There are hundreds of people doing the same thing around here. In the first place, you are writing instructions for someone else. The poor devil out in that field office has to take the first flack. You are more or less protected in the central office.

At last, after several years, Yarrow "felt I was accepted" (III).

It didn't mean that I knew everything that was going on. Probably at the end of, say, a couple of years. You usually feel accepted when you get your first promotion. I was fairly uncomfortable around here the first one and a half to two years. At the end of three or four years I pretty well knew what was going on. I still don't know what is going on here. You never do in a place this size. I don't think there is any one particular event [that symbolized my acceptance]. Probably you realize that you finally can do this kind of work. It is when you can take a project and can work it through on your own.

His first promotion was one of many, and he is now a deputy division director, managing one hundred fifty people, including programmers, analysts, clerical workers, and supervisors. He identifies with the organization, and others respect his seniority (6).

I have an important role to play here. I have influence in the area where I work. I am recognized as somebody who has a certain level of skills. I am fairly well thought of around this place. I think I am looked on as someone who contributed a fair amount of expertise to this organization over the years. I am someone who did a good job for the agency over the years. I am well thought of because of this. I can't think of any negative aspects to my career.

He has moved out of analysis and is primarily an administrator. Now his greatest satisfaction comes from helping others make their way into the organization (7),

helping to recruit new systems people and helping these people get started in their careers here. I get very little involved in technical aspects anymore. They try to place the people as best as possible—

get the new people on board—and shift our workforce around and get the tasks done. Reallocate people among tasks. Keep things on an even keel. There is budget work that is not the greatest fun in the world. [My greatest satisfaction] is working with the new people, and moving them into supervision, and to try to give them the basic guidelines and tools to provide them with the abilities and supervision.

Speaking as someone who has made it in the organization, he reflects on what worked for him in advising newcomers to

work very hard at first and get a good basic ground in what we are trying to do here. Apply yourself very diligently very early. If you don't do this, the people who can't get promotions are those people who don't have a good basic understanding of what is going on around here. The basic task. The big picture. Get yourself a good grounding of what the basic mission is here. You have got to move out of your own sphere of influence. How your component's activity fits into the big picture. Don't limit yourself to what you are doing at the time.

After floundering at the beginning, unable to make sense out of the huge organization, he understands and counsels others in seeing "the big picture."

Yarrow links his assistance to newcomers with the mentoring that finally relieved the pain of his early years. He plays with his initial injury in several ways. By giving others the aid he needed but did not get for a long time, he unconsciously takes active control over the situation he passively suffered earlier. By identifying with the mentor who eventually rescued him, he strengthens himself. His pleasure in inducting others expresses both his satisfaction in symbolically gaining control over his own overwhelming experiences and gratitude at his mentor's assistance. In his mind, mentoring is an act of loyalty to the organization; he is finally repaying an old debt. Though he does not say so, his actions also repair the organization. At least in a small way, it is no longer a place that injures newcomers. If he were once angry at the bureaucracy that did not care for little people, if he once harbored thoughts of getting back at it for what it had done to him, he no longer says so. Instead, he identifies with the organization, which he helps to be a good, caring place.

Mentoring as Compensation and Reparation for Not Being Helped Earlier: Harriet O'Neill

Sometimes workers develop interests in mentoring because of the opposite initial experience. No one ever helped them in their painful struggle with the new organization, and they want to mentor others as a way of becoming what they hoped for but missed.

Harriet O'Neill, for example, associates her interests in mentoring with her own initiation. Her first job after getting a degree in social work was clinical work in a federally funded health program. Over the next ten years she moved among several field offices of the federal agency and advanced into supervision. About fifteen years ago she took a promotion to headquarters in Washington and moved into personnel administration. In her initial confrontation with the central office, she recounts upending first experiences like Yarrow's (I).

> I was astounded by the physical size of the organization. Secondarily, I was astounded by the resources and the high grades, the big money that was being paid related to what seemed initially narrow responsibility. No consistency with someone out there who runs an office that serves a couple of million population.

Not only was the organization large, she recalls, but the language was new, assignments were ambiguous, and, particularly difficult to deal with, work led to few specific products.

It was bewildering to work through a role in the organization (II). Not only was her work ambiguous, but no one was particularly interested in either showing or telling her how to do her job. Her formal supervisor was no help:

> There was little structure, orientation to what was a different environment. What you picked up tended to be from peers. Most of the positions have a quasi-supervisory position, who reviewed your work, who was available, who, if you had a patient one, taught you things. For example, "This person you are writing to has a preference for these terms." This was survival. . . . I went into an abominable area. I had a manager who was a lovely man but a terrible manager. I had to do a lot of work. . . .
>
> The first experience was such a negative one, but I guess it happens often enough. There are some fairly well-prescribed parts of your work. There are certainly subjects that are yours to deal with. What is difficult, what you learn by trial and error, and by the grace of your peers, is how you function in this role. You may have writing skills, but you don't know whom you need to talk to. Whom to get approval or disapproval, not always a good sense of how what you are working on impacts the larger organization. [It would be helpful if there were someone who said,] "Until you get a grasp of generally, say, 99 percent of the cases, here is what I do. On the rest I play it

by ear." [Eventually] you get confident, so that you are not fum-
bling around. I don't think we have an organized program we
put people through.

She expected the veterans to take responsibility for inducting her
along with other new members. However, she reflects, perhaps her
"sheltered naive background" led her unrealistically to expect to be
taken care of.

I have an extraordinarily high awe threshold. I have always thought
that people who hold a position have certain characteristics, whether
they do or not. So when I came back here, I tended to hold certain
people in certain lights because of the jobs they held.

She expected those in high positions to act like adults. Instead, what was
most disturbing, they childishly did whatever they pleased.

Finally, "a year or year and a half" after she began working in
headquarters, she felt like part of the organization (III). There was
no specific incident so much as general impressions. For example, she
would say things in her area of expertise and find that others accepted
her views.

Nevertheless, as a result of her first experiences, she has always
thought about taking care of newcomers.

I am always very concerned when I directly supervise people. I am
very conscious of trying to go forth, of trying to get them involved.
. . . The only thing I would say is, before I die or retire, and there is
not a lot of pressure to do it now, I would really like to see the
agency get much more serious to structure training so that people
who make big moves like I did would get as much help as possible.

In the absence of any significant organizational change, she has
taken advantage of opportunities to make her own contributions to new
workers' security, to make sure they get the guidance she never received.
She says she always thinks about the early period when she sat around
and had nothing to do, where her idleness made her feel both ashamed
that she didn't seem useful and guilty that she was taking money for
doing nothing. When she became a supervisor, she went out of her way
to give new staff members training and meaningful work. "I think I have
projected into jobs where I am doing what the people who work for me
do a lot of work which is meaningful."

When asked what she does that best allows her to act on her interests
and abilities, she immediately mentions mentoring.

In the past, I mentored people in the [agency's] developmental program. It is good for me. It makes me take a different look at issues. Where do you want to go? What does it take to get there? What does it take to be a well-rounded person? And the individuals are interesting.

O'Neill becomes interested in mentoring as an appropriate developmental aim after she feels she has become part of the organization. However, her associations between her various mentoring and supervising activities and her first experiences show her mentoring to be a way of playing with the injuries of entry. Mentoring, in contrast with the childishness of her own early superiors, is an adult activity. She offers others the parentlike guidance that newcomers need and she never got. In particular, she contrasts the partial attention of her supervisors with her treatment of her protégés as whole persons. She is attracted to them; they are "interesting." When she thinks about helping them get started, she tries to interpret their work needs broadly. Crucially, becoming interested in them in these ways brings her back to thinking about her own goals and making herself "well rounded." Unconsciously, nurturing people with whom she identifies helps to make herself whole.

At the same time, especially when she participates in the department's management development program, she, like Yarrow, thinks of mentoring as a contribution to the organization. She repairs the organization that did not care for her by making it more caring. As a result of her efforts, it is no longer a callous entity toward which she or her protégés need feel angry, vengeful, or guilty about such impulses. By treating her injury and by making the organization less injurious, mentoring is, indeed, "good for" her.

Mentoring and Work Organizations

These people vary in the formality of their mentoring, its intimacy and intensity, and the relationship between mentoring interests and organizational membership. O'Neill is the only one who mentors others with official recognition, through the agency's management development program. In addition, she, like Yarrow, informally works closely with a few of the people she supervises and guides them in the organization and in their careers. Wilson, at least for now, looks for less intimate teaching relations with some of her supervisees. In her case, she is informally deepening one of her formal role responsibilities.

Some of the apparent difference in intensity between Yarrow and O'Neill's mentoring relations and Wilson's teaching relations seems related to age differences. Yarrow and O'Neill are twenty to thirty years older than the people they mentor, and probably parent-child feelings become part of their relations with protégés. In addition, as mentors, they represent and are gatekeepers into large organizations. Their resultant power and the greatness of what their mentoring can give adds to the intensity of the relations. In contrast, Wilson is barely older than some of her subordinates and younger than others. Her organization is small, with few levels of hierarchy, and most people quickly come to know one another. As a result, her teaching is likely to be less parental or mysterious and more collegial.

Yarrow and O'Neill think of themselves as mentoring others on behalf of both themselves and their organizations and feel that their activities help both newcomers and the organization. For them, mentoring interests follow, and follow from, their attachment to the organization. Yarrow identifies particularly deeply with his agency. Wilson, in contrast, thinks primarily of teaching and secondarily of becoming a member of any particular organization. Nevertheless, she has to become part of the agency before her supervisees accept her as a potential teacher.

All three stories show that mentoring is a developmental interest, dependent on other accomplishments, most immediately identifying with a collectivity, on behalf of which and into which one guides protégés. The collectivity to which Yarrow and O'Neill relate is some part of their formal organization. Wilson thinks first of a professional field, environmental planning, into which she wants to induct willing supervisees, though her membership in the formal organization gives her the authority to teach.

Still, as Yarrow and O'Neill illustrate, specific motives for mentoring often derive from someone's first organizational experiences. Those who become organizational members recover sufficiently from their initial confrontation to work through relations with veterans. Nevertheless, the memory of the injury may persist, and mentoring offers an opportunity to play further with it and repair it. By actively caring for another with whom one identifies, a mentor may heal the wound of neglect passively suffered earlier.

In addition, mentoring may be a gift to the organization. Even when one had a good mentor, one can never directly repay the debt by mentoring him in return. Instead, one strengthens the organization by making it a more caring institution. For those who suffered from a lack of guidance, mentoring repairs the organization by making it a nurturant place. Workers who struggled early on may feel angry and vengeful toward the organization or toward supervisors who never helped. In turn, they may unconsciously feel they succeeded in hurting the organization or the supervisors, and guilt may hold them back from acting as aggressively as their work requires. Mentoring may reassure them that they never really hurt anyone or anything, because, after all, an organization in which they mentor, must be a good, whole place.[3]

All these motives contribute to the pleasure of mentoring. Helping a young person with whom one identifies is deeply gratifying, as is growing into the position of someone who took care of one earlier. Repairing an organization that one imagined damaging satisfies by relieving anxiety.

MAKING SENSE: THINKING FOR ONESELF

Making sense of life's experiences is something one does for and by oneself. Others may provide a mirror or audience, but the final judge of the integrity of the themes is the one who crafts the story. In certain ways, this search for wisdom in the final stage of life resembles the search for basic trust in the first. Both are solitary activities. In both, the relationship between one's self and the world is, at best, ambiguous.

Although the older person examining life's experiences and recounting them to some of those who will listen seemingly occupies a world of many people, he is the only real datum and the only real audience. Moreover, it is the sense of leaving this life, perhaps going to another, but at least approaching something great and eternal, which inspires the painful search for wisdom. The old person is on the same boundary as the infant, where the world sometimes seems to be one body and sometimes two. The difference is that the older one is moving back toward the single-body world, while the infant considers emerging from it. This is life's symmetry.

How well the search for meaning goes depends on how well preceding developmental efforts have worked out. Erikson (1984), emphasizing the links among all the stages, notes that the first provides an important foundation for the last. Basic trust in infancy gives rise to hope, which by old age may mature into faith. If the infant can trust the world of the parents to be dependably nurturant, then in old age he will have faith in the basic meaningfulness of the world.

The search for meaning has no intrinsic relation to work. Work may provide meaning, for example, by showing that one can competently help others. But the search for meaning spans one's entire life—not only work, but also love, not only adulthood, but also childhood. Work may seem less important in this quest for those who have retired, especially if they were forced to do so.

Like mentoring, looking for meaning in one's work is subversive to organizations. It is a solitary activity, with loyalty only to oneself. Furthermore, it is motivated by a sense that mundane things and appearances matter less than the transcendent and the essential. In seeking these meanings, one must question what one has done and what others expect. At last one asks whether what the organization demanded was worth it, whether it meant anything. The search cannot avoid being seditious.

Seeking meaning is ultimately more subversive than any other developmental quest. For here the accomplishments of sublimation themselves
may be overthrown. Just as work arrangements may be questioned, so,
too, may the "polite" expressions of libido or aggression. Even if older
people do not act on all their new conclusions, they may be less loyal to
the sublimatory expectations of work than ever before.[4]

No organization hires someone solely because of his interest in making personal sense of life's experiences, though someone who matures and
rises in an organization may become a top executive or senior advisor
whose sense-making efforts also aid the organization. In the latter cases,
the work of organizational reflection may represent at least a subtle
change in role, requiring some reinitiation. However, most often, the
developmental aim of finding meaning in things, because subversive as
well as peripheral, remains covert. An individual tacitly initiates himself
into an organization by testing whether activities there help make sense
of life themes.

The following case studies illustrate the tangential relationship of
the search for meaning to organizational work.

Playing with Work to Make Sense of Her Life: Norma Sawyer

Norma Sawyer, now in her early sixties, has used her work to express
and reconcile major themes in her life. She began working for pay only
twenty years ago, when her husband left her after their children were
grown and she had to support herself. Although, as she acknowledges,
she was hardly in a position then to think about a career, let alone find
work that could begin one, she ended up taking jobs that made sense of
lifelong preoccupations. Drawn to nature and concerned about civic
affairs, for the past six years she has organized public participation in
environmental decisions for a regional planning agency.

Work became for her a second career, after raising a family. She had
to take courses to develop marketable skills (4) and to establish a viable
work role (5). Once she settled into her job, she was able to identify with
aspects of the organization (6) and nurture those who work with it (7). But,
crucially, even though she was thrown from the role of homemaker into
the labor market, these challenges at work were only new forms of developmental tests she had already satisfied. She had come to terms with
generativity in raising children (7). Even though her family experiences
were not directly transferrable to the world of work, her accomplishments
there gave her confidence and ability to move ahead on the job.

In a number of ways, she was ready to think about the meaning of
her life (8) when she began working. She had been abruptly ejected from
a career she had taken for granted, and she had to come to terms with
what had happened. At the same time, she was developmentally prepared

to examine the integrity of her life. Beginning work in her forties, she had to be concerned about work skills and work identity, but she also wanted to be sure her actions made sense.

When she entered the work world, she had some typically upending experiences, including a reprimand from a boss who felt she had been dangerously disloyal in some public comments. Nevertheless, she succeeded in proving her value and in being accepted. The account here focuses on how she now uses work to make sense of her life.

When Sawyer was growing up, she never expected to go to work. For a woman of her generation there were few models of women who had jobs; for her, "there was no working woman." Her mother raised children. Her father was a successful scientist and inventor who valued higher education. However, neither parent considered diverting their daughter from a traditional path. "My family expected me to go to college and get married for life!" Those women who failed to find husbands became teachers, but Sawyer says she certainly didn't want to be a teacher. Hence her major decision concerned what to study in college while waiting for a husband.

She identified with her father's scientific work, and her older sister had gone into astronomy. At a different point on the cosmic continuum Norma chose botany. She says hers was "a science-oriented family. . . . So I thought science was right." But, she reflects, she made her choice more on the basis of loyalty to her father than any consideration of her own inclinations.

> I went into science because of the model, not because I had a
> scientific mind. . . .I can't get away from the idea that science got
> me in my head, rather than my abilities.

And yet her particular scientific choice, botany, was not accidental, as her later activities suggest.

She enrolled in a women's college and married a man she met while there. During the next two decades she raised two children. Interested in public affairs, she volunteered with civic associations. Then her husband left her, and for the first time in her life, she had to work to earn a living. Despite her lack of choices, her first paying job made sense in terms of her interests. Concerned about nature and committed to civic responsibility, she found a job helping citizen groups become active in environmental preservation.

Although she has worked for three other organizations since then, each job represents a variation on that first one. Her work continues a number of her lifelong activities. Here it is useful to listen to what she says about herself.

If she had any choices earlier, she says, she feels she has few now. "I don't have an unlimited future in terms of more money, especially with the government. I don't think I will jump around much." She has an old bachelor's degree in a field where higher credentials are increasingly important. "The way to change at this point would be to go back to school and learn something else. But I'm sixty, right?" What possibilities does she weigh, at least in fantasy?

> If I were thirty years old, it would be different. I think your age makes a difference. If I were thirty, I would go back to school and become an engineer, because engineers here do well. If I were career oriented today, I would think about forestry, something that would get me outdoors. In 1950 the idea of my being a forester never crossed my mind.

To be financially more secure, perhaps also to pay appropriate homage to her father the scientist, she would become an engineer. But to suit herself she would become a forester. Forestry is a nurturant, even a maternal, activity, tending to the greatest mother of all, Mother Nature. It is a confidently caring activity. At least unconsciously, as Sawyer offers advice to herself at age thirty, she understands how to reconcile her various activities and interests: being a forester would make it possible to be a mother and to express her concern about nature.

Although forestry is a solitary activity, there is a complementary social side to Sawyer as well. She entered the 1960s in her early thirties and found the events of that decade extremely exciting. She liked the social activism of the period, where people who had previously accepted their world now discovered they could change it. Probably these public thoughts of hers mirrored private, even unconscious reflections on her own life. Her social interests involved the natural environment.

> I was very active in the sixties. We discovered Appalachia, the wetlands. The world was going to pot. I got involved with the Sierra Club. What people do is related to the world and us. I just like to see changes in public policy, and this involves people. I have done things like run for office, support candidates in elections. . . . I like seeing things happen.

She recounts a rich personal history of civic activism, with electoral campaigns, community organizing, service on boards, and "a lot of reform spirit." Her extensive voluntary activities of the 1960s presage her later employment, combining a concern about nature with a belief in democracy.

In her present job she does many things to promote public participation in environmental planning. She circulates information about
programs to citizen organizations and provides ways for environmental
groups to participate in public hearings and comment on development
proposals. She gets pleasure at work from

> my contacts with the public. I enjoy getting out and talking with
> the public and telling them what we are doing and bringing back
> their conclusions. There is job satisfaction. I can see things I
> have accomplished.

As part of her job, she staffs an environmental advisory committee,
serving the chairman and organizing periodic meetings. She says this
work really gives her an opportunity to play with her interests and
abilities. As a result of her enthusiasm, "Some of our quarterly meetings
are spectacular. . . . The last one come off beautifully." In her role, she
brings together not only her concern with nature and her commitment to
public participation, but also her nurturant tendencies. This part of her
job is like a professionalization of her role as homemaker.
What is gratifying about her work is that

> I get to see the delivery of services, to see if citizens like what we
> provide. As I go on, I get a better sense of what a government should
> be, and I don't think there is any difference between government
> and the people.

And yet she acknowledges "my function is odd for bureaucracy,"
which normally conceals decisions and excludes citizens. She doesn't
know yet, after six years, whether she is accepted as a legitimate
member of the organization, which employs her to satisfy federal funding conditions. But she identifies very strongly with her role, and she
feels confident that she is a member of the environmental community,
even if not of her agency. With pride she characterizes herself as "an
ombudsman for the public."
    Her complaints about salary and bureaucratic rigidity notwithstand-
ing, her work fits her. As possibly her last job, it makes sense of lifelong
concerns. Playing with the possibilities of her role, she has found professionally respectable and organizationally legitimate ways to express
her concerns about nature, promote citizen participation, and nurture
others. As a self-designated ombudsman, she maintains independence
on the organization's boundary. By shaping her work in a way that gives
meaning to her life, she has succeeded in initiating herself into the
organization on her own terms.

She is able to use her work to make sense of the public and private themes in her life (8) because she has found ways to satisfy the developmental prerequisites as well. She has exploited her botanical background and supplemented it with courses in public participation to develop a valued work ability (4), and she has created a work identity that satisfies both her employer and herself (5). In addition, her job enables her to identify with citizen groups, as well as an advisory committee (6). All her actions implicitly contribute to caring for nature, while her staff work specifically nurtures the committee (7). These accomplishments are both developmental prerequisites for and part of the work of finding integrity in her life. She has thus succeeded in avoiding the despair that could come from being a rejected wife and an older woman of little value to others.

Using the Job for Making Sense of Her Life: Edith Cone

Edith Cone's story is similar in many respects. She is also in her early sixties. She, too, grew up in a time and a family where women did not go to work. Like Sawyer, she lives alone in this period of her life, although she is recently widowed, rather than divorced. The big difference between the two is that Cone does not find her work to be a source of life's meaning. Rather, she has used things her job has offered her to make sense of her life outside of work.

Although her mother didn't work, at age fifteen Cone imagined she would become a teacher. However, when she graduated from high school during the Depression, she concluded that it would be hard on her parents if she did not go to work, instead of college. Her parents felt college was a necessity more for boys than girls; despite the hard times, if her older brother had wanted to go to college, they would have paid for him. She says, "If I had done things the way I wanted, I would have gone to college and gone into teaching." Instead, she took commercial courses for a year and went to work. She worked as a secretary until she got married two years later.

For the next eighteen years she stayed home, raising children, although she did a lot of volunteer work. She organized a nursery school and took part in other activities involving children. When her children entered college, she returned to the labor market to supplement the family income. She became a secretary again. For five years she worked with a garment firm, but staff feuds got to be too much for her. She was secretary to two men who didn't like each other. Alternately, they would come to her and say, "Do my work, don't do his work," and then pull the paper out of her typewriter. She waited until the factory closed for vacation, checked the classified ads, took a test, and got a clerical job with a state agency.

During the twenty years she has been with this agency, she says, she has worked hard at whatever she was offered. She was initially shocked by bureaucratic ways. For the first few weeks she sat at a desk with mail piling up, but she wasn't allowed to open it because she hadn't been oriented yet. She could not believe the do-it-tomorrow attitude she found. When she wanted to answer someone's letter after the afternoon mail had gone out, she would sometimes put her own stamps on the envelopes, just to make sure the correspondent got the timely reply he deserved. She has had difficult bosses and good bosses. She was particularly fond of one, an ex-colonel.

> He would walk down the hall thinking, not saying anything. In an hour, he would come up with something that no one could work out in three or four days. He said to me on the first day, "I will not always do what you want, but you can count on me to listen."

After about ten years, the governor reorganized the agency, and Cone managed to move from her secretarial position to a low-level administrative job, whose description had been tailored to her background. Then, two years ago, she accomplished an extraordinary feat, getting promoted to a major administrative position. Often she had wanted to take tests for promotions but was not permitted to apply because she did not have a college degree. This time, she says, thousands took the examination, she scored near the top, and she came out first in the interviews. She now runs a statewide regulation program, and she supervises several dozen secretaries doing what she used to do. With pride she says,

> This job was quite a promotion for me, a three-grade promotion. It was nice because I was deadended. I would not have dared not to take this job: I was a lot of "wrongs": perhaps the wrong sex, the wrong race, the wrong age. I felt that for my countrymen I had to do it.

To emphasize that she was the best choice, she talks with pleasure about the extra efforts she makes to help out the program's clients.

She says that work is an important part of her life, probably especially so since her husband died, and she has moved ahead in the organization. Nevertheless, over the years she recognized the importance of the college degree she lacked, and it made her think more and more about using her job to pursue the career she had wished for before the setback of the Depression.

She began taking work-related courses offered at the department by the community college. As if she really were in her teens again, she remarks that this effort made her mother swell with pride. College was a turning point.

The school experience showed me I could do it. I enjoyed competing in my fifties with younger people and sometimes coming out better. I regret very much that I didn't start earlier.

She is not sure her present job is her ideal job, but it challenges and gratifies these wishes for an education. She says with satisfaction that she has "to learn a lot of new stuff at an older age, and basically I have to learn it on my own. . . . I feel good that I have learned this job as well as I have learned it. I am successful."

At last, she became the successful college student she had wanted to be. Although the courses she started with were related to her job, she satisfied her work interests relatively quickly. After all, she was in her fifties, she already had a family, and she wasn't really preparing for a long work career. She began thinking more about making sense of her life, and she started filling in her education with courses about ideas and feelings.

She took a literature course that affected her deeply. After the instructor read her papers, he encouraged her to write and offered to help her publish when she was ready. Realistically, she will never be the schoolteacher she thought of when she was fifteen, but writing offers a chance to teach in a way connected with her contemporary concern with finding the meaning of her life. She can write about what she has learned from her experiences, and, by publishing her essays, she could teach others.

She says she "will probably work as long as God and the state let me," but some of the most important items on her personal agenda are things that her job has made possible but that she will take most advantage of after she retires. With a measure of self-deprecation outweighed by poorly concealed pride, she says she wants to continue on "to get my little A.A. [Associate in Arts Degree]." She remarks she does a lot of needlework. Once she retired and had enough free time, she could use this hobby to realize a bit of her teenage ambition: "I could probably teach that if I wanted to." But mostly, she reflects, getting to the point,

I'd like to write a little bit. Mainly essays on life, thoughts and feelings, et cetera. Which I have done already. I have never published. I have never gotten that far. . . .

But she has been in touch with the literature teacher who offered to help her.

Reflecting on her experience in the agency, she offers succinct advice to anyone starting out there. "Keep your creativity, and develop it." This is a distinctly Eriksonian proposition: take stock of who you are, and as you approach each new developmental challenge, take advantage of the world to continue growing. She did not have the career she wanted when she was young, but when she reached the agency later in life, she took opportunities that not only rewarded her financially, but also meshed with her earlier experiences.

Her first position in the agency did not require new job skills, though she and those orienting her wanted to make sure she could use them in the mode of the state bureaucracy (4) and would fit into the role of a state worker (5). With each of her promotions, she has successfully mastered new skills and new relationships. Coworkers accept her, and she feels settled in the department. Still, she identifies more strongly with her role and service to her clients than with the organization and adherence to its rules (6). She has no hesitation about overriding bureaucratic regulations when she wants something done for her clients; after all, she says smilingly, "I am the boss." In uncalled for and largely invisible ways, she gives of herself to both her program's clients and the clerical staff (7). She bends deadlines to get clients documents they need, and her past as a secretary makes her especially sensitive to the needs of clerical workers.

For many of the same reasons as Sawyer, Cone is increasingly concerned with making sense of her life—both her family career and her work career (8). She works because she needs the money, but also because she feels effective doing so. She is finding integrity in her later years. Although she might have despaired of never achieving her childhood ambitions, and although widowhood could have turned her away from the world, she continues to work in it and uses it to make her life meaningful.

Meaning and Work Organizations

Sawyer and Cone measure everyday organizational events against the expectation that work help them make sense of their lives. Somehow the mundane must bring them to the profound. Some events—for example, when Sawyer helps a citizen group get environmental protections into legislation—are exquisitely reassuring and gratifying. Others—for example, when Cone isn't allowed to open accumulating piles of mail because she hasn't been "oriented" yet—are absurd and exasperating. Cone tells this story with full appreciation of its nonsense, and yet—at least after awhile—she sees the humor in it as well. She can use this experience along with others to find meaning in her life. In her Gestalt, this bureaucratic inanity is the backdrop for her own intelligence, persistence, and integrity. Thus a sense of irony is important to the sense-making project.

Whether an organization makes day-to-day sense depends on a reasonable fit with personal expectations. Sawyer and Cone can take meaning from their work, despite their irritation with bureaucratic routines, because their organizations are "meaningful enough."[5] They can play with the organizational material they encounter—roles, relationships, and everyday events—to find ways of working that accommodate their biographies and the truths emerging from them. At their stage in life, in demanding the big picture be meaningful, they may be willing to overlook or give up certain incongruous but nonessential details.

The search for sense late in life is only a special case of a lifelong demand for meaning. As a child grows into an adult, his criteria for meaningfulness become more explicit. A thirty-five-year-old woman, for example, can talk at length about what belonging to a community means to her, whereas an infant has no words and only tentative stirrings of consciousness to decide whether its mother responds to it in the right way. Yet both want their immediate experiences to make sense. In the same way, every work expectation is a wish for social relations that will be gratifying because they are appropriately meaningful. The requirements of professional competence, for example, are in Latham's mind; he will develop a sense of work ability when he satisfies his own expectations. So, too, with Ransom and organizational affiliation or O'Neill and mentoring. Sawyer and Cone's hope of finding that work helps them make sense of their entire lives is only the culmination of a continuing quest for meaning.

The narrowing focus on the broader meaning of things is a developmental interest, succeeding and dependent on all other developmental accomplishments. More than any other adult activity, it is individual work. Especially for the many who are not at the top of organizations, making sense of things uses the materials of the workplace but does not necessarily attach the individual to it. For example, neither Sawyer nor Cone fully identifies with her organization. For both, higher values conflict with organizational loyalty. These are the personal truths that emerge from life's events. Sawyer articulates her truths in common political terms: protect the environment, and promote public participation. Cone speaks more simply in terms of helping those she is responsible for. Sawyer's truths tie her more tightly to a specific job, and she identifies strongly with its constituency. Cone's truths are transferable. Her job serves them, but she can serve them elsewhere. Cone is not as settled as Sawyer. She is still making sense of her life and weighing what is important for her to do. In her search she exploits opportunities the organization offers, but she is sure her job is only a way of discovering and getting to more meaningful activities yet.

Thus, finding meanings for life in work may not tie someone to an organization, though sense-making successes may increase a worker's investments in activities that coworkers see and appreciate.

MENTORING AND MAKING SENSE: POSTWORK AIMS

Mentoring and making sense differ from other developmental interests. Unlike the prework concerns, they may be consistent with organizational interests. Unlike the "work" expectations, satisfying them is not necessarily associated with organizational affiliation; moreover, they are relatively self-centered and less collectively oriented. They belong to a time in life when, both socially and psychologically, work loses centrality. They refer to a period when paid work in formal organizations yields, gracefully or otherwise, to other work—the work of preparing for posterity and the work of reckoning personal accounts. Everyday life may be just as active physically and mentally; it may be more complex socially. But the meaning of these activities changes. In the simplest of terms, producing things for strangers gives way to creating and strengthening relations with others of one's choosing: family members, friends, people in need, a community, or oneself.

People may join or, more often, stay in a work organization to satisfy these interests. However, just as work is not essential to satisfying them, they are not essential to the work of organizations. In a sense, workers with these demands tolerate other organizational conditions, while their coworkers, if they are aware of colleagues' mentoring and sense-making efforts at all, tolerate them as well. Although veterans initiate newcomers with an eye to their ability to work skillfully in appropriate roles and to cooperate sufficiently to get work done, they rarely have initiations for later interests. Workers with postwork expectations must initiate or reinitiate themselves.[6] However, even if they succeed, they may not become as deeply involved in the organization as they were or could have been earlier.

The next section looks at people whose work organizations have disappointed them. Chapter 7 examines prework expectations. Each in a different way conflicts with what veterans want. Each also represents a different retreat from the exercise of power in conventional organizational politics. As a result (as chap. 9 will discuss), each represents different problems in becoming intimately attached to a work organization. Chapter 8 draws general conclusions from all experiences of disappointment with organizations, including those that are eventually remedied, regarding the possibilities of organizational membership.

Part Four
Disappointment and Its Consequences

Working Without Belonging:
Fixation on Recognition, Autonomy, and Power

Workers whose sense of identity depends on getting recognition (1), autonomy (2), or power (3) make demands on organizations that veterans cannot easily agree to. The needs developmentally precede the establishment of work ability, elaboration of a work identity, or affiliation with an organization. When veterans ask them to work industriously, identify with a role, or collaborate with colleagues, they make requests with which these people can hardly comply. Hence, these people are unlikely to negotiate membership on their terms, and they are developmentally unprepared to attach themselves to an organization.

In addition, because they are concerned with issues linked to a period in life prior to the beginning of sublimation, they have not yet learned to sublimate their aggressive and libidinal wishes sufficiently to make compromises required for joining organizations. As a result, because sublimation is crucial for advancing beyond prework expectations, their difficulties in adjusting to organizational norms show themselves most conspicuously in problems with sexuality and aggression.

Expecting recognition, autonomy, or power is not unreasonable or uncommon.[1] What makes these workers' demands problematic is that for each this is nearly the only thing he wants; it is by far the most important reward each expects from work. Moreover, the demand is insatiable: work becomes a continuing search for means of satisfying this one aim.

Each of the persons described here is trying to make a meaningful work situation consistent with his or her sense of identity. All act in good faith. None is in any sense obstinate or perverse, refusing to do something he or she "really" could do. However, unconsciously, they are still concerned about being satisfied by very few people in a small world. In different ways, they are not yet ready to consider themselves cooperative partners in a complex social activity like work.

For reasons not fully clear from what they say, they are concerned with developmental dilemmas normally resolved earlier in life. Their particular orientations may not create difficulties outside work, and they may take advantage of social relations elsewhere to master developmental tests. However, their focal concerns pose problems at work, because they demand resources veterans normally cannot or will not supply. The workplace cannot give them what they need in order to grow.

As their stories reveal, each manages to make a place in an organization, but none succeeds in becoming or feeling part of one. They are on the payroll, but emotionally they do not join, and they do not become attached to either the corporate body in general or other workers in particular. They epitomize the condition of employment without membership.

These people differ from others in the intensity of certain expectations and their sensitivity to whether the workplace supplies certain rewards. They are very much like others in what they want—recognition, autonomy, and power. In exaggerated fashion, they illustrate what happens to any worker who cannot get the recognition, autonomy, or power he expects. The clearest consequence is an inability to enter, let alone identify with, an organization. Another result evident in their stories is difficulty exercising power in organizational politics. As chapter 9 will explain, these two problems are closely related: the unconscious dangers of politics can cause people to regress to seemingly safer early developmental concerns, where neither power politics nor organizational affiliation matter. Thus the three people here, in showing what happens when workers hold prework expectations, also reveal the consequences of any organizational situation that causes workers to regress.

RECOGNITION

Seeking Recognition Libidinally, and Playing Outside When the Organization Fails to Provide It: Susan Dorsey

Susan Dorsey has such strong wishes for recognition that she cannot adjust to the demands of her work organization and become attached to it. She expresses her need for recognition libidinally, often seeking more or less romantic responses from others, rather than the collegial cooperation that work demands. She has worked as a policy analyst in a small division of a state agency for approximately fifteen years. She says she originally wanted to develop her skills (4) and learn a job (5), and yet she has never really moved ahead in the organization. Her wishes for recognition (1) get in her way.

In her account of her organizational career she emphasizes her immediate disappointment with the director. Just out of graduate school, she had anticipated joining an agency where the chief would recognize her obvious professional ability and promote her. Instead, she found her boss indifferent; he treated her as just another new staff member among several whom he hired at the same time. They did not talk much during her early months at the agency, and he gave no sign of seeing her as especially talented. She quickly concluded that he would never give her appropriate recognition or the promotions she deserved. In fact, although she has had a variety of assignments over the years, she has not advanced much, and she blames the director's initial impressions of her.

Whenever she talks about getting recognition from the director or colleagues, she variously describes her relations with them as intellectual and libidinal. She observes that the organization is like a "family." The director, she says, reminds her of a grandfather, though he compares poorly with her own grandfather, who doted on her when she was young, recognizing all her accomplishments. Until the day he died, he was mentally alert and responsive. In contrast, the director lacks the sharpness of mind that would enable him to see her ability. She felt that not only was he indifferent to her work, but also he did not care about her.

From the moment she began, she tried to get to know her colleagues. She wanted to display her intellectual abilities, to prove to others that they needed her. At the same time, she began to socialize with other staff members. She accepted lunch invitations and joined sports activities. She also dated other workers. In recalling these early years, she emphasizes that staff members were broad-minded in accepting close personal relationships among coworkers.

There are signs that during this period both the socializing and some of her professional activities were similarly aimed toward romantic ends. Early on, she got to know a senior staff member who was quite helpful in orienting her to the department. She appreciated that he was very intelligent, "almost too bright," though, perhaps like herself, he did not relate well to others on the staff. Despite the apparent warmth of this relationship, she insists that "it was not personal," because the man was married. She wished others in the agency had his brilliance and interest in her without being married.

Her descriptions of her work efforts of the period call further attention to the apparent intermixing of professional and libidinal interests. She talks of "showing off" her "presentation skills" to colleagues and "using body language" to emphasize points at a staff meeting.

She began working with a man on the research staff in developing a proposal for suburban growth management. She liked analyzing the data, noting, "There is something very cathartic" about displaying it on a map. "It makes you hesitate to computerize it, because you lose the contact." She and the man brainstormed about issues, stimulating one another to think of new sides to the problem and possibilities for intervention. She says,

> I like having my mind challenged, plotting the strategies. I ended up going out with that person, because it was a turn-on. It did not last, because we were different kinds of people. But I have had some good individual experiences like that. If I ever look for another field, I'd look for something like this. I like talking with people and sharing things.

As she portrays the evolution of this relationship, the intellectual stimulation of professional collaboration led to romantic excitement, even though, she notes, they were quite different people. Still, she hopes future work will offer similar opportunities for intellectual exchange that could develop further.

As time went on, she exhausted the dating possibilities in the agency. She also began to feel her intellectual abilities were less and less appreciated. She says she is something of a perfectionist; ever since childhood, she "was always meeting or exceeding people's expectations." This is not always functional at work, where time limitations and political constraints call for compromise. On one occasion, she was trying to collect the last information needed for a study, and her supervisor told her not to, that the study could be considered finished without it. She was angry, because "it was more like reining yourself in when you don't have to." This episode reminds her of childhood questions about how much to achieve in order to get recognition without offending or shaming others.

Over time, new staff members were hired, and some were promoted while she was not. She still related poorly to her department head, and she often felt alienated from the staff as a whole. Professional life has not worked out as well as she had expected from her earlier experiences. "One thing I have brought from childhood is that your work will bring promotion because you have done something singularly well." In explaining her difficulties, she suggests that her intellectual accomplishments, rather than drawing others to her, may have put them off. "This is okay in school, but not in professional work."

In describing her present position, she reveals its pain. "It is not that people discredit me to my face, but I feel not valued emotionally." In an ostensible denial of linkages between work and love, she indicates that the two really are connected for her, and that work has disappointed her in this respect: "It is not that they have to love everything that you do, but they have to be aware of it." She emphasizes, "I can do credible work, but I am an outsider." In a possible unconscious double-entendre she hints at an unconscious meaning of being overlooked. "I don't think people know what to make of me." Even though she works competently, she cannot get the credibility that leads to sexual involvement.

In reality, whatever Dorsey's beliefs and misgivings about success at work, the director kept her on through a period of major staff retrenchment. However, she directed increasing energy to volunteering with community, civic, and religious associations. She observes that volunteering "compensates" for disappointments in her work. Voluntary activities are her own creation: she can choose what she does, she can enter and leave at will, and her actions have no consequences in her formal work world. Socially, each new organization provides an opportunity to meet and date people. She may get recognition from new contacts. In addition, these organizations, many of which are in fields related to her job, provide opportunities for professional success she does not get at work. She can have responsibility for whatever she volunteers to do. She can be accepted by others, can belong to these organizations, and can be central to them. The longer she stays in any organization, the greater authority she can assume. Thus she is able to advance in the voluntary realm, but she still has misgivings that echo the disappointments of her job. "Volunteering," she says, "is sort of like an alternative work setting that is not quite so pleasurable or social, because I am in a decision role. . . . It is lonely at the top"—others respect her ability but keep their distance.

Interpretation

The dominant theme in Dorsey's organizational career is her intense wish for recognition and her continuing failure to get it. Even though she performs more or less successfully in a complex organizational setting, her actions correspond to efforts at growth normally associated with earlier in life. Her apparent failure to find a consistent source of recognition (1) makes it difficult to be secure in such later developmental accomplishments as a sense of professional competence (4), acceptance of a work role (5), and identification with an organization (6). In addition, she has difficulty keeping romantic wishes out of the workplace and thinking more directly about instrumental relations with coworkers.

It is difficult to know why Dorsey searches for recognition as she does, and interpretation must be speculative. Some remarks about her childhood suggest that she unconsciously uses the organization to treat long-standing injuries and to grow from them. She says she has always had to work hard for recognition from adults, beginning in infancy with her father. She feels her father always gave more attention to her older sister, and her resentment still affects relations with her sister. When she went to school, her teachers did not properly recognize her academic successes. They labeled her an overachiever, implying that she was not as capable as she seemed. She offers a puzzled observation about her high school that also suggests a disappointment with recognition. She excelled academically and got some support for that. However, she doesn't understand why students didn't date much at the school. She implies that romantic appreciation would have been a fuller reward for her intellectual work.

Like most others in her high school, she went on to college, but her expectations of education and work were closely linked to her assessments of her parents. She says that her father never overtly influenced her aspirations and did not push her to go to college, although years later he confided that he had wanted her to become a scientist. She says her mother's lack of occupational opportunity strongly convinced her of the value of college, so that she could have choices her mother missed. At the same time, she had no clear idea what work involved. Her father told her little about his jobs and gave no distinct impression of enjoying them, although she recalls that he seemed to like some more than others. Like his wife, he had limited formal education, and he did not advance at work. Dorsey says that she concluded from this that she herself would not advance in whatever career she pursued.

She thus simultaneously idealizes her father and resents his shortcomings with regard to both recognition and work. Although he is the good father whose recognition will support her, he never responded enough to assure her that she could depend on him. Her sister, for one, got more. Her puzzlement about her high school experiences suggests a connection between this early disappointment and her later thinking about the rewards of work. She wanted special recognition for her new intellectual accomplishments; the idea of dating combined earlier wishes for a man's recognition with contemporary adolescent ideas of romance.

Her conclusion that she would not advance professionally because her father had not has no realistic basis. Although she thinks sympathetically of him as a man who did rather well at work with a limited education, in her mind he seems to hold her back. Perhaps she believes that if she outdid him, she would hurt him, and he would punish her by never giving his recognition. This may be why she "reins herself in."

These conflicting perceptions of her father could evoke ambivalent feelings toward him. Although she is attached to the ideal father, at least unconsciously she must resent the father who disappoints her. One can speculate that Dorsey transfers this ambivalence to other men. It could explain her intense search for recognition from her director and her quick—and angry—decision to give up trying to impress him. After all, her unfavorable comparison of him to her grandfather suggests that she wanted him to provide paternal—or, at least, grandfatherly—caring and regard. In general, these assumptions could contribute to her continual, unsuccessful efforts to get the recognition she wants.

Dorsey's organizational career may be seen in terms of difficulties sublimating romantic wishes sufficiently to adapt to working conditions. Her intense desire for the director to recognize her intellectual abilities presented demands he could not satisfy. She seems to have experienced his apparent snub as a reproach (a conflict between her wishes and reality) (Stage I in the sublimation process). Simultaneously, her romantically toned efforts to collaborate with new colleagues put forth expectations that they might not satisfy either. In turn, she may have felt her lack of a steady relationship also as a reproach of her wishes.

Perhaps her emphasis on perfection was a reaction to such a rejection (the beginning of an effort to resolve the conflict) (II). She would apparently disavow romantic interests in work and, instead, raise her standards still higher. In her account of the conflict over this approach to a project, she aggressively maintains her position in order to convince skeptics of her superior competence—and perhaps shame them for not recognizing it. As a new effort to succeed in the organization, this way of working seems to have failed in two ways. In reality she was not recognized and promoted, although she did survive layoffs. Unconsciously, possibly, she feared the consequences of shaming others by measuring them against high standards and vacillated about doing so. She might have experienced either reaction as a reproach for these defensive efforts to avoid the director's original rejections and romantic failures with colleagues. In addition, she eventually had met all eligible men in the agency without romantic success.

At this point, initiation into the organization required her to compromise by sublimating her romantic wishes—substituting related wishes and actions more productive at work (a realistic compromise) (III). This would mean two things. First, she would have to convince departmental veterans that she considered intellectual collaboration with them everyone's primary work interest. She would have to concentrate on doing competent work or carrying out her role without constantly asking or checking for tender approval. To do this, she would have to separate her perceptions of the director and others from those of her father and assess roles and responsibilities more realistically. This effort would facilitate work with other staff members by "neutralizing" relations with them. Second, she would have to find satisfying ways of expressing her romantic wishes. This would help her develop interests in work abilities and work identity. It would entail finding a substitute for erotic attachments to the men on the staff. It might also require finding ways to make up for any imagined damage to the director or coworkers in the process of rejecting them.

The world of voluntary organizations offers these possibilities. Within broad limits, Dorsey can make it whatever she wants, creating opportunities to satisfy her unfulfilled wishes. Her voluntary activities offer her the chance to play with the injury of organizational entry and find compensation that would permit her to become a member. In the voluntary world she can repeatedly recreate the situation that hurt her when she came to the state agency. Over and over, she can attempt to join and get recognition. In particular, she can try to find the romantic response she has not gotten at work. In addition, she may find opportunities to assert herself intellectually without being ostracized as she believes she was in the agency, and she could overcome her anxiety about working aggressively. The voluntary world provides an ideal opportunity for creating ways to master passively suffered injuries.

This play could help her join her agency in several ways. First, getting recognition, particularly romantic appreciation, in the voluntary world could increase her confidence that she will get recognition in the workplace. Second, the relatively safe circumstances of volunteering might enable her to succeed at tasks that are hard in the workplace, such as asserting herself intellectually. Third, this realistic success could assuage any fantasies that she hurts others by working aggressively. Fourth, most simply, any satisfaction from voluntary activities could provide sufficient compensation to balance her frustrations at work. By changing her expectations of the workplace, these developments would enable her to respond more realistically to it.

In the end, Dorsey succeeds partially. She participates actively in several organizations and gets recognition for her efforts. However, she has not yet found the romantic appreciation she wants. And she finds that, even in the voluntary world, she can be "lonely at the top." The satisfactions she finds in volunteering do not encourage or enable her to make the sublimatory compromises with her department that entry requires. However, they lead her to divert more and more energy from her job in pursuit of the pleasures volunteering offers.

In short, Dorsey's intense wish for recognition interferes with joining her work organization in two ways. First, she does not have the developmental security to meet veterans' "work" requirements of newcomers. Second, the injuries in her earlier life—and her wish to repeat and master them—tie her tightly to her past identity, as unsatisfying as it is, and do not allow her to change in ways a self-initiation requires. In particular, her demands for romantic recognition are so strong, that she cannot play with any transitional role in a way that satisfies veterans and herself and enables her to become part of the organization. Her voluntary activities represent an effort to go outside the organization to master the challenges of basic trust, recognition, and reciprocity, and thus perhaps to return as a changed person. However, such a strategy, which succeeds for Latham and Parsons, fails her. She finds pleasure to compensate for continuing organizational disappointments, but not enough reassurance to develop.

AUTONOMY

Conflict about Acting Aggressively to Assert Autonomy: John Hartley

John Hartley is more secure than Dorsey about recognition but has such strong—and conflicted—wishes to be autonomous that he cannot affiliate with his organization. Each encounter with a coworker becomes a test of his independence, in which he acts aggressively to show his strength. Equating collaboration with surrender, he cannot throw himself into work with others. In terms of ego development, his continuing doubts about autonomy (2) hinder his consolidating work skills (4) in an organizationally valued role (5) and joining the organization (6). His need for autonomy is so intense that he cannot compromise with colleagues and sublimate his aggressive wishes into collaborative intellectual attacks on policy problems. Although he does seem to have encountered some difficult coworkers, his obsession with being on his own makes it hard to distinguish instances of their collusion from his aversion to collaboration.

When Hartley started out at a federal health agency fifteen years ago, he was one of the first analysts in a new programmatic area. However, he was not among the small group who established the analysis section. This handful of people had struggled to create program standards and an analytic framework without any precedents or outside guidance. Not only the work challenges, but also the fact that most were young and just starting families, drew them together. They grew into a tight-knit group, gradually mixing social life with work.

Hartley came to the section when it was about five years old. In his early thirties, he had been working as a systems analyst in a manpower agency and was looking for more challenging work, "a job I could grow in." He requested a transfer to this group because it had a reputation for first-rate technical work. To his shock, however, he found the staff not only close, but closed. They often ate lunch together, but, he says, they left for lunch early and returned near quitting time, usually too inebriated to do any work. Not only that, but when they were gone, he was left to take messages for them, because the secretary would not answer the phone.

He attributes this situation to the section chief:

He was an individual who had a high school education and resented anyone who had higher than a high school education. His skills had never gone past the late fifties or early sixties. He would try to make as many problems as possible for you and then come in and try to look like he saved the day. This person ran a sweatshop and managed through intimidation. The majority of the people belonged to that clique.

Crucially, he says, "if you were not willing to join the clique and be part of it, you would be isolated and condemned. You had to join them totally or be isolated as an outsider." What would he have had to do to join the clique? "I would have had to go out and take the same lunches as them and buy the first couple of weeks. That would have done it. And go to their parties in the evening." All of this pointed out the lesson in governmental work:

> One thing you found very quickly in the government: if you want to go anywhere, don't emphasize individuality. Like the military, they want you to do the same they do. In the private sector I found you could at least be an individual.

It is impossible to know just how accurately Hartley recounts the situation. However, two things are clear. One is that he doesn't like what he found, despite the fact that his previous inquiries had led him to expect just the opposite. Second, he draws his conclusion from the situation very quickly, almost immediately writing off everyone—in ways reminiscent of Dorsey's instantaneous feeling that the director would never recognize her.

There are two ingredients to his reaction: one is what he expects of a work organization, and the other is what the veterans offer and demand. He wants to work autonomously, and he expects coworkers to be strictly businesslike and work alongside him without asking him to get involved with them. Not only do the clique members seem unprofessional, but they demand he be with them or against them. His expectations make him particularly sensitive to issues of autonomy, and their actions force the issue on him.[2]

The first theme in Hartley's story is his insistence on being independent, resisting the clique. In recounting his experiences, he presents a veritable chronicle of treachery and frustration. After repeatedly defending his integrity against the crowd, he complained:

> I was very resentful to a lot of people and told them how I felt. They were violating people's rights. They said, "Okay, you'll pay; you can't take us all on." I did take them all.

Not simply does he insist on being an individual, but he will be David to Goliath, and he will do battle with Goliath no matter how many times he is beaten.

For his part, he dug in in the trenches. He spent more and more time plotting battle with his adversaries.

I was totally by myself, and everything I had to do was cover my ass, and that used up two-thirds of my day. I am the type of person who realizes that I don't have to play the game. Then, everything I did, I realized that I had to cover myself. It caused certain personality changes. But you were always looking for something to be dropped on you. You were looking for someone trying to set you up. You were less patient with people making demands on you. No matter how much you accomplished, it meant nothing to you.

In the meantime, Hartley became involved in a number of special projects for other divisions around the department, and these people liked his work. After he had been in the section for a half dozen years, this success encouraged him to apply for a position in another division of the agency. In the context of his attitude toward members of the clique, this was either a very courageous or a foolhardy act. He scored well on the written and oral tests and then went for an interview with the deputy director—who happened to be one of the original members of the clique. A candid man, the deputy director took the interview letter from Hartley's hand, "threw it in my face, and said, 'If you think I will interview you for this job, go fuck yourself.' "

A couple of years later, he was called in on an especially difficult project in another division, and, he says, the deputy director promised him a promotion if he could handle the problem.

He said, "Okay, give me the paperwork [for the promotion]." Eleven months went by; he kept saying it was there. I told them [in Personnel]. I went up to Personnel. They never received the paperwork. I asked him why he did it. He said he'd never give me the promotion. I realized, hey, you're not going anywhere with these people.

One of the most conspicuous aspects of his career is visible only as the underside of the events he talks about: namely, he continues to do battle and lose. Although feuds and vendettas are not uncommon in bureaucracies, what stands out in Hartley's case is that, despite mistrusting "the clique," he keeps on doing battle with them and suffering defeat at their hands. It is as if he gains strength from these humiliating defeats. It is as if being autonomous and being victimized are somehow equivalent. He seems to value both kinds of separation from others.

A clue to this puzzle comes from a comment about how he feels at work. When asked whether he is different on the job than elsewhere, he says he is "a lot freer, friendlier, happier, content person when I am on the outside." He continues,

I am more serious, much more direct, more to the point on the work. My nature ... I am slow by nature. At work I am extra fast. That is against my nature. I do it without question. I am a slow person, and I enjoy work on the outside. Work [here] is against my overall nature.

He goes on,

If I became independently wealthy tomorrow and I could say, "This is it," I could tell them good-bye. I would never do another one of the functions I do at work. And yet I would be perfectly content with what I do outside. These skills were totally developed for one reason: the job.

Although the work means nothing to him, he says, he does what he does, which violates his nature, because the job requires it. Not only that, but he works faster than the job requires because a worker is supposed to work hard, even though people in the clique hardly work. The clue lies in his final sentence, which awkwardly turns to the third person and the passive voice to describe his developing work skills. This sentence only echoes another, in which he described his reactions to the confrontation with the clique: "It caused certain personality changes."

The passivity in these two statements contrasts starkly with his apparent protests against the clique. Indeed, if his comments are reread in the light of these statements, they seem more passive. They also seem more detached: even when he speaks in the first person, it often seems as if he is speaking of another person, as if he is not always "in" the actions he describes.

Thus he presents diverse images of himself: an individual, an independent actor, a passive object, an extra fast worker, a slow person by nature, a fighter against the multitude, and a humiliated victim. The contradictions point to an effort to disclaim action. On the one hand, he says he is furious about the clique's actions; on the other hand, he says that their actions caused his personality changes and that he works in ways that are not consistent with his real nature. If he does find the clique frightening, these conflicting statements could express an effort to disown his anger toward them, in order to avoid punishment.

But he seems to deny more than simply anger. Activity itself seems to be a question. Is he an avenger or a victim? Is he active or passive? Is he independent or under someone else's control? To put these questions differently, if he is so angry about his worsening situation, why has he remained in it for fifteen years? The deputy director does not control all possible moves Hartley might make. For some reason, Hartley chooses to remain in a situation where his activity and his independence are in question.

Now, once again, he has applied for promotion to another position. He says he is at the top of the priority list, and if funding comes through and if no one else appears who has better credentials and for whom the position would require less of a pay raise, he could get the job. He waits.

Interpretation

Susan Dorsey desperately wants recognition, and she cannot get enough from the organization to allow her to take a work role. John Hartley is concerned with the next developmental goal, autonomy, but his work problem is not that he wants more than the organization can give him; rather, he is not sure he wants any at all. One result is similar for him as for her: focus on a prework aim—here, autonomy (2)—hinders his feeling secure in job skills (4) that fit an organizational role (5) and identifying with a group of colleagues (6).[3]

Why he is so concerned with autonomy—also, why he vacillates about taking it—can be better understood in terms of his problems with sublimation. As with Dorsey, Hartley's organizational career may be characterized in terms of a failure at sublimation—in his case, of aggressive wishes. He expresses his aggression in two ways inimical to work. First, when he contemplates acting aggressively in the organization, as work requires, he thinks in terms of annihilating other people, rather than attacking problems in concert with them. His aggressive thoughts about the clique and those associated with it are so violent that it is difficult for him to consider influencing them strategically, much less collaboratively. Even if his allegations about the actions of clique members are true, he might work with or around them, exploiting them for some of his own purposes, if only he had a differentiated image of them and a moderated view of influencing them. He does have effective working relations with others outside his division, but his success there probably comes partly from the fact that he has only temporary relationships as an outside consultant.

Second, much of his aggression is not directed even toward the outside world, but against himself. In a way, his entire stay in the organization is masochistic. Even though the passing of years has broken up the control of the original clique, he repeatedly deals with people who will defeat him. Still today, the dominant themes in his work history are his humiliations. Although one might play with past humiliations by retelling them until they seem less traumatic, Hartley recounts these stories obsessionally: each represents a living grievance that doesn't seem to have diminished much with time. More generally, by directing his aggression inward and by working against his own acting in or upon the world, he renders himself passive.

These two ways of thinking about aggression go together. In the first, he sees much of the world populated by bad people, who would destroy him if he did not slay them first. He is a small good person in a dangerous world. In the second, he directs aggression toward himself. He is beaten, and he is humiliated. It is as if these latter thoughts are retaliation for the former, as if they are the work of his conscience punishing him for wanting to destroy others. In turn, the humiliating defeats enrage him and make him want to obliterate his oppressors. It is impossible to know which thoughts came first. At work, the clique seems to torment him first, and then he becomes furious. However, he might have brought an unconscious wish to be beaten or humiliated from his earlier life—perhaps as punishment for other real or imagined offenses, perhaps as a special way of being loved by a parent.[4]

Possibly Hartley's immobility is an unconscious attempt to avoid the seemingly inevitable guilt his actions would entail. Perhaps earlier in life he got stuck on the task of taking initiative without guilt and retreated from the test by regressing to an earlier stage. By then unconsciously failing the previous test (autonomy vs. shame and doubt), he would never again have to confront the challenge of initiative versus guilt. Thus his obsessive vacillation about autonomy (2) might represent a success—in defending himself against guilt (3). Without more information, it is impossible to be certain about the relationships among his motives.

In any case, his wishes aggressively to push others aside conflicted with the norms of the clique. Their hazing and punishment certainly reproached him for these wishes and encouraged him to sublimate them (I). Perhaps he directed his aggression toward himself, forcing himself to work faster than was natural for him, to defend himself from them. If he did his job extremely carefully, then no one could rightly fault him (II). And yet this course of action also failed. Members of the clique wanted him to come around, to recognize them, to engage them, and to work with them.

He still needed to find a sublimatory compromise in order to join the organization. He would have to learn to attack policy problems instead of clique members in order to seem safely competent and acceptable—if not to the clique, at least to others (III). In addition, rather than setting himself apart from coworkers, he should group himself with them and, if anything, concentrate on establishing their collective boundary at the edge of the organization. Then they would feel that he considered himself one of them and include him in work. These compromises with the veterans would depend on complicated, difficult compromises with himself.

He would have to set standards for his performance that allowed him to feel successful without feeling driven. This would mean finding a compromise between whatever ideals urge him to work "extra fast," the range of effort that would be acceptable on the job, and what feels consistent with his "nature." More realistic standards would relieve the shame he experiences before the ideals, as well as rage against them. At the same time, he would be less likely to doubt his autonomy or feel he must violently assert it.

Thinking more independently about what he expects of himself requires thinking differently and more flexibly about the aggression that work requires. To act autonomously, he needs to find ways of redirecting his aggressive wishes outward. The beginning of such a change would be to recognize that aggressive wishes are not automatically expressed in action, that thinking about aggression need not be dangerous. Furthermore, he would have to learn to see aggression not as action that inherently aims at total destruction, but as a way of asserting himself in different degrees, against various objects, toward a number of ends. If he could think of himself as acting without attacking others or provoking their retaliation, he would not be immobilized by anxiety about the consequences of acting. He could regard acting as a matter of deliberate, instrumental choice.

The resultant ability to act would affirm his autonomy. Newfound effectiveness would relieve the humiliation he now experiences when he tries to act and would reduce the rage his frustration spawns. Success would reduce his doubts about his independence and his feelings he must aggressively assert himself. He would be freer to attack the materials of work.[5]

However, like Dorsey, Hartley is unsuccessful in playing with the injuries of entry to find compromises that will initiate him into the organization. He repeatedly talks of the defeats of his first years, as one might do eventually to weaken the grip of the pain and move on. And yet he recounts the initial insults in stories still ringing with violence, as if their retelling is meant to maintain an inequitable account, rather than set the account to rights or write off losses. He seems unable to give up the humiliation and move on to work in this way.

At the same time, while contrasting the pleasure of his outside life with the pain of work and insisting that work means nothing to him, he works "extra fast" on the job. Perhaps this is his best effort at compromise: by working in a way that goes "against [his] overall nature," he succeeds in both doing his job in an acceptable, even praiseworthy manner and continuing to direct his aggressive wishes at himself. He masters injuries of work by actively inflicting them on himself. And yet the injuries continue, now insidiously his own project. He does not manage to inflict the pain on others or relinquish it.

If Hartley got the promotion he has applied for, he would no longer be subject to the direction of anyone associated with the clique, and, indeed, they would have to negotiate with him for certain kinds of analysis only he could offer. It would be sweet revenge. As a fantasy, the new job playfully treats and compensates for the initial injuries. Earlier thoughts of escaping through promotion may have been similar, play intended to ease the trauma of being part of the organization. At the same time, even the fantasy incorporates some of the problems of real-life action: its prominent feature is separation from the clique, more than joining new colleagues. If, in fact, he gets this promotion, play will have turned into instrumental action, even if fifteen years have passed.

Hartley's concerns about autonomy interfere with his entering the work organization in several ways. In general, his concentration on the prework issue of autonomy (2) interferes with his feeling secure about his competence (4) or his role (5) and moving on to feel part of the organization (6), any of which veterans would appreciate. His specific conflicts about autonomy also get in the way of identifying with the organization. His aggressive wish for independence leads him to do much more to separate from others than to form connections with them. His opposing wish not to be autonomous, both in itself and as a source of conflict, inhibits his acting and makes it difficult to do work flexibly. He is so fixated on the question of autonomy that he cannot make the change in identity that initiation entails. In particular, he is unlikely to move on from the initial confrontation to a transition because he assumes that any "working through" will be a "working over." If he gets the promotion he talks about, he may have the chance to enter a new organization, confront new veterans, and initiate himself on different terms.

The contrast between Hartley's isolation and Dorsey's gregarious-ness illustrates differences between aggressive and libidinal wishes in organizations. Libidinal wishes lead toward connections with coworkers. Although these wishes may allow cooperation, if they are not sublimated, they may lead to too much closeness to permit independent judgment or a choice of how and with whom to collaborate. At the other extreme, aggressive wishes lead toward separation from coworkers. Although these wishes may allow independent initiative, if they are not sublimated, they may lead to too much distance to permit sharing and comparing infor-mation or cooperation and teamwork. In both cases, if sublimation does not take place, workers will not have the intellectual or social flexibility required for collaborative problem solving.

POWER

Aggressively Trying to Control Others Without Conflict, and Playing
Elsewhere When It Is Impossible: Michael Anderson

Michael Anderson also has problems sublimating his aggression, but the ego developmental challenge he faces is different from Hartley's. Anderson wants to find ways of exercising power over others without confronting them, because he fears they would punish him. These efforts to exercise initiative without guilt (3) hinder his feeling secure about his work skills (4), taking an organizational role (5), and identifying with the organization (6). Although he has worked competently for nearly twenty years as a transportation planner with a county planning agency, he says he has never felt like a member of the department or been accepted as one by others.

The department offered him his first permanent job after graduate school. He began with ambitions of designing an extensive modern transportation system in the developing county. He received three promotions in his first four years and even acquired administrative responsibilities. Nevertheless, almost from the beginning there were signs he was not fitting in.

At the time he was hired, his director needed technical support for discussions of transportation policy with the county executive and council members and took Anderson to meetings with him. Typically, Anderson would offer impassioned arguments for rational transportation planning, and the director would assert his position that the planning department had to be involved in any decisions about new roads or mass transit. When they presented a proposal, Anderson would begin with a "youngster's" "overly enthusiastic," but knowledgeable, argument for a proposal, after which the director would give a "less knowledgeable" but "more mature" overview of the issues. As Anderson frames it, he would provide "content" and "excitement," and the director would impart his "authority and "control."

After about a year of these meetings, however, the director stopped inviting Anderson along. Anderson regards this action as a violation of a "deal" he and the director had. Anderson has some realistic explanations for the severance. He recognizes that the director sometimes grimaced when Anderson made his enthusiastic presentations, and it is possible that the audiences regarded him as hopelessly idealistic, not attuned to suburban politics.

However, he also interprets the break in terms of a failed father-son relationship with the director. He recalls,

It was like I was his nephew, and he was my father. . . . We were never pals, but in a work sense we were pretty interdependent.

He goes on,

[The director] really then and continually wants me to be his son. This is something that I wouldn't give him after that deal fell through. He always talked down to me. . . . He doesn't know how to lead other than being in the father role. [This is a problem] for those people who will not give him sonship or daughtership. Those people who work with him do this unconsciously. I need the equivalencyship which is not part of sonship.

Here Anderson insists that the director was the one who wanted to treat him as a son, that he had no wish to see the director as a father. In fact, Anderson suggests, his desire for equal status was probably a cause of their breakup. And yet his characterization of himself as like a nephew is ambiguous. Although a nephew is not a son, a nephew is a closely related member of the younger generation. Thus there is a hint that Anderson may have had filial feelings toward his director and that these feelings may have influenced Anderson's actions toward him.

Consistently, when Anderson talks about the requirements for organizational advancement, he offers an image in which, indeed, leader and subordinates are related as father and sons—and, moreover, their relations are rife with mutual hostility and murderous aggression. Speaking of his own failure to get ahead, he refers to something he has recently heard about

wolfpacks, the social structure of coyotes. Males get born into a pack; you have a whole litter. You have men who will never be leaders because of their biology, their genetics. And you have some more aggressive cubs, and they will do whatever they need to do to become leaders. And they have to eat the pack leader. And he never gives up until he can't resist any longer. I think I was born in that other group. When the puppies are born, they do all sorts of things to give the dominant male his rights, and they will do all sorts of growling, and the puppy will turn over. There are linkages back and forth between humans and coyotes. Somehow I must not ever have given my bosses that yelp and stomach up, and they sensed it. And I never got that membership and support that I needed.

In this portrayal of the organization as a jungle, Anderson affirms that a leader is like a subordinate's father, and he ambiguously denies that he has harbored aggressive feelings toward his director. Organizational entry entails baring one's most vulnerable part to a powerful superior. Success is equally gruesome: killing—and eating—one's boss. The bloody story of wolfpacks is certainly no realistic version of bureaucratic life; instead, it may be interpreted as a fantasy account of his ambivalence toward superiors. The two types of puppies each express different feelings toward a father, or leader. On the one hand, there are cubs who want to advance, as he did when he began work in the organization. They must want to devour their leaders in order to move ahead. However, as soon as he makes this observation, he refers to cubs' needs to show full respect to the dominant male, who will attack them if they do not obey. It is as if he first admits his own aggression toward a boss, then senses the danger of doing so and projects this aggression onto the boss, and finally advocates passivity as the only protection from reprisal. After all, he notes, he was born into the group of cubs that are incapable of attacking the leader. Significantly, in this denial he does not say that he does not want to attack his superior; instead, he says that his biology prevents him from doing so. Thus, whether he harbors any animosity toward a fatherlike boss or not, he is genetically innocent: no one could reasonably even imagine that he wants to harm his superior. Nevertheless, his comments seem to be a tacit admission that, indeed, he has thought of his director as fatherlike and has wanted to challenge his position and authority.

On another occasion, when describing the limitations of organizational life, he acknowledges that "control is the big issue in my life": he would like it, but he doesn't want to pay the consequences of having it.

> My powerlessness has reduced the potential value I can give to the county. If I had the ability to accrue power, I'd do things of larger scale, larger area, and more institutions. This is why I feel hungry for power, why I miss the power I'm not being allowed to have. When I have power, I don't control people. Control is the big issue in my life, but to participate in power involves control, and I don't want to be controlled, and I don't want to control.

In a repetition of the language of the jungle, he admits he is "hungry" for power. But at once he insists that when he exercises power, unlike the leader of the wolfpack, he does so benevolently: somehow, he does not control people. Then he goes on to deny that he really wants power, because "participating in" it involves not only controlling others, but also, inevitably, being controlled. He tacitly reasons that if he exercises power, those whom he controls will resent him and strike back, and they will punish him for what he has done. Significantly, in the final sentence, he associates participating in power most closely with being controlled and then moves immediately to deny that he even wants to control. As in the description of the jungle, he avows interests in controlling others, but then denies them, as if to avoid inevitable punishment or guilt.

The interplay of these themes—the paternity of leaders and ambivalence about acting aggressively—can be seen in Anderson's initial actions in the organization and in his reaction to the breakup of his "deal" with the director. His early "excitement" in meetings with the director probably expressed pleasure in accompanying a benevolent leader who guides. In addition, it may have reflected aggression toward both the director (in acting ambitiously) and his audiences (in telling them what to do without consideration for their political constraints). He may have confused showing the director his abilities, with showing up the director. After all, he not only contrasts his "youngster's enthusiasm" with the director's "maturity," but also insists that he alone had the requisite knowledge for decision making, while the director had only the brute authority of his bureaucratic position.

Anderson reacts desolately to the director breaking off their "deal." Probably he experiences it as the director's reaction to his aggression. He says he has such strong feelings of betrayal from the early period that he has never discussed his disappointments about the "deal" with his boss. At the same time, he is certain that the director's initial impression of him as overly enthusiastic and undisciplined has haunted him throughout his career.

In evaluating his work, Anderson emphasizes that many of his proposals have been accepted and are concretely represented by roads and the expansion of a mass transit system. He says other staff members like working with him, although he has one peculiarity that sometimes leads them to pass him over for other transportation planners. He is extremely meticulous, taking far longer on projects than anyone else. When time is important, other planners cannot afford to call him in.

About five years after his "deal" with the director broke down, a new deputy director came to the department, and Anderson hoped for a fresh start. He felt that he was first in line for an opening as head of transportation planning. However, the deputy director, criticizing his work style, passed him over. Anderson immediately concluded that he had no possibility of advancement in the department. He abruptly purchased an old houseboat and turned his planning interests to its renovation. He could design and execute the construction of the boat without contradiction from others, and he says that it became his real "passion." The houseboat, he says, has become the "center" of his life. While he continues at the planning department, he has withdrawn from it emotionally.

Interpretation

Michael Anderson, like John Hartley, has created a dilemma for himself. Hartley wants autonomy but fears its consequences. Anderson wants power but wants to avoid the dangers of acting aggressively toward others. He has made a number of important technical contributions to his department, but he spends much of his time thinking about and trying to solve developmental challenges normally associated with earlier in life. His inability to exercise initiative without guilt or fear of retribution (3) makes it difficult for him to think more carefully about how to make his expertise useful to specific clients inside or outside the organization (4), to take a clear role in planning projects (5), or to identify with the department (6).

Although, like Hartley, he fears the consequences of acting or thinking about acting aggressively, he defends himself differently and is more successful in taking initiative in the organization. Hartley retreats from the dangers of initiative by denying his autonomy to act. Anderson pretends others do not exist. Specifically, he acts as if others, such as county politicians, do not have interests that he might offend and that they might defend. Unconsciously, this attitude may represent a covert attempt to annihilate those who exercise power and could control him. However, in reality this denial of frightening situations makes him politically naive and lessens his chances of wielding power. Moreover, his repeated ambiguous comments about his interests in power suggest that he does not even succeed unconsciously in banishing thoughts of those who will punish his aggressive wishes.

What Anderson says about his director suggests that his apprehension about aggressively taking initiative is unconsciously linked to thoughts about attacking and being punished by his father. It is difficult to know what connections he makes, but comments about his childhood show that, at the least, he identifies with his father's own conflicts with authority. In describing his family, Anderson sketches people for whom social relations were often problematic. He regards himself as similar to his father, who was typical of many men in the family. He says his father was brilliant but could never take directions from anyone. He finally settled into a position with a regional corporation as their traveling troubleshooter. He would circulate among branch plants, "doing wonders" on problems no one else could fix. In this way he solved his own problems with authority: he could work for an employer but never stay in one place, subordinate to a single boss. Several other brothers and uncles similarly are itinerants: they are bright and professionally successful, but they travel and work for a number of clients, thus avoiding the strains of a relationship with one boss. Although

Anderson identifies with his father's problems with authority, he is exceptional among the men in his family in remaining with one employer for such a long time.

Thus, Anderson's father provided a model of a man who would flee authority, rather than confront and acquire it. In addition, Anderson's relations with his father may have contributed to making aggression toward authority a central problem in his life. His father died when Anderson was an adolescent. Although it is impossible to know the specific meanings of this event, adolescence normally is a period when children contest their parents' legitimacy as models of development. In wishing to overthrow parental authority, adolescents symbolically want to kill their parents, to destroy mental images of them as moral guides.[6] For adolescence to be successful, children must challenge their parents and wrest developmental freedom from them without destroying them. The actual death of an adolescent's parent would be terrifying. Not only would a child lose his loving and supportive parent, but he could unconsiously imagine he was responsible for killing the parent.

Such a failure at adolescent development might lead a son such as Anderson to regress to the work of the Oedipal period, to reassure himself that there is a way of acting aggressively without destroying his father or bringing the world down on his head. If he were unsuccessful, he might continue to link each thought of taking initiative with killing his father, fear annihilating punishment for it, and anxiously deny or repress any aggressive wish. Such vacillation between aggression and guilt could immobilize him and prevent him from taking initiative later in life. At the same time, he might make extraordinary efforts to restore the father he imagines having destroyed. One way to do this would be to see organizational leaders as paternal, as if doing so might deny the reality of his father's death and free them both.

Anderson's career in the organization can be seen in terms of his failure to sublimate aggressive wishes sufficiently to adapt to working conditions. His enthusiastic demands for closeness with the director, intertwined with aggressive challenges to his authority, contributed to a growing conflict with the director. When the director revoked the "deal" to collaborate, Anderson seems to have felt reproached for his expectations of the director (I). Following this, he became an extremely meticulous worker. This style can be considered a compromise, in which he can defend himself against charges of aggression while doing his assigned work and maintaining his independence (II). If he works so slowly, no one could even suggest that he is acting aggressively toward anyone. If he works so carefully, no one could challenge his competence. At the same time, he can covertly exercise aggression against others (by making them conform to his painfully slow pace), but in a way that appears wholly innocent (after all, he is simply giving proper attention to details). This defense against punishment often works, but, as he notes, it eliminates him from urgent projects.

The deputy director criticized Anderson's working style while passing him over for transportation chief. Anderson undoubtedly experienced this rejection as a reproach of the defense he had carefully crafted. At this point, he needed to find a more realistic compromise. He would have to recognize the extent of his aggression, realistically assess the director's personality as well as requirements for working with others, accept the legitimacy of others' needs as well as his own, and offer staff members collegiality without hostility (III). This compromise would not only encourage others to accept him, but would also help him to work with others. First, by responding to realistic task requirements, he could direct his aggression against projects, rather than against colleagues. Second, coworkers' support for his efforts might reassure him that he could act aggressively without harming others, thus reducing his conflicts and anxiety about aggressive wishes. Third, related to that, he could unconsciously repair any imagined damage to the director or colleagues.

However, Anderson could not find any version of an organizational role that would enable him to make these compromises and, at last, admit himself to the agency. He did not give in on his aggressive wishes—he could not divert them from directors, politicians, or coworkers toward projects. He gave up on the organization and created an arena where he could express his aggression with less conflict.

Work on the houseboat provides a parallel enterprise in which he may succeed in ways the organization let him down. This project permits him to attempt playfully to treat and compensate himself for the injuries of trying to enter the organization. He can design and build whatever he likes, without being subject to others' schedules. With the boat he has become the master-builder he imagined being for county transportation. The project is a "center," a source of security that balances his marginal position on the job.

Unlike Parsons, for example, who succeeds in initiating himself by turning to an outside activity that parallels his job responsibilities, Anderson never comes to feel part of the organization. The houseboat project is a failure at self-initiation for some of the same reasons it succeeds in defending him from the anxieties of aggression. Like Dorsey's voluntary world, his play world is pretty much what he wants it to be. He fashions it to be like the organizational domain he wanted, one in which he could exercise aggression without fear of retribution. He succeeds by creating a world in which no one else has authority—because there is no one else. Consequently, once he turns outward from the department, he never has the experience of acting aggressively toward anyone with authority, let alone the experience of doing so safely.

Anderson's intense wishes to take initiative and exercise power without guilt or reprisal interfere with his joining the organization in two ways. First, he lacks the developmental security to meet veterans' "work" requirements. Second, whatever leads him to act aggressively toward people with authority has become an integral part of his identity, and he has difficulty changing in ways a self-initiation requires. In the language of separation and individuation, his initial confrontation with the organization forces him to differentiate himself from his graduate student status (I), but he only halfheartedly practices an alternative agency role (II) before turning outside without having come to rapprochement with veterans (III). The world of the houseboat may bring him satisfactions that compensate for the disappointments of the agency and help him stay there, but it does not yet treat him for his original injuries or help him develop further.

DEVELOPMENTAL PROBLEMS IN INITIATION

These people contrast clearly with others described earlier. They do not become integral to their organizations, nor do they feel like members. To the contrary, they are outsiders, who see the organization as either ungiving or threatening. They are in more or less loyal opposition. None of these people describes work or the organization with pleasure. Their jobs are a struggle—to ignore insults and somehow get something done. Unlike others described earlier, these people share little, if any, purpose or interest with their organizations. Although none might use such a phrase, there is an important sense in which working in the organization is for each a psychic life-and-death battle. Under these conditions, it is hardly surprising that none gives in to veterans' initiatory efforts or initiates him- or herself.

Much of the explanation for their strained relations with their organizations has to do with their initial expectations. The people in chapter 5 all wanted work organizations to help them develop, consolidate, or maintain at least work ability (4), a work identity (5), or an organizational affiliation (6). A number of them used the organizations to satisfy their original expectations and then advanced to others. In contrast, Dorsey, Hartley, and Anderson want organizations to satisfy such prework demands as recognition (1), autonomy (2), and power (3).

None of these expectations is inherently inconsistent with becoming part of a work organization. Members legitimately and successfully seek recognition for their work, autonomy in doing it, and power to implement it. Furthermore, they are likely to get along with coworkers when they also have interests in exercising work abilities, taking valued work roles, and affiliating with an organization. Dorsey, Hartley, and Anderson, however, each want *only* one of these prework rewards. They set membership terms few work organizations could satisfy.

David Ryan, described in the first two chapters, provides an instructive contrast. He clearly had strong interests in exercising power and controlling others (3), but he also developed work abilities (4) and a work identity (5) consistent with the organization's mission and structure. Moreover, he was able to make a realistic assessment of his opportunities for initiative in the organization. Dorsey, Hartley, and Anderson have such single-minded interests that they cannot realistically appraise their organizations and veterans' expectations.

The reason they continue to make demands that insure their failure to join up has to do with the nature of these expectations. Concerns with recognition, autonomy, and power are normal for infants and children. They will spend as much time as they need on each of these tasks until they master it. For example, a young child may repeatedly see or arrange encounters as a test of his independence until he grows confident of his autonomy. Normally, children resolve each of these dilemmas in turn and move on to adolescence and adulthood.

Personal identity is shaped by the characteristic ways an individual deals with these developmental challenges. Some adults, for example, may be especially sensitive to questions of trust, while others may look first at issues of power. Nevertheless, most adults are sufficiently secure with these matters that they have the cognitive and emotional flexibility to assess contemporary situations realistically. When adults are still centrally concerned with early life dilemmas, this is a sign that they never succeeded in mastering infantile or childhood feelings of mistrust, shame, doubt, or guilt. The older they become, and the more time they have invested in one of these challenges, the more difficult it is for them to consider others. When they approach organizations, they are relatively rigid single-issue negotiators.

These workers have especial difficulty coming to terms with organizations because of the nature of libidinal and aggressive wishes associated with the early developmental stages, before children have learned to sublimate the wishes. Adults whose identities are strongly tied to those stages cannot draw on much successful experience in compromising their wishes to adjust to the social world. In Dorsey's case, her romantic and sexual interests partly serve her wish for recognition but also discourage others from treating her like a colleague. For Hartley, aggressive thoughts about others and aggressive attacks on himself combine to immobilize him from acting autonomously. Anderson's passive aggressiveness, intended to avoid frightening consequences of exercising power, hinders him from asserting himself and eliminates him from urgent projects. Each uncompromisingly continues to act in ways that make them insensitive to organizational work demands.

Not only are these people unresponsive to veterans' expectations, but they make feeble efforts to initiate themselves on their own terms. Latham and Parsons, for example, play with the injuries they incur in confronting their organizations. Each in a different way manages his own working through with organizational veterans. Latham chooses a succession of roles, some formal and some informal, each one presenting only the developmental challenges he is ready for. Thus he plays with different roles until he and veterans can agree he fits in. Parsons combines overt, explicit efforts to meet veterans halfway with outside efforts to improve his work abilities and change his way of thinking about himself in order to become a member. The latter activities, though outside the organization and at least partly unconscious, are designed to enable him to make his way into the department.

In contrast, Dorsey, Hartley, and Anderson react to their initial confrontation with their organizations by retreating. They design playful activities to treat and compensate themselves for the injuries of their entry. However, in each case, these activities are external to the organization, and their main aim is to repair the individual alone, not to fix the relationship with the organization. Unconsciously, each may be attempting to restore or create a relationship with the organization, but, in contrast with Latham and Parsons, what they expect of a relationship is too far out of touch with organizational reality to fit.

In the end, each has difficulty differentiating him- or herself from a past identity — unrecognized and untrusting; ashamed, doubting, and afraid; or powerless, guilty, and fearful. They practice new, organizational roles without conviction. They warily, tentatively, occasionally approach veterans hinting at rapprochement if only they can be accepted in their prior identity, but their terms are too unfavorable to veterans or the organization to be agreed to. As a result, they create no new identity to consolidate. It is not that they act in bad faith, but their identities are so fragile, that they are unable to risk attaching themselves to a collectivity.

CONCLUSIONS

People with prework expectations face more difficult odds than those with "work" expectations. As the examples in chapter 5 show, "work" expectations do not ensure entry, but they promote it. Without them, workers have much less chance getting in.

Some of the problem of prework expectations is statistical. People looking for these conditions are deviants, seeking roles few organizations offer. There are top executives, for example, who insatiably seek adulation, who assiduously avoid making decisions while blaming others, and who covertly force others to conform to their demands.[7] However, organizations selecting new members, especially for positions where personal contact and collaboration matter, particularly at lower hierarchical levels, rarely deliberately offer such opportunities.

More broadly, much of the problem of prework expectations is inherent in the nature of work, which, as Freud argued, requires the individual to be able to adjust to the needs of particular colleagues and the requirements of a tranquil society in general. In short, it is not simply a statistical accident that few organizations are open to newcomers with prework expectations. Whatever Dorsey, Hartley, and Anderson's idiosyncrasies, they demonstrate many of the problems that arise when newcomers want work to give them recognition, autonomy, or power above all else.

These three show us the personal distress that comes when someone works in an organization but cannot identify with it or become attached to colleagues. Nevertheless, they are all productive workers. Although civil service positions give them job security, Dorsey and Anderson work in places where many have been laid off. Their bosses decided they were more valuable than a lot of other staff members. Their efforts make a difference. Anderson points to many projects that used his ideas. Hartley has letters of appreciation from clients.

Their situation brings to light a peculiar condition. Legally and financially, they are employees of their organizations. But psychologically, they do not belong to the organizations. Nor do coworkers regard them as significant parts of the organizations.[8] We may characterize their position as employment without membership; they are formally part of an organization but not close to it. And yet they are not indifferent to their organizations. Much of their daily lives, even outside work, is shaped by their disappointed reactions to the workplace. They are not members, but they are certainly not detached. Though they are not invested in their organizations, they are committed to getting something from the organizations. Something keeps them from resigning and going elsewhere.

Unless one denies them any freedom of action, and unless one assumes they have no real employment alternatives, one must say they stay out of hope, the yet unfulfilled faith that work will give them what they want. In the meantime, they hold back from the organization because their identities are safer outside.

And yet, for all their peculiarities, they have similarities to other workers. In their own painfully conflicted ways, they argue what others often say as well: committing themselves wholly to a work organization would curtail their individuality and independence. Their needs for recognition, autonomy, and power are only more intense than others', not different in kind. Might not the disappointments that injure them and hold them outside of organizations be indicative of others' smaller, less noticeable injuries, which in some way hold them back too? Chapter 9 explores this question. Before that, the next chapter analyzes the different ways workers deal with the disappointments of organizational entry.

Disappointments Remediable and Irremediable: Playing Toward Membership or Withdrawal

People want to grow and express themselves at work as elsewhere in their lives. They share Freud's hope that work can be "a path to happiness." Unconsciously, they want to use work organizations to develop their ego identity. They expect that joining will allow them to retain the core of their identity while they choose compatible elaborations from work roles. Although they are willing to compromise, they want to go on getting the aggressive and libidinal rewards they found in the past.

The last three chapters portrayed workers' attempts to enter organizations. Some initiate themselves by negotiating successfully with veterans. They take an organizational role that allows them to develop, and they find acceptable ways to sublimate their aggressive and libidinal wishes. Others do not join, either because they cannot find a role compatible with their developmental aims, or because they refuse to sublimate certain wishes. They work for organizations, but they don't belong to them. The earlier chapters have shown how newcomers react to deprivations or disappointments in the initial organizational confrontation by creating activities that provide rewards the formal workplace denies. This chapter analyzes the variety of playful responses to membership requirements, reasons for different reactions, and the consequences of different choices.

PLAY: EFFORTS TO CREATE THE IDEAL ORGANIZATION

Play is a means of mastering passively suffered injuries by finding symbolic equivalents that can be actively controlled. At work, it expresses an organizational critique. It tacitly declares that an organization should meet certain expectations, for which it attempts to enact the conditions. Thus play is a continuing effort to create the ideal organization. Unconsciously, workers cannot accept anything that denies them what they need to grow. Consequently, play is a dominant influence on organizational behavior: workers act purposefully to create relationships that satisfy developmental needs. Not all these needs can be met. Some are inimical to work altogether, others do not fit specific organizations, and still others are irreconcilable with conflicting claims from other workers in a given organization. Disappointing, injurious initial experiences may evoke reactions that influence how workers think and act for as long as they remain in an organization.

Organizational play may be categorized according to its aim, its location, and its success. Play is a normal part of self-initiation efforts, whereby newcomers manipulate the work role until they find a configuration that admits them to the organization and satisfies developmental needs. This is *initiatory role play*. When newcomers find it impossible, they may create or select outside activities to help initiate themselves into the work organization. These efforts are *initiatory outside play*.

When these efforts fail or incompletely deal with injuries from organizational conditions, workers may use their formal role to devise informal activities to compensate for the injuries enough to enable them to stay in the organization, even though they do not identify with it. These activities are *compensatory role play*. Sometimes workers fail to find any way, inside or outside the organization, to initiate themselves and also find no compensation within. In these cases, they may devise outside activities to compensate. This is *compensatory outside play*.

When workers can neither initiate nor compensate themselves, they may use outside activities to escape from the organization. Although they continue to be employed, they are weakly tied to the workplace. These efforts represent *escapist outside play*.

These labels describe workers' *intentions*. Each type of play may or may not be successful. Whether it succeeds depends on the realism of the worker's play plan, his ability to execute the plan, and the availability of other people and objects to fit the intended scenario.

None of these play types is inherently associated with specific developmental expectations. Everyone at first attempts initiatory role play, even if only briefly. The demands most likely to succeed are related to work ability, work identity, and organizational affiliation, though these may require initiatory outside play as well. Prework and postwork requirements are less likely to be satisfied and may lead to either compensatory or escapist play, just like frustrated "work" expectations. The following examples illustrate the types of play.

Initiatory Role Play

Charles Latham provides an example of successful initiatory role play. He came to the organization interested in affiliating with it, but he needed to solidify his professional competence and establish a professional identity before he could embrace colleagues and the agency. He played with available roles to negotiate three successive developmental dilemmas. He worked out an extension of his formal role by joining interagency social service projects so he could get past the physicalist bias of his department. Then he was able to develop skills in social planning and elaborate an identity as a social planner. When he had succeeded at these aims, he took the community planner role and used it to work through his estrangement from physical planning colleagues. He overcame his initial sense of being "a bastard child" and became an integral part of the organization.

Harry Jackson encountered so many obstacles in his work, that just getting his job done was initiatory role play. He joined a state economic development department in his midtwenties. He wasn't sure if he wanted to make a career in the field but was interested in trying it out. Immediately, he found people were "rigid, difficult, insensitive, and some were rather cold."

> People had their own personal files and kept them locked. You had to go through a long story, what you wanted, why you wanted it. It was like there was a scarcity of things—yellow pads, information, program plans. . . . It was hard doing your basic job, working with people on the staff. My first chief—it was hard for me to get information from him to do my job.

The veterans deliberately tested Jackson.

> You needed to prove yourself, put in time, replicate positive behavior over a period of time. If you were sent on a mission—to get a map, which is what you do when you start out; Did you do it? Did you get the right map? Did you get the right scale? Did you return it? Could you do it again? They didn't send everyone for a map. . . . They would only send people who were reliable and got the right map. I used to prepare memos for capital transfer. There is a date when it has to be received by the governor's office; there is a whole sequence of things that have to happen. People who were in charge didn't trust anybody to do it.

"Some people perceived all this as a racial thing," he adds, referring to his race, "because black people were new to state bureaucracy. That is not my perception. It was just part of operations." Whatever their motivations, his new coworkers succeeded in making him feel like an outsider who had to prove his competence to show he was a professional.

Another comeuppance offered a clue about making it. One day he routinely asked the man in charge of supplies for a magic marker, only to be questioned about why he was coming back for a new one so soon after getting the last one. Was he wasting supplies? He discovered that the old man had an

> ornate, elaborate system of giving out supplies. This was crazy, but I learned from that you should not be wasteful. The best way not to be wasteful is to develop a personal system that will control your consumption of things.

After coming to the organization on a look-see basis, after confronting a battery of tests, after receiving no welcome, nevertheless, he decided to stay. After resenting others' coldness, rigidity, possible hazing, and possible prejudice, he aggressively threw himself into work. Taking the role offered, he worked hard so that others had to accept him. He sublimated his anger into work discipline, mastering the challenges and making the bureaucratic rules his own. At the same time, he could feel he was competent and had a role in the organization without embracing those who did not obviously want blacks or him. Gradually he convinced others and himself that he fit in. After ten years, when an administrative position opened up, he decided he wanted it, because he did identify with the department, and he was promoted.

Latham and Jackson play with frustrations of "work" expectations and succeed in initiating themselves. People with postwork developmental expectations also react to disappointments or injuries in their initial confrontation by playing with roles. However, their satisfaction may not involve identifying with the organization so much as becoming enough a part of it to use it for transcendent personal purposes. Organizational affiliation may be secondary to mentoring others or making sense of life experiences. Still, their actions are initiatory role play because they use formal roles to bring themselves into the organization.

Ralph Yarrow and *Harriet O'Neill*, for example, show how initial concerns about being taken care of can turn into interests in mentoring others. Although they came to their agencies to expand their work skills and move into new roles, they were overwhelmed by the size, complexity, language, and impersonality of the organizations. Even after they had been promoted several times, they never got over the feeling that the organizations were cold, uncaring places. Once they got administrative positions, they used them to mentor junior staff members. O'Neill even signed up to develop new managers. Both she and Yarrow speak of these mentoring interests as compensation for how they were treated. Although mentoring was not central to the work of either, both used the formal role to make up for earlier injuries and, after a number of years, identified more closely with the organization.

Norma Sawyer wants to use work to make sense of her experiences. In her play she responds more to injuries earlier in her life than to initial organizational events, but her success commits her to her job responsibilities. She uses her public participation role to admit herself to the organization on terms that affirm her identity. She consolidates her concerns about nature and public affairs. In addition, after being deprived of a work career earlier in life, she demonstrates by her competence that she could manage one. Centrally, she willingly carries on activities that had earlier displaced this career. As a wife and mother, she was responsible for taking care of a husband and children. Now, as staff to the advisory committee, she makes extraordinary efforts to care for committee members and the agency's clients. Actively choosing what she had passively accepted is central to her finding integrity in her combined family and work careers.

Initiatory Outside Play

All these people succeed in playing with a formal role to create a relationship with an organization that satisfies them and makes them welcome to veterans. Sometimes, however, newcomers cannot use the formal role in this way. Some role enactments enable them to grow, others comply with veterans' demands, and still others do neither, but none does both. Newcomers who still want to become members may turn outside to find an activity that transforms them and makes initiation possible.

Everett Parsons illustrates this search. He came to the planning department looking for professional success as an architect. Instead, he found that others ignored him. Nervously, he tried to interest them, but without success. Then he began painting as a way of mastering rejection of him and his graphic abilities. Painting allowed him both to work through his feelings and to develop drawing abilities that would improve his work. By going out of the organization in this way, he was able to return and enter.

Marilyn Hayes also went out to get in. In her first seven years with a large city planning department she held a series of positions: research, long-range planning, and community planning. Although she believes she did each job well, she still didn't feel part of the department. If anything, community planning made her more of an outsider. Caught in the dilemma of serving both city government and neighborhood groups, she was fiercely loyal to community associations, and other staff members came to question whether she was with them. After three years of this she was tired of fighting with coworkers whom she expected to support her, and she wanted out.

Rather than quit, however, she got the agency director to assign her on loan to the mayor's office. Two years there changed her and enabled her to return to the planning department with acceptance, eight years after starting out.

> All of a sudden, I just woke up, and there I was [accepted into the department]. It was after I went to the mayor's office and came back. And then I was accepted here. I felt more confident of myself after I survived in the mayor's office. I was working in a very sensitive area. . . . After surviving in that situation—it was demanding— once I felt that I could do that, I felt I could do anything. I was more confident. I spoke up more about what was good for me.

Work in the mayor's office transformed her and perceptions of her, by allowing her to play with the issue of loyalty to city government while teaching her the two lessons of initiation rituals. The mayor's chief advisors taught her substantive knowledge in urban management and regional governance, matters of importance back in the planning department as well. At the same time, they challenged her to represent the mayor's position in negotiations with businesses and community groups. She found she could establish a working relationship with the top city authority, which oversaw the planning department itself, while supporting citizen participation in decision making. Finding a way to be loyal but responsive to the public in the high-pressure, powerful mayor's office, she was ready to return to community planning or other roles in the planning department. Her survival of mayoral politics convinced veterans in the agency that she was "reborn," not only more competent and a professional, but also more authoritative and more responsible—an independent person whom, nevertheless, they could accept. When she returned to the planning department, her earlier anger at colleagues was supplanted by aggressive work with them.

Compensatory Role Play

When manipulating the formal role fails to provide a way to organizational affiliation, members may look for compensation—not just for an injury in the initial confrontation, but for the general disappointment of not becoming part of the organization. Workers often look outside for this compensation, either because they are too angry at the organization to invest in any of it or because it just seems too alien to them. Sometimes, however, people who are in, but not of, organizations use formal roles to exact compensation.

Phyllis Jones started work with a federal housing agency as a secretary sixteen years ago.[1] She needed an income to support her children and wanted something that challenged her abilities and gave her a place to belong. Relatively quickly she found that she could do some of the analytic work assigned to others, and she gradually gained some technical responsibilities. She eventually became the director's secretary. And yet she observed a number of discrepancies in the organization. Some of the technical people, most of them men, really were not capable of doing their work. Some of the clerical people, most of them women, could have learned those jobs, but management would not give clerical staff technical training. Whether sexual discrimination was at the root of this or not, the result was that responsibilities were not matched with abilities.

Despite her advancement and limited involvement in technical work, Jones regarded the overall situation as one of organizational "dishonesty." When a new director came in and moved her to a lower, primarily clerical position, she felt stuck. The wall between clerical and analytic work hurt her by ignoring her work ability and ruling out the possibility of establishing a consistent work identity. She liked the income, but she began to channel her energy toward finding compensatory rewards, informal sources of competence and a work identity.

She began to organize dramas where she could successfully direct others' actions. Here we may recall Erikson's (1977) observation that children practicing a sense of industry often do so by playing organized games, through which they discover successful methods of following rules to goals. Adult workers who feel their organizations deny them the opportunity to work competently may invent side-games in which they can practice their skills. Jones gives an example. If she could not move men with her intelligence, she would affect them with her feminine charms.

> As a woman, I can get things done that men can't get done. Men basically want to help women. There are women in my section who can't get things. I have no problems with that. I do have problems with some women who have gotten into higher positions simply through physical use. I wouldn't do that. I have no problems using my God-given abilities, because men want that. Men don't get that same feeling helping other men. (Baum 1987:95)

She organized a network of "friends," on whom she can prevail for various favors. The following example involves getting assistance that is necessary for work, but her pleasure in the incident comes from creating a setting she can control, not helping an abstract organization.

> I am only limited by the people whom I know, unless I maintain a growing span of friends that includes the newcomers. I recognize that. I make a point of meeting people, getting them to know and

like me. When the office next to us moved, they took one of the girl's partitions. It happened that I am friends with the branch chief. I said, do me a favor, et cetera. We need the partition. We need to separate smokers from nonsmokers. He said, by Monday you will have a partition. He is a new friend. I have new friends in the Director's Office. There is something in the human psyche that denotes authority. People assume that I have authority that I didn't know. There is something about my demeanor that denotes authority. (Baum 1987:96)

In play like this, Jones creates something like an ideal organization, and she is its director. She knows what should be done, and she has the authority to get men to do it. These activities are extensions of her formal role, though few are essential to doing her job. None of this effort leads to professional or organizational advancement, but it establishes a domain for competence and an identity that compensate sufficiently for limited formal opportunities to keep her in the organization.

Compensatory Outside Play

Outside activities offer many opportunities for compensation for initiation injuries. *Leonard Davis* and *Susan Dorsey* are two of many people who volunteer in organizations similar to their agencies. His activities let him play with the possibilities of being competent and holding respected roles. Hers allow her to experiment with responsibility and authority and to find recognition and companionship. *Michael Anderson's* houseboat gives him opportunities to play with authority and to find ways of implementing his designs without opposition or guilt. All get gratifications they consider unavailable in their organizations and can more easily continue on the job.

Some find participation in young people's athletics similarly rewarding. For example, *Clarence Fisher* went to work for a county planning department thirty years ago. The agency was small, and he worked in a lot of areas. When builders came to the largely rural county proposing housing, he got involved in trying to hold developers to long-range plans. However, as building accelerated and the county became more of a suburban extension of the central city, development became a complicated political game. The director hired new people to negotiate with builders, and these people closely supervised negotiations with developers. Fisher, now reduced to working for these new senior staff members, lost most of his earlier influence. On top of that, he was upset to see technically reasonable positions given away in political negotiations.

Along the way, he became involved in refereeing sports, and gradually it became a year-round activity.

From the middle of January to the first of September, I am a baseball official, an umpire. I attend class two times a week until March. I work for high school, from [age] eight to ten on up to unlimited ball. From March to the end of May, it is high school, college, or whatever they assign to you. In the summer I work with the Bureau of Recreation.

He says this work has helped him put his children through school, but it is worth more than that.

It is like a relaxation. You see some of these kids who start when they are small, and you see them two to three years later, and you see how they have improved. Some of the coaches don't know anything about it but try to teach the kids. I used to work football, basketball, and baseball.

Refereeing is "like a relaxation" because it allows him to play with issues of authority over which he has lost control at work.

Planning—it is the same as officiating. You have some rules you have to take care of. You see the development of the county. Here you see the development of the kids. But if you try to fight the rules, that is when you mess up. Both in sports and planning.

On the playing field he has found a way to exercise unquestioned authority and promote development. This satisfaction compensates him for his loss of authority and marginality at work and helps him put up with negotiations over which he has little control.

Escapist Outside Play

When not even outside activities can compensate for the disappointments of an organization, workers may plan for escape. They ponder settings that would include what their job denies them to create an ideal, imaginary, workplace. Imagining this other place requires working through the problematic conditions of the real work organization. For example, if efforts to take initiative are repeatedly rebuffed, workers must think about this situation until they can picture an alternative, in which they could take initiative, perhaps even turning others down. By contemplating a place where they can actively control what in real life they passively suffer, they get pleasure denied them in the organization.

The escape plan may be pure fantasy, with no bridge to anything real. A worker may at some level know this, especially if the fantasy is part of a conscious daydream. In such a case, even though the content of the plan is escape, its function is primarily compensatory, maintaining the worker in a disappointing position. However, insofar as the worker takes the plan seriously at all, it points a more or less realistic route out of the organization. Simply by indicating an intention to leave, by providing a mental retreat across the organizational boundary that originally inflicted pain, the plan provides temporary relief. Its execution promises release.

Escapist outside play often involves thoughts of going into private business. *David Ryan* has actually purchased a service station, and the only uncertainty is when he will retire from his federal job. This dream-turned-into-reality permits him to do what his job does not: accrue capital and pass on his accumulated worth to descendants.

Adam Wilenczik says that his salary as a federal auditor carries him until he can establish a private accounting business. He likes financial management, but he is uncomfortable in the auditor's role. He takes orders from a director, and he has to wield authority against people who dislike him. As a private consultant, in contrast, he would be the boss, he would work only with clients who want to see him, and he would help them make money, not take it from them. He gets little pleasure from his federal job, but

> on the private job, the attitude is so much better. You in turn are the boss. If you want to see someone on Tuesday night at eight o'clock, you can say, come over. If you want to see TV or play with your kids at nine o'clock [,you don't have to see anyone]. And people have a better feeling for you. When you are auditing, you are a pain. When you work for the feds, the check will be the same, no matter how you work. If you invest people's funds, you get the return for your own. I help people plan their finances. [About being the bad guy,] I know I am going to do it. It doesn't matter. It is a problem for them. It will embarrass a lot of people. In private work you see people once in six to twelve months. It is really great. You don't have to ask people for money. You just show them how to spend their money better. I also help people with life insurance. Get out of the stupid insurance business, and get into the investment business. I find it very enjoyable. I am not the typical stockbroker, asking people to invest a quarter-million dollars. With the government you really can't have this feeling.

As an auditor, he feels guilty about exercising authority and hurting people. If he ever moved full time into his own investment business, he could, instead, nurture people who are his peers, and he would be the center of a good and caring, if small, organization.

Others' thoughts of going into private business are amorphous. Some involve fantasies of getting rich selling beauty and cleaning products.

Brenda Lasser, a fifteen-year veteran in a state housing department, describes a variation of this:

> When I leave from here, I want to go into my own business. I am setting this up now. Nothing to do with housing. I want to go into import and export, [because] I like to travel. I have seen, I have brought back things that people want. I see a lot of consumer items. I just want to test the waters. This is a new ambition, ever since I went to Europe three years ago.

Like all plans for private entrepreneurship, these thoughts emphasize independence and personal expression. As Ryan points out, the results, whether success or failure, would be immediate, not limited by bureaucratic regulations.[2]

Others express similar escapist wishes in terms of finding a new profession, often the law. *Frederick Lincoln* attends law school at night while working with a suburban planning agency. He makes a common complaint about his job, which "constricts" him:

> There are definitely certain groups that require unreasonable things, and I would like to be able to tell them, but the political realities are such that I can't. This is one of the things that I detest about planning. I feel it is too closely tied to the political process and prevents us from making technically optimal decisions.

He believes that, when he becomes a lawyer, he will be able to take reasonable positions without political opposition. And, he says, he will be able to wear a "white hat." In this fantasy he will always be right, never encounter conflict, and be free of guilt. This image of the law, the opposite of planning's frustrations, avoids injury and satisfies desires for recognition, autonomy, and authority. Becoming a lawyer may disillusion him once more, but going to law school is a plausible plan for escape.

These are the primary themes in most escapist outside play. Although those who think of escaping are a long way from organizational affiliation, they are reacting to conditions that most workers, even intimate members, resent from time to time. In their complaints, they reveal some of the roots of what Freud called the "natural human aversion to work."

WHAT DOES THE ORGANIZATION DEMAND OF MEMBERS?

All acts of play respond to injuries people suffer when they encounter organizations. Those who eventually initiate themselves are more successful in treating their injuries in ways that compromise with veterans.

Nevertheless, even their play shows that few people readily fit into organizational conditions. The unsuccessful are most outspoken about what does not feel right, but nearly everyone who enters an organization must change some. People describe what is expected of them in the following ways.

Playing a Role

Most people believe they are different at work from how they are outside.[3] When they are at work, they play roles. They follow formal rules, suppressing their personal preferences when they conflict. They relate to other people strategically. Elsewhere, they say, they are more spontaneous.

A traditional argument for formal rules is that they enable managers to judge subordinates' work without becoming emotionally involved in personal lives and possibly making organizationally irrational decisions. A federal budget officer accepts this requirement as part of his role:

> To a large degree, you've got to play a role when you are in a certain level job. There are some people who can turn on and off a spigot. [They understand] the reactions of the employees here. Sometimes you have to play a role. You have a job as manager, and there are some things that you have got to have done. Sometimes you will not keep people happy. But if you keep personalities out of it. Sometimes there are unpleasant things that have got to be done. You have to structure yourself. . . . I don't mind playing the role, [on a] nonpersonal, a business basis.

A program manager equates impersonality with professionalism: "Most of the time, I am more professional on the job [than elsewhere]. I . . . play by the rules. I attempt to adhere to rules and regulations."

A community planner, whose work requires him to balance the concerns of his employer with the interests of neighborhood associations, explains how he must contain his natural reactions and calculate what he says in terms of his organization's aims:

> When you are a community planner, every time you open your mouth, you have to think, this is the City talking. You have to be careful not to give your own opinion. You just give the official City line, which is the appropriate thing for a City employee to say about this issue. I give up my reactionary [spontaneously reacting] position. There are certain things I know as a public person I have to do while I think, "Why in the hell are you calling me about this?" But I know it is something I have to do. Be more diplomatic.

I am a lot less conservative privately than I am publicly. Some of my positions would not be the compromises we have to make. You can't take anything personally on this job—for example, in reaction to criticism of a project you worked on. Become tough skinned real fast because your feelings could be hurt real frequently.

Two middle managers speak of themselves as if they are different persons at work and at home, more formal at work, more spontaneous at home. The first says that, despite his efforts to be the same in both places, his staff tell him he is different:

I don't think I am [different at work than at home], but everyone tells me I am, so it must be true. When I come to work, I put on my work face, because I am a supervisor. My wife works in another state agency in this building, and she knows I don't like her coming over here and talking to the people who work under me, because I have to throw her out after fifteen minutes. I am more formal at work than I am outside work.

He indicates that work responsibilities take precedence over friendly visiting, even by his wife.

A second manager is not surprised at all. At work she must always be dispassionate, in contrast to what she can do at home.

I am two different people. On the job, I am always in command. I never lose my cool. People see me that way. If only they saw me at home, where I lose my temper! I wish I could keep my cool at home and keep my control. At work things are more predictable. I am very organized at work. I am not very organized at home. Home is the place where I crash.

Treating people strategically, rather than personally, is the essence of the contrast between work and home, a policy analyst argues:

You tend to react, relate to people in the office, the bureaucratic situation, in more of a formal way. I still try to be a nice guy. I have a hard time coming down on people. This is the difficulty. I am more relaxed at home, more myself at home. I sort of enjoy what I am doing now. I get along with people. You have to do a job. You go home and are looked at as the head of the household, and you can lay down the law. There are certain ways you have to relate to people in order to get them to follow through. You have got to pamper people a lot of times. There is a strategic way of acting, and there is a formal way of acting. I don't think there are too many people who can go into bureaucracy and act the same as at home. You have to follow a pattern.

These workers describe formal organizations that resemble the Weberian ideal-typical bureaucracy (Weber 1967), and they report that they try to follow the rules. Nevertheless, they emphasize that to do this is to act unnaturally. How do they feel about making this compromise to fit into organizational roles?

Benefits of a Role

The federal budget officer says that he benefits from putting on a role: it protects him from guilt. If he judges a subordinate adversely, he can take comfort in believing it was the role, and not he personally, that acted. The community planner, even though he chafes at the constraints of his role, suggests that it protects him from shame and anger. If neighborhood residents or developers attack his position or projects, he assumes that they are reacting to him only as the city's representative, not personally. He can also accept some of their criticism, convinced that, if he were freed from the role, he would act differently. One of the middle managers generalizes that putting people in roles benefits everyone by making organizational life relatively peaceful and predictable.

Thus these workers argue that roles protect them and their organizations from dangerous unconscious thoughts. They can act in aggressive ways their job requires—for example, in appraising subordinates' performance or in taking positions against opposition—without provoking overwhelming opposition or inhibition. If others get angry at what they have done, they can treat the role as the actor and deflect hostility toward it. If their actions hurt someone, they can avoid guilt in the same way; indeed, they can even join the aggrieved party in attacking the role.[4] If their performance is poor, they can avoid shameful self-criticism by blaming the role, and they can join their critics in doing so.

This conceptualization of action makes life amicable in two ways. First, the convention that roles act but people don't reduces legitimate interpersonal aggression. At some point, "reasonable" persons, no matter how injured or disappointed they are, have to accept the "fact" that what has happened involves only involuntary role behavior, that, no matter how painful it was, it involved no personal malice or ineptitude. Second, insofar as this framing reduces hostility between aggressor and aggrieved, it allows them to unite, even to care for one another, as joint victims of the role.

In these ways, the rules governing roles encourage conscious and unconscious mental processes of splitting, denial, and projection.[5] Workers can think of their destructive actions as split off from who they really are; they can deny that they intend to hurt others or that they have done so; and they can project harmful intentions onto the role. Thus they can think of themselves—and encourage others to think of them—as good while assigning bad qualities to the role.[6] Workers and their clients or constituents can care for one another as good in the shadow of their bad roles.

This conceptualization of roles is an important part of the compromises of sublimation required for work. Someone who wants to act aggressively can do so acceptably in an organization by molding inert materials, attacking abstract problems, or ordering and taking action against other people. The risks of reprisal and guilt are greatest with other people. Hence a convention that attributes excesses or failures to a role is important to the sublimatory compromise. "He's a mean boss, but being the boss requires him to be mean, and it even brings out some of his meanness." Reasoning like this excuses a lot of aggression by associating it with a legitimate role.

And yet this convention, as much as it gratifies individuals and, in particular, contributes to organizational peace, is a fiction. If only unconsciously, workers know what they are doing when they hold this view. They still recognize that they are the ones who do harm and fail, and they are still angry at others who hurt them. Furthermore, many workers are quite conscious of what is involved in cloaking roles in these arguments. They cannot avoid accepting responsibility for their actions— or blaming others for theirs—not only because they do not believe roles act autonomously, but also because they want credit for acting competently. They cannot convince themselves that they are responsible for only the good they do. Consequently, they do not succeed in avoiding feeling guilty, ashamed, or attacked.

In addition, many workers do believe they could do better, ethically and creatively, if only they did not have to accept the rules of the roles. They recognize role playing as a condition for organizational peace and, therefore, employment, and they do take advantage of it when it helps avoid guilt and shame, but it does not come naturally. Because roles often do not feel right, these workers have difficulty with sublimatory bargains that require exchanging spontaneity for role performance. The policy analyst, for one, knows he is more relaxed, more himself at home.

Inhibition and Anxiety

In fact, many people characterize themselves at work in his terms. They say they are inhibited and anxious. Like the community planner, they do not react spontaneously, but watch and control themselves. At the same time, they vigilantly observe others, to protect themselves from attack.

It is not accidental that workers mention these two experiences—being inhibited and being anxious—together. Freud (1963 [1936]) argued that they are integrally related. Speculating on why they commonly appeared together, he originally suggested that, when people restrained themselves from acting, the unreleased energy caused anxiety in its search for expression. Later, he concluded that the opposite relationship was more likely. He observed that the experience of anxiety is a signal of danger impending from a contemplated course of action. The danger may come from outside (for example, opposition from other people or physical objects) or within (for example, aggressive or libidinal wishes so strong as to outweigh realistic, prudent appraisal of actions or so directed as to arouse shame or guilt). If the ego heeds the warning, it may choose the defense of inhibiting the action.[7] Thus inhibition is a reaction to anxiety, which, in turn, is a response to perceived danger.

This relationship explains why the policy analyst feels more relaxed and more himself at home. His home is relatively unthreatening, and, consequently, he can feel free to act spontaneously. Conversely, he and others may feel inhibited and anxious at work because the organization contains a number of threats, and anxiety continually warns of the dangers of unregulated action.

When workers question the reasonableness of a role, they lose an opportunity for sublimating their aggressive or libidinal wishes in an organization. If they have no plausible place to redirect these wishes, since the wishes don't go away, safety requires them to inhibit the wishes, to keep them from open expression. The alternatives are not only guilt and shame, but also reprisal, and, above all, questions about organizational loyalty and belonging. The following comments fill in this picture.

A senior advisor to a deputy secretary in a federal agency describes her general self-restraint at work:

> There are some considerations that come into play here. ... I am only responsible for myself personally on the outside. On the outside there are a lot of experiences that I can react to any way and walk away from it. Here I have to live with it. So I have to temper my reactions.

A state health planner argues that organizational membership requires inhibiting expressions of sexuality:

> I am more inhibited on the job, more in control than with close friends of mine. For example, using [sexual language: I] don't do that on the job. Being a woman, this is more important. If you want to be taken seriously, you don't kid about sexual things. You don't

want to encourage any reaction on that level. So I inhibit my female-
ness. It is reality. There is nothing regretful about it. I guess there
was a little disappointment that some people are mean and cruel. . . .
It is disappointing that you can't trust people. This is reality.

Others describe organizational constraints on aggression. A public
information officer uses screaming as an example and says that she is
free to scream when she feels like it only at home. A data analyst
mentions cursing and says that he is "more likely to cuss someone out
outside than in-house [at work]." An environmental worker links his
inhibition of aggression to tension on the job:

> I am more wound up when I am in here. I don't know if my
> temperament is that much different. I guess I am more wound up
> here because I have less control of what stimulus will hit me on a
> particular day. Whereas on the outside I can lay back and tell
> someone to go to hell. In here I can't do that. This is a professional
> position. [Outside] I'll take my chances. If I have a conviction, I
> will not necessarily worry about the consequences on the outside.
> But here I have to make these considerations all the time. And it
> makes decision making more complicated.

In describing his anxiety at work, a regional planner speaks of "an
extra rigidity or fear of being trounced on here." A transportation analyst
says this attitude makes people constantly wary and tense.

> I am probably more tense, more paranoid, hopefully more aware
> of what is going on. Your decisions and actions are being judged by
> other people. So you have to be real cautious. . . . Maybe a sense of
> tension always makes people work better. And it is much more
> evident in private industry, as I was mentioning to a friend who
> works for [a utility company] when we talk. We were college stu-
> dents together. We discuss how the kids are. Then we discuss a
> professional question. I can actually hear his voice change. I don't
> think I do this to him.

Thus, workers recognize the requirements of sublimation for organizational membership and the risks of expressing aggressive and libidinal
wishes spontaneously. Bureaucratic conditions, which demand role conformity, may lead workers to exaggerate the dangers of individuality.
Ambiguities in bureaucratic relationships make it difficult to assess
others' authority realistically. In order to have reassuring predictability,
workers unconsciously fill in pictures of colleagues by drawing analogies

to others whose authority they have experienced, such as their parents. When people transfer assumptions about parents' power and abilities to bosses and colleagues, their coworkers appear more demanding and more punitive than they really are (Baum 1987). Still, when workers unconsciously expect others to act in these ways, they often tacitly encourage them to become what they seem to be. For example, a boss may unconsciously decide, "If nothing I do changes their seeing me as arbitrary, then I will be arbitrary."[8]

When workers say they feel inhibited and anxious at work, they refer to not only how they express libidinal and aggressive wishes, but, more generally, how they express themselves. Each developmental stage making up a personal identity depends on establishing social relations where it is possible to act aggressively, libidinally, and effectively in ways that promote growth and that others accept. When workers speak of their inhibitions and anxieties about the consequences of doing what they feel like doing, they refer to these compromises as well.

In each case, they calculate whether asserting themselves, demanding what their development requires, will jeopardize their membership. If they ask for less, others may accept them. If they can ask for less, they may be able to consider themselves part of the organization. Barry Landsdowne, for example, restrains himself from using his positional authority to tell others to do what he thinks they should do because he wants to be accepted as a newcomer. Susan Dorsey says she holds back on being as competent as she can be for fear she will outshine and offend others and be ostracized. David Ryan tempers his desires for a transmissible estate as long as he can so he can be satisfied with the job his organization gives him.

When workers believe they must choose between personal development and organizational membership, they contemplate their choices anxiously. They restrict not only their actions, but even the possibilities they consider. Workers who speak of donning a "work face" or being "two different people" acknowledge that they give something up. They also signal that they don't take their role fully seriously and may not take responsibility for their actions. In addition, they make it clear that they resent doing something unnatural for so much of their lives.

PLAY AND ORGANIZATIONAL BEHAVIOR

Thus workers may react to organizational demands with anything from close identification to cynical detachment. When people come to organizations, they normally try to join through initiatory play. By overt and tacit negotiation, newcomer and veterans may agree both will benefit from an addition to the membership. However, even if veterans are accommodating, playing any role demands concessions. Descriptions of the changes required indicate the difficulty and complexity of even successful initiatory play. Moreover, they suggest that many who appear to fit in still hold something back. Perhaps they don't identify with the organizational mission. Perhaps they question the gains from acting as if they are something they are not quite. For these reasons, even successful initiatory play encompasses a range of relationships.

If newcomers conclude that they cannot initiate themselves, they turn to either compensatory or escapist play on the basis of their reaction to the failure to attain membership, their assessment of the relative desirability of the current job compared to alternatives, and their perception of the available fantastic and realistic resources for changing the situation. Compensatory play, because it keeps the worker on the job, serves the organization better, although escapist play may gratify the individual more. If escapist play is pure fantasy, nothing else can equal its pleasure. If, on the other hand, it involves realistic plans for changing jobs or life situations, it may lead to new work requiring a new initiation.

In short, people do not choose one type of play or another arbitrarily, but as part of conscious and unconscious planning to satisfy their needs. Crucial to their decisions is the fit with the organization. Initiatory role play is possible when the fit is close and both newcomer and veterans are flexible. An intelligent, mature worker can try to make an informed choice of organizations. However, both choice and information are limited; in addition, some role requirements are nonnegotiable. In the end, an organizational neophyte can only respond reasonably to veterans' demands. In other words, managers and other veterans share responsibility for newcomers' choice of play.

An important lesson of workers' stories is that much of organizational behavior is play—in the sense not of unending fun, but of efforts to treat injuries incurred in early organizational contacts. These activities continue until the injuries are soothed. Initiatory play eventually comes to an end. However, even when successful, it may last for years, and it may become necessary again as needs or circumstances change. Compensatory play and escapist play go on for as long as a worker remains employed.

Compensatory and escapist play dramatize the meanings of all play. So long as a worker contends with the demands of initiation, he does not fully invest in organizational assignments or even personal work. Play is essentially self-centered: it is an effort to preserve one's identity in the face of threatening organizational demands. Even initiatory play, which rests on an intention to come to terms with an organization, expresses ambivalence about the organization and maintains distance from it until the moment of conciliation.

Two types of sociological studies support this view of organizational behavior. Reichers (1985) reviews literature on "organizational commitment," defined as identification with organizational goals, which is part of what is here called organizational affiliation. Various studies show that when workers do not feel strongly committed to an organization, they not only show up for work less, but also lower their performance when they do come. Cherrington (1980), cites a study of construction workers that found that they spent only 51 percent of their time in activities related to formal job responsibilities. The other 49 percent involved coffee breaks, late starts and early departures, waiting, and "personal activities." This latter category includes activities characterized here as role play. The organizational commitment studies indicate that workers who do not feel part of an organization do not put themselves out for it. Cherrington's findings suggest, further, that such workers turn to alternative activities for success, compensation, or escape.

Organizational behavior that is playful is meaningful, and it is intentional. It is not random or accidental. Nor is it simply perverse, unreasoning rebellion against the constraints of adult work life. Neither is it simply an accumulation of amorphous adjustments to working in groups.[9] A basic component of organizational behavior is individuals' conscious and unconscious efforts to restore their integrity and to grow in the context of work requirements.

The very first circumstances of organizational entry—even the attention a chief executive gives a job applicant—have far-reaching impacts on workers' careers and organizational life. They affect not simply whether newcomers become members committed to organizational purposes. They influence also whether employees turn outward toward colleagues or remain primarily concerned about themselves.

Part Five
Organizational Membership
Problems and Possibilities

How Organizational Politics Hinders Organizational Affiliation

The people who have shared their work stories show us there is no universal experience of joining organizations. Some describe themselves as members. Not only do others accept them, but they have succeeded in using working conditions to develop themselves. A small group talk further, of social or psychological intimacy with the organization. They feel close to coworkers and identify with collective aims. On the other hand, there are many who feel little attachment to an organization, including a number who are only employees, not even members. Many of these are newcomers engaged in yearslong negotiations over membership. Some, such as Parsons, Hayes, and Thomas, will eventually become members, while others, such as Landsdowne, Anderson, and Davis, never will. For much, if not all, of their employment, they speak of the organization as something alien, not a social body of which they are part.

The reports of working in organizations without belonging to them, even if unsurprising to many of us, would puzzle others. Members of traditional societies, for example, would not understand them. Their initiation rituals work because everyone feels the power of the community in each of its embodiments, and rituals can transfer bonds with the larger society to any of its smaller units. New members would have no question of their identification, for example, with a hunting group or a women's group. In modern society, in contrast, institutions are discrete. The work group has no relation to the kinship group, nor, for that matter, does it have any overt religious functions. The faith invested in any spiritual being and the loyalty tied to a family do not readily go over to a specialized work organization, which is impotent to invoke or evoke either of these emotions.[1]

Societies differ, and even human "nature" is not invariant. Nevertheless, it would be strange if people who spend much of their waking hours five days a week working together were only indifferent to one another. Intimacy is a normal developmental interest for adults, and organizational affiliation—caring for coworkers and identifying with an organization—is one opportunity for learning and expressing it. The family, where many people spend less time than on the job, neither satiates needs for intimacy nor prevents turning to work as well. Physical closeness and interdependence at work give modern workers an opportunity for emotional closeness and tacitly ask them whether they want it.

There is another group, who may not be puzzled but are directly concerned about the stories of indifference to the workplace. These are the managers who talk of "corporate culture." They see workers' desiccated organizational ties but insist that modern organizations, indeed, can have the intellectual and emotional cohesion of traditional societies. They cast the psychological questions of this book in social, economic, and policy terms. They believe the success of organizations as intelligent and efficient collective bodies depends on workers' membership in, and intimacy with, the workplace.

The crucial link between the social conditions of work and feelings of membership and intimacy lies in organizational politics. Some of the strongest feelings people express about work organizations are anger about "politics." For them, office politics just pushes them away from the office. Their job, they say, would be pretty good, if only it weren't so political. But because it is political, they try not to take it as seriously as they would like to. This chapter looks at themes in discussion of organizational culture and then analyzes how conventional organizational politics hinders membership, intimacy, and the establishment of a coherent culture.

ORGANIZATIONAL CULTURE

Much of the sociological literature on organizational socialization reviewed earlier rests on the assumption that workers and managers share interests and that, therefore, organizational membership is nearly inevitable. The literature on organizational commitment, examining the correlates of identification with organizational goals, recognizes that intimacy and membership depend on workers' perceptions of and feelings about working conditions. The organizational culture literature most readily treats organizational identification as problematic (e.g., Pettigrew 1979; Deal and Kennedy 1982; Martin 1982; Peters and Waterman 1982; Martin, Feldman, Hatch, and Sitkin 1983; Smircich 1983; Naisbitt and Aburdene 1985; Peters and Austin 1985; Pondy, Frost, Morgan, and Dandridge 1983; Schein 1985; and Schwartz 1985.

Chroniclers of "excellent" corporations report that workers' collective commitment to an organizational mission is central to success.

However, the growing interest in organizational culture reflects more than new sophistication about workers' motivations. It also expresses deepening disquietude about something that can no longer (probably never could) be taken for granted: workers' commitment.[2] Hence the concern about "organizational culture" represents an interest in promulgating beliefs that will draw workers to the workplace.

The talk of re-creating organizational culture includes romantic nostalgia, fantasy, and calculated efforts to increase productivity. Yet, regardless of the motives, those interested in culture need to understand that it is more than abstract ideas that someone may dispassionately accept or discard. It is a system of beliefs that must both sound logical and feel reasonable. Intellectually, these beliefs must make sense of work activities and fit in with other parts of workers' lives. Psychologically, they must call for social relationships and commitments congruent with the emotional attachments of which workers are capable.

Changes in work have weakened traditional organizations' success in satisfying the first condition. The growing complexity of production and organizations makes it increasingly difficult for a worker to identify the outcome of his work. Organizations produce things, but individuals do not. Moreover, as more and more workers perform services rather than make goods, even the nature of the product is unclear. Neither an employer nor a worker can be as certain of productivity in health care or finance, for example, as in auto manufacturing. Increasingly, products are ephemeral. Many services consist of transitory relationships: many goods are quickly consumed or broken. Under these conditions, workers find less ready evidence that the organization is a place where they can be competent and feel grateful for the opportunity.[3]

Nevertheless, formal mission statements may apparently satisfy the first condition: what they say "sounds right" to workers. And yet the words don't "feel right." An integrative culture depends on workers' belief that they share the economic interests of coworkers and the organization. But, in addition, workers must feel that they, colleagues, and the overall enterprise grow together and strengthen one another. Then they willingly collaborate and assist one another. They feel close to one another, and work relationships shade into social relationships. In addition, workers feel close to the organization, identifying its welfare with their own. In other words, the psychological requirements for an organizational culture are those of organizational affiliation.

If managers talk or write simplistically in promoting "organizational culture," their motivations seem clear: they want loyal workers. And yet the ideal of a unitary organization may attract workers, as well. Realistically, they may want to affiliate with an organization, but this relationship depends on satisfying a series of difficult developmental prerequisites. Workers who cannot satisfy these requirements may turn to fantasies of a primitive merger with an organization where development is not necessary and failure never occurs.

In this fantastic organization, all would be close; indeed, all would be one and the same. Distinctions between managers and subordinates, the top and the bottom, would be gone. And because all would be one, everyone would be omnipotent and omniscient. Furthermore, all would care for one another; indeed, the great organization would care infinitely for everyone. This common fantasy, which Schwartz (1987a and 1987b) characterizes as an "organizational ideal," corresponds to and has origins in an individual's ego ideal. Infants have the narcissistic fantasy of being one with a powerful, loving, and perfect universe, and the memory of this becomes the basis for efforts later in life to reestablish the experience (Chasseguet-Smirgel 1985 and 1986). For example, an artist may create a work that restores this feeling of perfection. Alternatively, and commonly, people may idealize organizations and identify with the fantasied institutions. Thus, someone who identifies totally with an organizational ideal can feel loved and protected by a powerful entity. Significantly, this attractive fantasy corresponds—and responds—to many managers' presentations of an integrative corporate culture.

The core of this fantasy, as well as the ideal organizational culture, is the possibility that the individual and organization can be powerful together, without conflicts and without anyone acting aggressively. This wish is the key to many complaints about "politics." Acting politically means acting aggressively: separating oneself from others and engaging them in conflict. While some complaints about "politics" refer to realistic obstacles to work, others register objections to a reality that interferes with the ideal. They unconsciously dissent from a world where people are separate and different, where they are in conflict, and where harmful outcomes are possible—where, in short, the fantasy of unity with the organization is clearly impossible and where they must develop and act aggressively in order to get work done and identify realistically with a workplace.

AGGRESSION AT WORK

Acting competently, holding a work identity, and affiliating with an organization depend on continuing success at tasks associated with these and previous stages of development. These accomplishments require sublimation of libidinal and aggressive wishes. This includes acting assertively enough to complete tasks but caringly enough to do them with others.

Most of the everyday language of work emphasizes its aggressive components. Even though managers may have an easy time with workers who care for the organization and harbor no aggressive wishes against it, they also want subordinates to "work hard" and to "attack problems." No one says much about libido on the job. Few talk of caring for colleagues. Many say cooperation is desirable, but, when pressed, quickly give it up for getting things done alone. The most common expression of libido at work is a highly attenuated interest in "getting along" with others.

Thus managers confront a dilemma: to encourage sufficient aggression to get work done, but to elicit enough caring to ensure that workers don't hurt one another and feel loyal to the organization. Workers, in turn, unconsciously face the quandary of acting aggressively enough to be competent without feeling guilty or anxiously awaiting reprisal.

Yankelovich and Immerwahr's (1983) survey of American workers provides evidence of this dilemma. Eighty-eight percent say they want to work hard and do the best they can on the job, and more than half say they have an inner need to do the best job regardless of pay. Nevertheless, 75 percent say they could be significantly more effective on the job, and half say they work just hard enough to avoid getting fired. In other words, workers say they want to work aggressively but hold back. Some explain they don't get paid any more for doing more. Others, pointing to the dilemma about aggression, say managers provide little incentive to work harder.

The frequency with which people talk of working aggressively shows how close to the surface their aggressive impulses are. Workers sublimate them enough to do their jobs but under stress could revert to harmful actions. Unconsciously, they are anxious about the security of their sublimations. At the same time they are poised to defend themselves, they also worry that such a response would undo them. Realistically, this means they might embarrass themselves by acting inappropriately for their role. Unconsciously, they fear the greater danger of losing a range of sublimatory accomplishments, including carrying out any work roles or mastering any work abilities. Worst of all, they imagine jeopardizing the Oedipal bargain and reencountering the Oedipal father.[4] Although conditions that unsettle previous developmental achievements are normally upsetting, the strong aggressive component to work sharpens the unconscious dangers of regressing.

AGGRESSION, POWER, AND POLITICS

Politics is a realm in which people act aggressively, strategically promoting their interests to influence the allocation of resources. Even though political activity may help get work done, many people see it as extraneous to working, even antithetical to it.[5] Often for them "politics" is a screen for talking about aggression that upsets them, and "power" is a common name for aggressive wishes and acts.

Every organization requires political procedures, for solving certain problems. The "politics" to which many workers object represents a particular type of politics: win-lose interpersonal conflict, based on the assumptions that people have irreconcilable interests and that solving problems requires defeating, rather than joining, others. Realistically, some who complain about organizational politics describe procedures interfering with their professional autonomy. Others, however, are expressing a general discomfort about getting involved in political relationships. Some dislike politics because it demands abilities they lack. They have difficulty conceptualizing issues in terms of interests or are poor strategizers. Others feel uncomfortable confronting people, especially those who oppose them, and particularly those who seem powerful. This unease may discourage developing political abilities or thinking politically. It points to a number of unconscious problems with the exercise of power—aggressive thought and action.

The Developmental Character of Politics

In general, politics may be defined as the exercise of power to promote interests,[6] but there can be as many types of politics as there are types of power. The most common conception of power portrays independent parties asserting themselves to defeat one another. This is the principle of politics in a world of scarcity and conflicting interests. It is a zero-sum politics: when one party wins, another must lose.[7] Normal organizational politics is an example.

Arendt (1958) has conceptualized power differently as the ability of different parties to achieve something together they could not accomplish individually. This power governs a politics concerned with creating new possibilities in a world where resources may be scarce but where some interests may be joined and new resources created. This is a win-win politics: victory is only collective, and one party's loss defeats all.

Significantly, different persons conceive power differently and practice politics differently in the same situations. McClelland's (1975) study of the experience of power finds that there are four "power orientations," which vary according to two dimensions. The *source* of power may be external (another person or a principle) or internal (oneself). The *object* of power, similarly, may be external (influencing or controlling another) or internal (controlling or strengthening oneself). Figure 5, adapted from McClelland's work, shows the four power orientations.

Figure 5. Classification of Power Orientations

	Source of Power	
	Other	Self
Object of power		
Self (to feel stronger)		
Intention:	"It" (God, my mother, my leader, food) will strengthen me.	I will strengthen, control, direct myself.
Action:	Being near a source of strength. I	II Collecting, accumulating information, things.
Other (to influence) IV		III
Intention:	It (religion, laws, my group) will move me to serve, influence others, to do my duty.	I will have an impact or influence on others.
Action:	Action on higher principle or purpose.	Competing with, affecting others.

Adapted from McClelland (1975), p. 14; reprinted with permission from Baum (1987), p. 63.

    In analyzing the characteristics of people he has studied, McClelland concludes that the four orientations correspond to stages in Freud's model of psychosexual development and Erikson's model of psychosocial development. The Type I power orientation ("It strengthens me") resembles the infant's oral concerns with being fed by a nurturant mother. In Erikson's terms, it relates to a search for a trustworthy foundation in the world (1). Someone who as an adult still seeks assurance of the world's trustworthiness is likely to take this orientation to power. Not only does the orientation provide security, but it also represents the only orientation of which such a person is capable. It expresses a wish to feel powerful by working for someone who is powerful and, therefore, can be trusted to provide a secure world. By seeking satisfaction in the closeness of loyal service to someone strong, this orientation may be particularly helpful for someone who advises an elected official or top manager.[8]

    The Type II power orientation ("I strengthen or control myself") corresponds to the young child's anal concerns about being able to control the accumulation and elimination of personal products. Psychosocially, it is a quest for independence and self-control (2). An adult who is worried about autonomy is likely to take this power orientation. It expresses a wish to feel powerful by being independent, free of contact with others and not bound by their interests or actions. It may encourage an interest in data collection, for example. By accumulating and managing information, someone may gain a sense of control over the objects the data represent without directly becoming involved with them.

The Type III power orientation ("I have an impact on others") corresponds to the phallic interests of the Oedipal period. This is a time when the child wants to show off his endowments and defeat the same-sex parent and win the opposite-sex parent. Erikson observes that the child must eventually find a way of taking initiative without suffering guilt (3). Adults who have not fully resolved the Oedipal dilemma may unconsciously exaggerate the danger of conflict and the likelihood of reprisal or, alternatively, the chances of success and resultant guilt. They are likely to take this power orientation. It expresses a wish to feel powerful by doing battle with others and vanquishing them. This is the power orientation most closely related to conventionally defined "politics," where one party tries to defeat another to gain the latter's holdings. This orientation can be helpful to strategists and community organizers.

The Type IV power orientation ("It moves me to serve or influence others") is most complex, depending on successful development from latency through adulthood.[9] It begins with the latency youth's identification with the parents' moral norms, the identification with the imagined aggressor that settles the Oedipal struggle. In Erikson's terms, this is a time of interest in internalizing culturally valued technical norms (4). In addition, the power orientation builds on the adolescent's developing interests in genital mutuality. Physiological satisfaction in this project requires social interaction by more or less equal parties. Psychosocially, these and other adolescent experiments should lead to the creation of a secure identity (5) and the initiation of intimacy (6). This is the basis for the Type IV power orientation: reciprocal interaction among people who understand who they are and accept others as their equals. The orientation may help planners who make recommendations on behalf of a public interest they discern in the interactions of groups, mediators who look for ways of reconciling conflicting parties, or managers who act on collective interests rather than personal loyalties. Type IV corresponds to Arendt's view of power.[10]

Although only the Type III power orientation is normally associated with "politics," each of the four leads to a specific type of politics, as figure 6 shows. The Type I orientation encourages a politics of subordinacy, in which people look for others on whom they can depend. Although some who become consultants hold this orientation, when people talk of "the politics of advising," they usually refer not so much to the (Type I) personal efforts to establish a relationship with a client as to the (Type III) self-interested, often conflictual interactions between an advisor and a client. An example of the Type I power and political orientations is Susan Dorsey, who wants to be powerfully recognized by a wise and fatherly boss.

Figure 6. Relations Between Power Orientations, Developmental Stages, and Politics

Power Orientation	Corresponding Stage of Development	Likely Politics
I. "It will strengthen me."	Trust vs. Mistrust	Subordinacy
II. "I will strengthen myself."	Autonomy vs. Shame and Doubt	Isolation
III. "I will have an impact on others."	Initiative vs. Guilt	Interpersonal conflict
IV. "It will move me to serve others."	Industry vs. Inferiority Identity vs. Identity Confusion, and Intimacy vs. Isolation	Collaboration

The Type II orientation, in contrast, leads to a politics of isolation, in which people try to become self-sufficient by accumulating as much as possible. Although some who analyze data hold this orientation, most conventional talk of "the politics of information" refers less to the (Type II) self-oriented activities of gathering information than to the (Type III) conflictual interactions of requesting and resisting its dissemination. An example of Type II power and political interests is John Hartley, who measures his power in terms of his independence from others.

The Type IV orientation, corresponding to Arendt's concept of power, leads to a realistically sophisticated collaborative politics, enabling workers to promote interests and resolve conflicts while maintaining an attachment to coworkers and the organization. When the ability to be intimate undergirds problem solving, people feel that they can assert their interests vigorously but securely, that others, including those with more or less power, will continue to support them despite disagreements over real conflicts, and that colleagues will look for cooperative solutions for problems. Because (Type III) conflict is a common definer of "politics," this (Type IV) consensus-building is often characterized as "apolitical." "Professionals," for example, often couch their actions in terms of the "neutrality" of serving a "public interest" or such general principles as "rationality." Sally Ransom offers an example of someone who thinks of Type IV power and politics in terms of making decisions on behalf of overall organizational goals.

Finally, the Type III orientation leads to a politics of interpersonal conflict, in which people try to defeat others to get what they have. The interpersonal focus distinguishes Type III politics from Type II, which emphasizes independence, and Type IV, which is suprapersonal, serving abstract principles or large groups rather than specific individuals. The conflictual basis of interpersonal relations distinguishes Type III politics from Type I, which emphasizes harmonious dependence. Thus, this conventional politics involves a view of power distinct among four possible types. Although Michael Anderson fails in early attempts to intervene in taking a Type III power orientation, his descriptions of organizational advancement make explicit common assumptions about relations in Type III politics.

The distinction between everyday "politics" and Arendt's model is a contrast between the third and fourth power orientations. However, these are not simply alternative choices, because, McClelland discovers, the four orientations are related as developmental stages. Learning one depends on mastering others preceding it. For example, just as Erikson observes that confronting the challenges of initiative and guilt depends on establishing autonomy, McClelland finds that someone cannot practice the Type III power orientation before mastering the Type II orientation. Similarly, someone who is not secure in the Type III orientation cannot understand or begin to learn the Type IV orientation. This means that those for whom the conflictual politics of the Type III power orientation represents the edge of their development are unable to conceive of or participate in the cooperative politics of the Type IV orientation.[11]

The developmental relationship among power and political orientations means that the more advanced a person is, the larger his repertoire of actions. Although any of the orientations may be appropriate in specific roles or situations, effectiveness depends on being able to choose the most fitting one at a given moment. For example, Type III political action may be necessary at certain times, but only someone with a Type IV orientation is able to choose between that and alternatives including mediation.

Because power orientations are expressions of personal identity, the orientations and stages of development are reciprocally related. For example, someone who has not found ways of taking initiative without guilt will not be secure with or competent in the Type III power orientation. Conversely, someone who has trouble with conflict in the Type III orientation will have difficulty moving beyond autonomy to guilt-free initiative, as well as meeting later challenges.

Political situations present tests corresponding to different stages of development by requiring a power orientation for success. People are especially likely to interpret situations in terms of the orientation matching their most secure stage of development. However, other actors or institutional norms may encourage or force acting differently. For example, someone who is comfortable with intimacy may attempt to enact a Type IV orientation by mediating a conflict between organizations over scarce grant money. However, if the grantor is willing to give money to only one organization, or if none of the organizational directors is willing to compromise, then the would-be mediator may get drawn into Type III politics, siding with one director against others.

The consequences of success or failure in a political situation are the same as those in other situations where stages of personal development are tested. Political success will reinforce accomplishments at a corresponding stage of psychosocial development. Failure will unsettle achievements at the corresponding stage, as well as subsequent ones. Unconsciously, the individual will then regress, giving more attention to situations that reinforce the successes of the previous stage and trying to practice in situations that build up the recently upset accomplishments.

The Regressive Effects of Participation in "Politics"

This perspective helps understand workers' complaints about "politics" and their indifference to organizational affiliation. Commonly, people refer to a specific type of politics, Type III. They say it is self-interested, rather than collectively oriented. It is concerned with winning, rather than collaborating. It is devious and circuitous, rather than direct and straightforward. It is selfishly calculating, rather than disinterestedly rational. It favors collusion over competence.[12] This "politics" holds out two dangers, reflected in the complaints. It induces people with advanced development to regress in order to participate. More generally, it entails expressions of aggression that make people anxious and encourage them to defend against attack rather than assert their interests. This section describes the regressive pressures, and the next examines the dangers of aggression.

For those who regard their work in terms of a Type IV orientation—who see themselves acting on general principle, serving collective interests, or mediating conflicts—Type III politics asks them to act in ways consistent with an earlier developmental orientation. As the example about grants suggests, an actor with a Type III orientation makes it difficult for others to maintain a Type IV orientation, because there is no commitment to reasoning together and collaborating. It is tempting—and may become strategically necessary—to step down from the Type IV position.

Sometimes people with Type IV orientations engage in Type III politics while continuing to think of the possibilities for Type IV politics. They do not regress, their previous development is unaffected, and they act relatively effectively. However, "politics" may regressively affect both power orientations and identity development. A Type IV orientation depends on a secure sense of industry, a coherent personal identity, and comfort in intimacy. Because the Type III orientation corresponds to earlier efforts to free initiative from guilt and reprisal, adults may unconsciously experience the conflicts of Type III politics in terms of the family conflicts of childhood. As a result, they may reexperience guilt and fear about asserting themselves and have to learn once again to take initiative. This challenge pulls them back from later developmental stages and may temporarily undo or unsettle previous achievements. Realistically, adversaries in Type III politics may threaten someone's position, income, or power. At the same time, involvement in this political process unconsciously endangers his sense of competence, identity, and ability to be intimate, as well as generativity and ability to make sense of things.

These threats to personal identity help explain why relatively few workers, even those who are members, feel part of their organizations. Continuing involvement in Type III politics makes it difficult for someone to be close to or care for coworkers or to identify with an organization. When workers conceptualize most of their relationships in terms of calculated triumph over rivals, they have trouble thinking of coworkers as persons whose welfare they share. Superficially, people might observe that they are so annoyed by "politics," they don't feel part of the workplace. This statement describes an unconscious connection: "politics" makes intimacy difficult.

The Damage of "Political" Aggression

All politics are expressions of aggression, in attempting to influence, move, shape, or harm others or the self. Each is an effort to establish or maintain a boundary between the self and others or in-group and outsiders. In different ways, Freud (1962 [1930]) and Klein (1975b [1932] and 1964 [1937]) argued that social life depends on opportunities to balance aggression with expressions of love and caring in acts of sublimation.

Freud emphasized the social gains from sublimation. Civilization is possible, he said, if individuals can relinquish destructive expressions of their aggression and direct sufficient libido toward society to value and maintain it. Klein called attention to the personal benefits. Every expression of aggression, beginning with the infant's fantasy of harming the mother and thus losing her, arouses the anxiety of being punished and losing a parent's love. To avoid this, the infant must learn to think of acting in a way that combines libido with aggression. The love repairs the imagined injury and permits a compromise, which satisfies aggressive aims but avoids guilt and retaliation. Society is possible, Klein argued, when people have opportunities to find these compromises. Instead of confronting a world of imagined retaliators and abandoners, people will be able to live relatively peacefully with more or less loving others.

This requirement extends into every developmental stage and social institution, including work. Clearly, when people complain about organizational "politics," they are talking about the problems of aggression at work. Because Type III politics is developmentally related to Oedipal struggles, participation in it may unconsciously evoke memories of childhood anxiety about aggression. For adults who have not successfully resolved the Oedipal conflict, each new relationship recalls the earlier struggle and presents new challenges to make symbolic peace with parents. Even those adults who have succeeded earlier feel the need to make reparation for any aggressive impulses.

Thus, workers' complaints about "politics" express not only resistance to regressing, but also anxiety about the consequences of unrepaired aggression. Managerial exhortations to work hard call for aggression without providing opportunities for caring for others. Emphasis on economic efficiency gives individuals credit for producing in quantity, but not for making good, valued objects.[13] Organizational "politics" similarly encourages individuals to set themselves off from others and fight them without compromise. As a result, even when some people benefit from strategic action, engagement in "politics" unconsciously makes many people anxious about aggression not balanced by caring.

When workers complain about the "politicization" of their organization, they may refer, realistically, to efforts of elected officials to dominate what were once autonomous professional decisions. In addition, they may hint at the unconscious dangers of an organization that gives workers few opportunities to repair the imagined damage from normal aggressive work. When workers think in terms of individual achievement, and when they concentrate on attacking coworkers, they become anxious about being hurt or hurting others, they become isolated, they fear embracing an organization containing so much unsublimated and unrepaired aggression, and they are unlikely to feel part of the organization.

Self-restrictive Defenses Against the Dangers of "Politics"

Sublimation may be thought of as a successful defense against threats. Its compromises avoid dangers but also satisfy the originally risky aims. It is play that succeeds. Other defenses involve unsuccessful efforts at compromise and play. *Denial*, for example, may avoid recognizing dangers, but the threats remain. Moreover, the surest way to ignore hazardous realities is to give up the original aims that led toward them. Consequently, for however long people succeed in avoiding these realities, they do so at the cost of restricting their domain of action. *Repression*—unconsciously choosing to remain unaware of or to forget external realities or feelings— has similar costs and limitations. The realities or feelings remain, and avoiding them requires limiting the scope of one's actions and one's intentions. Similarly, in the case of *regression*, danger may be avoided, but at the cost of surrendering the original aims. People who resort to regression as a defense act as if they were less mature and, thus, less potent and less dangerous to those who might frustrate or punish them. In the process, however, they deny themselves the abilities that came with growth and thus limit their repertoire and domain of action.[14]

Workers who feel anxious about Type III politics may defend themselves in several ways. Some, for example, continue to work and act aggressively but try to deny that they do harm or risk reprisal. They may also try to repress any guilt about damage or anxiety about retribution.

Others unconsciously regress to a Type II power orientation and argue cynically that "politics" is immoral and dangerous. They will work well but independently, so that they don't have to deal with coworkers, owe them anything, or risk losing to them. Some rationalize their actions in terms of a pseudo-Type IV orientation. They say they are serving "technical rationality," "economic efficiency," or "the public interest," and that their positions should overrule the selfish actions of "politicians." Claiming intellectual superiority, they almost magically expect power without making contact with coworkers.[15]

A still more regressive defense is fantasizing that the organization is a strong, intimate place where caring pervades, "politics" is absent, and aggression is unnecessary. People may express longing for this organizational ideal in wishes for an integrating culture. Regression to this Type I orientation is usually less consistent than the Type II defense with getting work done because it deprecates the aggression work requires. It depends partly on a magical belief that, if a worker holds back on acting aggressively, identifying with the organization and managers will provide the power to get work done. This premise, as well as that underlying Type II, imply that development is not necessary to work.

These defenses all retreat from realistic relationships with coworkers and an organization. By protecting workers from dangers of aggression, they require holding back from aggressive action, not simply in social relations, but also in work itself. In addition, these regressions in power orientation have regressive consequences in personal development. They redirect concern to problems of aggression and initiative, autonomy, or basic trust and make it difficult for a worker to maintain a sense of competence. Crucially, workers are developmentally unable to feel secure being close to coworkers or identifying with a real organization.

In short, conventional "politics" often confronts workers with a difficult choice: in order to try to promote their interests and get work done, they must risk regression. Not only do many workers realistically or fantastically fear others' power to harm them, but they are anxious about the possibility of regressing. They fear losing the mastery, sense of identity, and possibilities of intimacy that have come with their past development. Those whose development is insecure find work and "politics" especially threatening and may choose the safety of withdrawal, caring less about work or the organization.

POLITICS AND THE ORGANIZATION

The unconscious meanings of Type III organizational politics both attract and threaten workers. People may be drawn to Type III situations—indeed, may even create them—because of their connections to Oedipal situations. For those who have not completely resolved earlier Oedipal conflicts, Type III politics provides an opportunity to reenact earlier positions. Symbolically, attacking a political adversary may provide the satisfaction of assaulting an undefeatable Oedipal parent. Type III situations also may allow someone to discover both political and Oedipal compromises.

At the same time, Type III organizational politics presents unconscious dangers. It threatens workers' most mature developments, from making sense of the events of a lifetime all the way back to establishing competence and sustaining a work identity. In addition, it engenders anxiety about aggression that normal work activities cannot relieve and may even compound.

Regressive defenses against these dangers not only intrinsically reverse development, but also imply that development is not necessary for joining an organization. In particular, identification with an organizational ideal makes intimate membership in a perfect organization effortless. All one need do is think of oneself as united with organizational principles or managers who represent them. Although these defenses bring pleasure in retreat from threats, they defeat any interests in becoming part of a real organization.

If organizational affiliation means identifying with a setting so seemingly full of dangers, it is clear why many workers want no part of it. Even membership without intimacy may entail negotiating with people who seem treacherous. Despite these risks, nevertheless, workers do join organizations, and some of them become intimate members. However, a number of people choose half-measures. If they care for colleagues, they may insist that these relationships have nothing to do with work. Alternatively, they may go out of their way to distinguish their own unit from the rest of the organization. Although the organization is dangerous, they say, their own section is a good place to work, where people look after one another. Perhaps management's espoused organizational mission is hypocrisy, but they feel their colleagues are honest and dedicated. These assessments may be realistic, in that many workers eventually find comfortable niches. However, the moral dichotomization of organizational realms may also reflect unconscious defenses against the dangers of being in an organization.[16] If people believe they work in oases of caring, protected from aggression, they are freer to affiliate with some part of an organization.

Play is a normal sign of civilization. Work, like so many other activities, becomes possible only when individuals find ways of reconciling their wishes with those of others. And yet the extent of compensatory and escapist play stemming from efforts to join work organizations measures the consequences of "politics." Some of this activity is the relief of those who are miscast for most organizations. Still, for others it is an attempt to assert developmental needs against the regressive pulls of Type III politics. It is balm against the failure of defenses that do not become sublimation.

In the face of "politics," workers look for outside domains where they can act aggressively with safety, because they fear the consequences of doing so inside the organization. Elsewhere, not only might they win for a change, but they may have the opportunity to engage in Type IV politics as well. In either case, they expect the outside world to offer a chance to repair any unwanted damage from their actions. In other words, they turn outward to find opportunities for caring, not only to mediate their aggressions but for its own sake as well.

Under these conditions, workers will have difficulty developing or engaging in sophisticated, realistic (Type IV) politics for resolving conflicts. They will also have difficulty creating or responding to any sophisticated, realistic organizational culture. Instead, they are more likely to insist on an organizational ideal that may serve managerial fantasies as well as their own and yet engages no one in the real work of the organization.

Worker Development and Organizational Development

In studying the meaning of organizational membership, we have inquired about the emotional status of the workplace. What do people expect in it and of it? What are they prepared to do to get what they want? What will they do if they fail? These are not new questions, but we have examined a normally hidden dimension of them. We have asked whether people unconsciously demand of work organizations certain things that are at least as important as the formal matters of employment contracts.

THEMES AND LESSONS

The Centrality of Developmental Plans to Organizational Behavior

A central theme in workers' stories is that people expect to grow in organizations. They approach work with the intention of using it to promote their development. Consciously and unconsciously, they try to create the ideal organization from what they find. If the organization disappoints them, they do not give up, but continue to try to establish conditions for their growth elsewhere. Thus, even "private," "informal" activities may be concerned with creating a good work organization.

Workers' stories give the following picture of organizational encounters. People approach organizations with a combination of conscious and unconscious demands. These expectations pertain to the content of work and working conditions, as traditional studies of work satisfaction tell us. In addition, crucially, these demands concern the conditions for entering an organization and becoming a part of it. Organizational membership brings employment and income, but it also requires giving up independence and accepting a new identity. Although formal negotiations involve only the former, every worker wants it all: employment and income and independence and pretty much the same identity.

Identity is the key to workers' negotiations with work organizations. What Erikson has called the stages in psychosocial development, workers experience as an agenda for everyday activities. They expect their social encounters to help them meet one challenge and then progress to the next. They do not simply wait passively, but move actively to create the situations they think will help them grow. Work is a central part of this program. Not only is work itself integral to development, but the workplace is an arena where adults may fashion their identity in other ways as well.

Thus workers are rational planners: they want to promote their personal development, and they consciously and unconsciously design ways to use work settings to carry out an unfolding agenda. Accordingly, organizations—even the same organization—may seem quite different things to different people. But for all of them, these meanings are far from frivolous.

Whether people succeed in becoming members of work organizations depends on how veterans receive them. Adjustment to job responsibilities may be the easiest part. And yet there are people who do their job well, but still don't fit in. They are *in* the organization, but not *of* it. Organizational entry is a complicated negotiation. Both overtly and in a deep unconscious way, veterans want newcomers to give up past claims of authority and status and to submit to being remade by the organization. Consciously and unconsciously, the newcomer knows what is demanded and prepares a defense, a strategy of appeasing demands for transformation while preserving past identity.

The ensuing negotiation is a deadly serious dance, in which veterans insist that personal identity be subordinated to the organization and newcomers insist that the organization is only a constituent of personal identity. The new worker experiences the organization's conditions as not simply a request to give up an established identity, but also an insistence on curbing aggressive and libidinal wishes. The balance of power in this negotiation varies, although in most cases the organization is stronger. The outcome depends on the newcomer's ability to use the organizational role as a transitional object, to find ways of both fitting in with the veterans and promoting personal development.

Play is the essence of this negotiation. If role play succeeds, the newcomer becomes an organizational member. If not, he may continue to play with the role or may play with the disappointing conditions of entry to find compensation or escape, some psychic gains to balance the costs of continuing to work in the organization. This negotiation may be relatively quick, but it often takes years. Moreover, personal development, as well as promotions, administrative changes, or reorganizations may start the initiation process all over again, with new expectations and no certain outcome.

Crucially, the incidents of the first confrontation between individual and organization set the terms for all subsequent relations. This point cannot be exaggerated: the first contacts between the newcomer and the workplace lay the groundwork for all later organizational behavior. Successful entry leads not only to job satisfaction, but also to acceptance of much that takes place in the organization. Frustration or disappointment in entry marks the columns in a tacit ledger, in which subsequent events are taken as confirmation of fundamental organizational debts.

Although many factors influence the outcomes of entry, certain developmental expectations are especially compatible with the demands and offerings of many organizations. The "work" aims of work ability and work identity fit especially well. So does organizational affiliation, though fewer workers consistently look for it. Nevertheless, although all "work" expectations are developmentally equivalent, they differ in content, and some match particular organizations better than others. The prework aims of recognition, autonomy, and power, if they dominate a newcomer's developmental agenda, are likely to interfere with becoming part of a work organization. The postwork aims of mentoring and making sense of life's events may fit in some organizations but be incompatible with others.

Resulting Organizational Relations

Workers' stories reveal four relationships with organizations. Some people talk of *membership with intimacy*. This is what Bellah, Madsen, Sullivan, Swidler, and Tipton (1986) mean by considering work a "calling": work ties the individual to a community and is inseparable from the individual's life as a whole. These people consider themselves members of their work organizations, and others seem to share this view. They take their work seriously, and they also take the organization seriously. They identify with its mission. In addition, they feel close to other workers. They consider many of their colleagues their friends, and they link coworkers' success with their own. These workers experience the deepest involvement in organizations. Developmentally, they are most likely to be concerned with organizational affiliation.

A second group speak of *membership without intimacy*. They are like those who, in Bellah's terms, regard work as a "career": it is a matter of progressing through an occupation, without ties to any community. Like the first group, these people have succeeded in getting enough from the organization to feel like members, but they do not identify with it. They take their work seriously and appreciate working conditions but believe they contribute much more to their accomplishments than the organization does. They may endorse formal organizational goals, but they emphasize that their own activities make up the real work of the organization. If they are close to others around them, they are likely to think of them less as coworkers who are friends than as friends who happen to be coworkers. Being at work is pleasant for these people, but they don't feel that their satisfaction depends on the organization. Developmentally, these workers are most likely to be concerned with work ability and work identity.

A third group describe *engagement without membership*. They are *employees* trying to become members. They think of work as at least a career, perhaps even a calling. They want something from the organization but haven't gotten it yet. They take the organization seriously as a place that can help them grow, but they haven't succeeded in negotiating entry. People with prework expectations are particularly likely to be frustrated by an organization, but this status includes anyone still involved in initiation efforts. If they succeed, depending on what they want, they may become members with or without intimacy.

A final group refer to *disengagement*. They are *employees* who regard work merely as what Bellah calls a "job": a way to make money. They are not members of the organization, and they expect nothing from it other than a paycheck. They may be disappointed and disillusioned. Prework aims may especially lead in this direction. Alternatively, they may have had no illusions or hopes in relation to a work organization. Some people who are concerned about their generativity or integrity may not believe they can satisfy these interests in the workplace. In any event, all these workers share a utilitarian view of the organization.

All these workers become veterans, and they eventually face other newcomers. Their role in later initiations depends on their relationship with the organization. It is helpful in this connection to recall the stages of an initiation. The initial confrontation, or separation, strips the neophyte of past characteristics that make him dangerous to the collectivity. The following transition, or working through, gives the initiate an acceptable new identity, which is subsequently incorporated, or integrated.

A veteran who has become a member participates in all stages. He can show and teach a neophyte what membership is. In contrast, someone who is only an employee lacks the experience of membership to transmit. Nevertheless, an employee trying to become a member has stakes in encouraging others to take membership seriously. Their progress confirms his faith in the possibility and value of joining. In addition, an organization in which more people are members is more receptive to everyone seeking entry. Moreover, acting as if one were already a member inducting others may help initiate someone trying to become a member himself. Only a disengaged employee has no stakes in others' membership.

Still, all workers can be threatened by an outsider. Members watch for dangers to both the collectivity and themselves. A disengaged employee may not care about threats to an organization short of those that would close it down. However, he shares one concern with others: the newcomer should not disrupt established routines and relationships. Thus even a nonmember may participate in initial stripping activities, though he may take aim at different attributes than veteran members.

From the stories here alone it is impossible to say much about the distribution of these four types. Clearly, those who are intimately members of work organizations are a minority. Many consider themselves members without expecting intimacy. Many others yet are in, but hardly of, their organizations, for the moment or for a long time much more loyal to themselves than to those around them. Although workers' expectations have a strong influence on their eventual relationships with organizations, organizations characteristically differ in their workers' typical relationships. Some are intimate places to work, while workers in others are more likely detached or disengaged. This fact is an important reminder that veterans' actions affect whether and how newcomers join organizations.

Disappointment: Causes, Meanings, and Consequences

When new workers fail to become members of work organizations, part of the fault is their own. They look for conditions the organization cannot provide, they want to join without changing, or both. And yet, because entry is a negotiation, veterans—both policymakers and co-workers—share responsibility. They reject an applicant who deviates too much from their patterns. They may say the newcomer would not fit into routines. More seriously, they know his way of doing things could raise troubling questions about how they have been working all along.

A newcomer may have "work" expectations, but they may clash with veterans' interests. For example, someone who wants to collaborate challenges people who are used to working alone. In general, veterans will resist a new worker whose expectations are more advanced developmentally than organizational norms. For example, someone interested in mentoring threatens others in an organization where workers mistrust authority and jealously guard their domains. Not only would veterans consider the newcomer's wishes disruptive, but, because of the developmental difference, they would hardly understand what the newcomer wanted.[1]

Veterans and newcomers together work in more or less bureaucratic organizations, which, many stories suggest, intrinsically upset or hinder the personal development initiation and membership require.[2] Normal bureaucratic politics arouses anxiety about aggression and encourages defensive retreat from work. In particular, by shaking workers' confidence they can take initiative without guilt, "politics" unsettles workers' sense of competence, work identity, security in intimacy, and higher developmental achievements. People focus efforts on exercising initiative, often to the detriment of working.

Even those who work in bureaucracy without regressing often report that they outgrow their organizations. Most often, they do not find generative or integrative possibilities at work. This divergence of interests is often considered an argument for early retirement: let older workers go from the world of work to other places where they can nurse the concerns of their final years. Yet this policy denies the centrality of work to people's lives and development. It means not only that adults would have to develop wholly new relationships to continue growing, but also that they would have to deny work meant to them as much as it did in order to move on. In addition, it deprives organizations of people who are experienced, concerned about creating relationships among workers, making their successes available to others in the future, and thinking about the meaning and direction of work and the enterprise.

These disjunctions dramatize the difference between modern and traditional societies. Traditional rites of passage build on one another and, consequently, are powerful. In contrast, entry into a modern work organization is not a precursor or successor to other initiations, but only one of a number of more or less independent beginnings. Few people believe having a job or working for a particular organization fundamentally changes who they are.

Nevertheless, the overt meanings of traditional rituals may persist in modern workers' unconscious fantasies about organizations.[3] The initiation rite that inducts a young man into a men's work group, for example, utterly transforms the youth. He must give up past license and accept new discipline. Except under the most carefully circumscribed conditions, he is never again allowed to act in the ways of his youth. Both psychologically and socially, the conversion is traumatic, and rituals are designed to smooth his passage.

And yet the youth gains tremendously from his new identity. Centrally, he has a place in the society. He matters. More than that, the society takes care of him. He is a worker (as well as, later on, a husband and a father), and daily interactions and ritual observances support him in carrying out the obligations he cannot avoid. Socially and emotionally, he is at one with the society. While he has little choice about enacting his role, he gains strength and security from identifying with the society.

Many characteristics of the inclusive traditional society are found in the organization ideal (Schwartz 1987a and 1987b). Though consciously workers may criticize real shortcomings in the workplace, unconsciously they fantasize that their organization is perfect, powerful, and loving. Beyond whatever satisfaction they find in their work, they love an organization for what they imagine it could be and hate it for some of its

realities. When this fantasy makes workers optimistic about the possibilities of growth in organizations, it motivates them to take realistic
steps to become members. The clearest sign of this is workers' efforts to
join organizations by creating ideal organizations in play.

The will to grow is inherent in living. Adults want to develop ties of
intimacy, pass on their accomplishments to successors, and make sense
of their lives just as urgently as infants want to find the world a trusting
place, become autonomous in it, or take guilt-free initiative. When adults
don't find opportunities to practice their aims, they die a little. Instead
of intimacy, they find isolation; not generative, they become stagnant;
without integrity, they become desperate.

Workers hate an organization that disappoints their expectations.[4]
Inevitably, every real organization fails to match the ideal. Organizations
make mistakes and fail. Managers are not loving parents. Much work is
humdrum, few projects are identified with individual authors, and most
products are ephemeral. Common organizational conditions frustrate
developmental ambitions. Organizational politics pulls individuals back
from advanced achievements to renewed insecurities about initiative
and guilt. No matter how much the infant in the adult yearns for
immortality, work cannot provide it.[5] People who cannot find ways to
grow at work, who find it only continually disappointing, hate the
organization for the repeated injuries it inflicts. They are likely to retreat
from it to fantasies of the organization ideal, where identifying unthinkingly with the boss or corporation offers the illusion of perfection
without development.

When workers turn to fantasy or other defenses, they sever realistic
ties to the workplace and thus make it difficult for managers to direct
them. An integrative culture motivates by tacitly promising adherents
the rewards of the organization ideal. However, it promotes powerful
collaboration by setting forth compelling, reasonable goals and by
describing realistic ways of accomplishing them. It tells people how they
can develop and how they can act aggressively and libidinally while
working. At the same time, it must be supported by working conditions
and politics that enable and allow these accomplishments. Whatever
interferes with membership not only curtails individual development,
but also limits the energy and intelligence available for organizational
productivity. Thus both personal development and organization development depend on successful initiation and self-initiation.

DIRECTIONS FOR CHANGE

Both public and private organizations must be productive: work
organizations have to work. However, dominant managerial assumptions

about how people should be organized are self-defeating because they frustrate workers' interests in developing and lead them to withdraw. Workers' stories reveal the eventual meanings of organizational designs. The costs are both emotional and financial.

Both personal growth and organizational productivity call for re-thinking the purposes of organizations. The expansion of service work means that more work consists of creating and guiding personal rela-tionships (e.g., Bell 1973; and Hage 1988). Work ability increasingly includes being secure in the closeness of relations with colleagues and clients. From an organizational point of view, work ability often depends on intimacy. Hence managers have stakes in helping workers become comfortable with intimacy. Thus, personal development must be a pri-mary organizing consideration, neither a residual concern nor a reluc-tantly conceded "constraint."

Workers, managers, and policymakers must ask directly what an organization should provide to enable a reasonable range of individuals to develop work abilities, work identities, organizational affiliations, mentoring relationships, and meaningful overviews of their lives. They must consider what relationships among workers are necessary for individuals to master each of these challenges. In addition, they must seriously examine organizational initiation. How should veterans receive newcomers so as to allow a variety of applicants to become members without losing what they value in their identity?

Integrative Organizational Culture

These questions may be discussed in terms of culture and politics. The problem of "corporate culture" is how managers may evoke workers' loyalty in a way that motivates them to work hard. Administrators cannot significantly change workers' inner lives, but they can shape the conditions to which workers respond. In particular, they may succeed to the extent that they satisfy the unconscious requirements for intimacy.

To begin with, a culture is not simply a set of rules like work proce-dures, nor is it merely a compendium of stories managers repeatedly tell. A culture comprises values and norms that affect people because the ac-companying actions make sense and feel right. Hence, efforts to "create an organizational culture" depend on changes in day-to-day activities.

In addition, contemporary work, a growing part of it intellectual and interpersonal service activity, must make new sense in two ways. The traditional work language of "production" and "productivity" does not obviously fit what many people do. They "produce" insights, decisions, or personal relationships, but none of this is the same as producing an automobile, a prototypical work image. People have difficulty measuring themselves when they spend their days attending meetings, talking on the phone, and exchanging memoranda. Administrators need to reconceptualize what workers do in terms that reveal the value of their activities.

At the same time, day-to-day activities must make workers important. They need recognition for specific efforts, such as authorship on reports. They need to see consequences to their actions, by participating in and observing decisions about whether and how their efforts are used. They need to be associated with things that last, whether tangible products or programs or organizations themselves.

These changes require the creation of Type IV politics. For workers to act with the maturity needed to identify with coworkers and an organization, they must participate in a collaborative politics that enables them to discover and serve collective interests. They need ways of expressing real differences and resolving conflicts that allow them to remain connected to coworkers and invested in collective work.

Type IV Politics

Type IV politics has five characteristics. First, its power orientation is to serve others besides oneself. People may act interestedly but must have a commitment to reaching decisions on abstract principles or collective interests. Second, psychologically, it depends on and serves personal development. This is one of the abstract principles (as well as a collective interest) that must govern actions. Third, in particular, socially as well as psychologically, it supports intimacy and loyalty to the collectivity. Fourth, it promotes work that is collaborative, in which people jointly choose and control tasks, as well as take responsibility for each other in carrying them out. Fifth, to serve these ends, it encourages open communication about situations, interests, and conflicts.

Human relations theorists, using their own language, have argued that such politics increases organizational productivity in two ways. First, if workers cease thinking of one another simply as rivals and begin to wonder what new projects they could carry out cooperatively, individual and organizational innovation is likely. Second, workers' participation in decisions about products, projects, or procedures invests them in their work and motivates them to do it well.

Type IV politics is a politics of personal development. It requires— and thus promotes—a sense of competence, a coherent identity, intimacy, generativity, and finding meaning in life's events. For example, as collaboration creates new productive possibilities, it offers workers the opportunity to feel competent at an expanding range of skills. In this way it makes available a broader repertoire of work identities. In addition, workers are more likely to feel that these identities are part of a community bound by intimacy, interests, and ideals. Members of such a community are especially likely to seek and offer mentoring relationships, and the community becomes available as a group to whom workers may pass on some of their work accomplishments. Above all, these relationships endow work activities with many rich meanings. Whereas Type III politics focuses workers on problems of initiative and guilt, Type IV permits them to pass that test and move to higher levels of maturity.

In addition, Type IV politics is a politics of reparation. Its overarching aim is to serve and strengthen others, and its method is collective action. Both types of mutuality permit—and require—that people replace or supplement aggressive, destructive wishes with libidinal, caring wishes. Collaboration creates or reinforces the conviction that the satisfaction or pain of one is a gain or injury to all. Equally important, the more workers find ways of working together, the fewer will be the instances in which they attack one another in the pursuit of separate interests.

Type IV politics cannot eliminate all conflicts of interest, but it lessens hostility between individuals and groups in the work organization. Not only does it reduce actual assaults, but participation in it unconsciously helps people repair injuries they imagine inflicting while working aggressively. The resultant increase in security fosters both individual growth and social solidarity.

This politics also affects the initiation of new members. Workers in an organization that recognizes, accepts, and attempts to reconcile differences regard newcomers differently than employees or members of a Type III political unit. Any boundary crossing is unsettling for both outsider and in-group. Most newcomers differ in some way from veterans, and each party will still regard the other anxiously. Organizational initiations will continue to follow a three-stage sequence as newcomer and veterans negotiate relationships. However, where Type IV politics is possible, veterans are likely to feel less threatened by new entrants and to treat their differences less severely.

Political Change

With any innovation, some will gain more than others, and those with stakes in present arrangements will oppose change. Many at the top of bureaucratic hierarchies are likely to resist politics that admits more participants. Those adroit at Type III strategies will not readily acquiesce in more deliberative and collaborative decision making. Furthermore, some will argue that Type IV politics is impossible, utopian and not worth trying. They may mean that they have never seen an organization different from their own. They may also be unconsciously asserting their developmental position: a Type IV power orientation may be beyond their present ability.

Even those who appear to lose under Type III politics may gain enough from it to resist change. Most people unconsciously consider

Type III a natural way to resolve differences because it corresponds to the assumptions and strategies of family Oedipal battles. Not only are the rules familiar, but they seem to promise eventual victory. Moreover, the predictability of the rules, even if they consistently lead to defeat, is reassuring. In addition, Type III norms avoid the risks of close confrontation. One does not have to reveal one's needs to others, approach others intimately, or suffer the shame and pain of not getting what one asks. Holding back from Type IV politics shields one also from the risks of winning: changing position, gaining authority, and acquiring responsibility for others.

There is no simple program for transforming organizational politics.[6] Policymakers and managers are central to any reform effort, because if they do not want Type IV politics, it will not emerge. They often benefit most from conventional Type III strategies, but they have two incentives to innovate. First, organizational norms that cripple workers' development limits productivity. In addition, managers have their own developmental needs, which Type III politics limits.

Type IV politics is not a fixed outcome to be achieved, but a way of thinking about problems and making decisions. It can be implemented only by implementing it; in other words, the first steps in introducing Type IV require acting in a Type IV way. Hence, the most important requirement for creating Type IV politics is a commitment to experimenting with organizational policies, structures, and work. Administrators can use their positions to legitimize experimentation and provide the trust and security it requires. By doing this, they make mistakes acceptable and encourage open examination of problems, interests, and ideas.

The principles that should guide experimentation are those discussed in connection with organizational culture. Above all, managers should recognize developmental interests and accept them as legitimate expectations of organizations.[7] They should encourage subordinates, veterans and new workers both, to do the same. This includes reconceptualizing the needs of newcomers, as well as what the organization can offer them. This perspective departs from the view that workers' concerns are unrelated or hostile to corporate purposes, a noneconomic diversion which, at best, must be tolerated. Managers who recognize and accept new workers' developmental needs can negotiate and satisfy them more knowledgeably and explicitly.

Despite our cultural mandate for economic selfishness, people hesitate to pursue psychological self-interests. They seem childish or secondary to the business of getting ahead. Or else they seem impolite and are promoted only covertly, often shamefully. For example, workers may enjoy recognition but regard it as egotistic. They may enjoy mentoring but regard it as unimportant or unseemly. However, exercising power, for example, is not necessarily selfish or sadistic; it can be a means of personal growth, part of an integrated identity, and a way of solidifying group interests. Intimacy at work is not necessarily misplaced or self-indulgent; it, too, can be a means of growth, part of an adult identity, and a source of organizational cohesion.

Individuals have limited choice of work organizations and limited information about working conditions, initiation requirements, and resources for personal development. Nevertheless, if people considering employment know what they need from organizations to consolidate and continue their development, they can analyze the possibilities more self-interestedly. In negotiating both formal agreements and tacit psychological contracts, they can more knowledgeably seek what they require. They will have a broader picture of their work interests and be better able to evaluate how well they fit with an organization at any time. They can measure both their economic prospects and their psychological opportunities. They will consciously better understand whether their personal development is consistent with remaining in an organization.

Administrators must experiment with a wide range of organizational policies, beginning with the conceptualization of work. Although technical requirements for tasks vary considerably, much more work could be defined and organized in terms of collaboration. Not only can planners, for example, work in teams, but planners and implementors or direct service workers can work more closely. If responsibility is assigned to groups, people will think more about what they can do with, rather than against, around, or aside from, others. The need to cooperate encourages people to talk more openly about problems and proposals. In general, it encourages people to develop to the point where they are capable and comfortable in collaboration.

At the same time, supervision and evaluation must take into account not only contributions to organizational productivity, but also progress in individual development. This does not mean that managers take over the roles of therapists, nor does it mean that they reward and punish people for their personality orientations. It also does not mean that managers become involved in subordinates' growth efforts wholly unrelated to work. Rather, worker and supervisor can discuss how the former might practice certain developmental tasks (for example, exercising authority or supervising others) while doing organizational work. The worker can discuss with the supervisor what tasks, if any, he wants to work on, and they can plan how the supervisor will support developmental efforts. Together they can decide how to evaluate the subordinate's work.

Managers cannot agree to everything workers want, but such discussions open up personal development as a legitimate organizational concern and follow principles of Type IV politics. Not only may workers and supervisors talk about getting recognition or having autonomy, for example, but these consultations give workers recognition and assume their autonomy. Not only may they talk about learning intimacy, but they may find some together.

Still, even when administrators better understand workers' needs and want to satisfy them, organizational structures constrain what they can do. Hierarchy limits possibilities for recognition, autonomy, and initiative, choices of work abilities and work identities, and opportunities for mutuality, mentoring, and making sense of events. It encourages shame anxiety and defensiveness. Type IV politics requires more egalitarian psychological and social structures.

Although few administrators can change entire organizations, many can make partial reforms, altering policies or structures within units over which they have control.[8] Experimenting with Type IV politics requires considering organizations themselves experiments.

CONCLUSIONS

We began with the question why people work. We looked in particular at what people expect of work organizations. Most people work at least for the money. But many people also boast that, although they could make more money elsewhere, they prefer the job they have. They may like it because they feel competent at it. They may enjoy the camaraderie. They may take satisfaction in opportunities to serve others. They may find ways to express themselves creatively at work. These interests and rewards are all much more complex than the simple exchange of money.

The question why people work is not an idle one. We ask it because we feel people often work despite a sense that what they do is alien to them, that it harms them in some way. When we wonder why people work, we really want to know whether it is possible for someone to grow through work, whether in particular a person can grow in a work organization. This is the theme of Studs Terkel's classic book, *Working* (1975), which he introduces by saying,

> This book, being about work, is, by its very nature, about violence—to the spirit as well as to the body. It is about ulcers as well as accidents, about shouting matches as well as fistfights, about nervous breakdowns, as well as kicking the dog around. It is, above all (or beneath all), about daily humiliations. To survive the day is triumph enough for the walking wounded among the great many of us. . . .

It is about a search, too, for daily meaning as well as daily bread, for recognition as well as cash, for astonishment rather than torpor; in short, for a sort of life rather than a Monday through Friday sort of dying. Perhaps immortality, too, is part of the quest. To be remembered was the wish, spoken and unspoken, of the heroes and heroines of this book. (1975:xiii)

We hesitate to find that work allows anyone less than he wants, for that conclusion threatens and haunts us all. If we see that someone else's job is unfulfilling, even oppressive, we ineluctably turn back to our own work. Do we enjoy it? Even if we enjoy it, is it good for us? Are we growing? Could we have grown more elsewhere, if only we had made other, perhaps more courageous, choices? These are deeply troubling questions. In part, they are queries about the human condition, and some of the answers are inevitably disappointing. We never know everything, and we make imperfect choices with the hope that there will be no unpleasant surprises. Periodically we play with the fascinating but unsettling question of what we would have done in some then if we had known then what we know now, and we usually quickly put the question away in exasperation over deciding who we would have been if we had known then what we know now. The premises are slippery.

And yet the questions about work may pain us more because we regard work as a social arrangement, one over which we have some control. We cannot choose which cosmos to inhabit, but we can select an organization to work in. And we believe, particularly deeply in America, that work is what we make of it, that it is our measure. Thus, no matter what our political or sociological sophistication, we tend to blame ourselves for the problems in our jobs—not simply if we don't get rich, not only if our products are imperfect, but even if working conditions grind us down. No one forces you to work here, the boss would say.

These feelings affect the reading of such a book as this. Reports of animosity between workers and organizations depress and discourage the reader. The impatient reader flips to the end to look for a chapter on remedies, quick or even gradual fixes. Others may put the book aside as a reminder of something they don't want to think about.

The findings here really are mixed. Organizational work is a compromise. A few people can just walk into an organization and fit into a job. The usual explanation for their easy accommodation is that they either do not take the job seriously or else do not take themselves seriously. Otherwise, adjusting to work is a matter of negotiation.

In the end, some people use organizations to grow. They overcome any initial disillusionment and then learn skills, take roles, make careers, and even become attached to the organization. Perhaps they are especially lucky in the organizations they go to, but they also make careful choices. In addition, they are adaptive. This means not that they freely give in to any of an organization's demands. but that they find compromises between these demands and their own.

Those who are less successful hold aims that conflict with adapting to an organization. They may be highly individualistic, more concerned about getting or knowing things for themselves than collaborating. Or they may be concerned with relatively private relationships, with one or two others. rather than the larger numbers of an organization. Those who have trouble adjusting to organizations fall into two groups. One group remain firmly bound to early developmental aims and have difficulty relinquishing them for organizational membership. The other group have already succeeded in working in organizations and are outgrowing them. After the complicated activity of organizational membership, they are looking for something more circumscribed, which may require withdrawing from the organizational center.

These findings are mixed in that some people succeed in making terms with organizations, while others do not. They are mixed also in that success is not a once-and-for-all matter. While some personal growth is necessary for joining most organizations, more personal growth may be an impetus to leave. There is no ground for saying that only the mature fit into organizations or that those who do not have only themselves to blame. As the stories reveal, maturity is multifaceted, and there are many ways to grow.

Whether we regard this finding as an indictment of our society depends on what we expect of work organizations. If we want everyone to have a workplace where he can become a member, then the society is failing. But, for better or worse, this expectation may be unrealistic. Some people—perhaps especially those who focus on early life needs—may be difficult to fit. They may find more satisfaction—even growth—in other spheres, outside work.

A more specific conclusion we can draw from these interviews is that few contemporary organizations can accommodate lifelong personal development. Bureaucratic organizations, pursuing predefined goals through standardized procedures, cannot automatically suit older workers who are concerned about mentoring, passing on what they have learned, and making sense of their work and other experiences.

We might decide that sensitive earlier retirement policies are in order, to ease more mature workers from work into other institutions that could more easily accommodate them. Yet such a policy would be economically difficult. In addition, it would be cruel to people who want both to work and to grow. Moreover, it is based on the false premise that current divisions among institutions could not change, that work, for example, could not become a realm for both productivity and generativity.

Hence, these stories of work point to an alternative conclusion, that we must redesign work organizations, to correspond to and satisfy the range of developmental needs normal people experience. This does not mean that civilization can be rendered free of discontents. But it does mean that work organizations, where most people spend at least a third of their waking hours, could be fashioned better to satisfy needs for intimacy, generativity, and integrity.

To say that workers might find intimacy in organizations does not mean that they would merge unthinkingly, unconsciously with organizational leaders or their policies. Nor does it mean that they would surrender their privacy to controlling supervisors or intrusive coworkers. Rather, it means those who want intimacy at work might find closer connections to colleagues and a sense of strength and purpose from realistic identification with reasonable organizational aims and leaders. Organizations would gain from authentic worker loyalty. More broadly, society would be strengthened by deeper ties between persons and institutions. Most importantly, human beings could grow together in ways probably unprecedented.

There are no easy prescriptions for transforming organizations with which this book might conclude. Clearly, any change in organizations requires fundamental changes in our individual and societal thinking. For a beginning, we may look nearby, at the stories recounted here. Just as they remind us what people like ourselves want from work organizations, they show us what we must think more seriously about. Each story is a tale not only of efforts to adjust to an organization, but also of an attempt to enact an organization that permits growth. Truly, each of these people tells us that the way to improve work life begins with taking ourselves more seriously.

Appendix: The Research

PSYCHOANALYTIC RESEARCH

This research examines organizational entry and membership with a two-part conceptualization. Erik Erikson's developmental framework offers a view of the substance of entry negotiations. The three-stage social and psychological initiation and personal change processes suggest a model of the structure of negotiations.

It should be clear that no study can "test" such a conceptualization of organizational entry, in any brute sense of confirming or rejecting it. To begin with, there are a great number of "variables," many of them obstinately resistant to "operationalization"; it is not clear what the variations or "ranges" of the variables are; and any study of the "effects" of variations in all would be next to impossible. Fortunately, however, such a conception of research is inappropriate. Here we are concerned about the meanings of social relations, which do not have simple causes and effects. Research into these meanings can be disciplined, but its requirements are different. This study tests the framework just described by determining whether questions and analysis guided by its concepts produce coherent, plausible stories, or descriptions and explanations, of becoming a member.

Still, the coherence and plausibility of stories that include unconscious content are slippery matters. Unconscious ideas, by their nature, are things we do not want to think about, because they make us anxious. Hence, we resist remembering them, much less saying them. What, if anything, we tell about our unconscious thoughts to such relative strangers as psychoanalysts or researchers depends on what we know and imagine about them. We may construct stories of our lives that are cohesive and compelling but that also avoid painful truths. In fact, the force of such stories may even be their warning not to take them at face value. What, then, does a student of the unconscious do?

The structure and length of traditional psychoanalysis are designed to do the best possible in reaching some truth under these conditions. To facilitate recollection of forgotten and repressed unconscious experiences, the analysand lies on a couch, facing away from the analyst's gaze, and attempts to observe "the basic rule" of uttering every thought that comes to mind. The analyst speaks mainly on occasions where interpretations may shed light on the analysand's assumptions about the analyst, which, in turn, may be transferred from relations with parents or others earlier in life and, generally, where interpretations may help elucidate the past.

Analysis takes place four or five hours a week and may last for several years. The frequency is necessary to establish a close and eventually secure relationship in which the analysand may experience and grow to examine an intense relationship with the analyst. The duration is necessary because of all the unconscious obstacles people place in front of recalling painful memories. If enough time elapses, an analysand may become comfortable enough to recall, then relate, and then analyze important experiences. But, at least as important, years are necessary because many early recollections may be not simply incomplete, but completely distorted. The passage of time may enable analysand and analyst to discuss the various accounts and come to some shared conclusions about their accuracy.

Freud likened the progress of analysis to an archaeological expedition: one digs through traces of the recent past eventually to reach their foundations in the distant past. However, Spence (1982), writing of psychoanalytic evidence and interpretation, argues that such an analogy is misleading. He distinguishes between historical truth and narrative truth. The former is what we conventionally mean when we refer to the "truth" of a story: it is a veridical account of what happened in some past time. The latter is an account of the same period that makes sense of remembered events in contemporary terms. It is what we have in mind when we say a story is "good" but not necessarily fully "accurate"; the core of the story conveys an important truth.

Spence draws this distinction because many psychoanalysts, as well as historians, following some version of the archaeological analogy, have confused the two truths, inferring the first from the second. But, furthermore, he argues that historical truth is an inaccessible ideal. Many events of infancy occur before consciousness and language and cannot be recalled in later life. At best, observers of infants may draw their own adult inferences from what they see. Beyond this basic abyss between experience and description, Spence notes that each of the acts a growing person takes to defend himself from thinking of an unpleasant experience becomes a barrier to the accurate recall of the events involved. One's developing account of one's life becomes a record shaped by variously accumulating self-deceptive distortions, which, if effective, prevent one from even recognizing that certain memories are only caringly constructed fabrications. To the point, those events that have created the most difficulties for contemporary life may be least accessible to investigation.

Spence is right about the elusiveness of historical truth. Narrative truths may correspond to historical truths, but their relationship is probably unknowable. Spence's argument is right, but it is risky. If analyst or researcher gives up efforts at the rigor implied by the apparently scientific activity of mental archaeology for the license implied by the artistic activity of constructing stories, it is easier to accept accounts that a priori "sound right" despite weak empirical support. An analyst's authority by itself may persuade both analysand and analyst where the evidence is incomplete or contradictory. A researcher analyzing data in isolation is susceptible to similar self-deception. Recognizing these dangers, Freud (1963 [1910]) warned against "wild analysis," glib speculation from fragmentary material. As a precaution, both psychoanalyst and researcher must be especially careful to distinguish preconceptions from evidence.

At its best, the psychoanalytic method provides checks against fantastic conclusions, but traditional psychoanalysis cannot be transferred intact into social research. Limitations of time, money, trust, and courage prevent that. Research into people's unconscious lives can be only psychoanalytically informed research. Interviews may be designed and conducted with the guidance of specific assumptions and hypotheses about human development and mental life. However, questions must be indirect enough not to arouse anxiety or encourage defensive responses. Still much more than in the clinical setting, a researcher is unlikely to gain much from asking a stranger directly about early childhood experiences, unconscious reactions to other people, or such charged matters as the exercise of power or experience of intimacy. Once the researcher collects the stories in the interview, the psychoanalytic framework offers hypotheses for interpreting them by constructing a larger account that seems to fit them all.

CONDUCT OF THE STUDY

In studying workers' efforts to join organizations, I was interested in their overt actions; the conscious and unconscious thoughts and intentions associated with these actions; and coworkers' actions, the network of social relations, and the organizational culture that constitute the individual's workplace environment. It is easiest for people to talk about what they did over a period of years and how they thought and (perhaps) felt about events. It is more difficult for them to interpret others' actions, including their motivations. People give the least explicit information about the unconscious meanings of their own or others' actions.

In order to explore these matters, I designed and conducted interviews with the basic conceptual framework as a guide to asking and interpreting questions. Talking with people, I looked for similarities between what they said they wanted from work organizations and, for example, what Erikson says people expect of others over their lifetime. In particular, I looked for correspondences between the course of organizational careers and the sequence of development Erikson observed. Did people seem to be describing their careers in terms of a series of Erikson's developmental accomplishments? Did blocks in their careers seem to involve difficulties with particular developmental tests? I asked questions designed to elicit unconscious issues as well as conscious thoughts or overt events.

I talked with fifty people in semistructured interviews organized around the course of an organizational career. We usually spoke for two or three hours, occasionally longer. For most of these people, this was as much time as they would spare for an interview. The brevity of the contacts limited the amount of information collected, but I benefited, as many interviewers do, from the privileges of the stranger (Simmel 1950 [1906]). He offers interest and intimacy but promises not to linger and to move on. Many people spoke relatively freely of defeat as well as triumph, of private thoughts as well as public acts.

As we talked, I listened for remarks suggesting that childhood events or unconscious aims may have influenced people's actions as adult workers. The interview with Charles Latham illustrates this process. Several times he characterized his agency as a "family," and, as we talked, I asked questions to explore how earlier family experiences may have influenced his expectations of the organization and his relations with others in it.

I tried to test the hypothesis coming to my mind that his apparent ambivalence about joining the agency reflected not simply a developmental plan but also conflicting childhood feelings about authority and affiliation aroused in his family. He was the second son, the second of nine children in a large extended family. I was curious, for example, whether his family position had led him not only to love, but also to resent, those who are around before he is, those who compete with him for attention, or those who bring others onto the scene. Such questions are theoretically and practically significant because they concern patterns of early life influence on adults' organizational expectations and careers.

In analyzing people's responses, I considered three contexts. The first is the interview as a whole: what the person said about himself and apparent themes running through the statements. For instance, Latham's mixed wishes to join the organization and his disdain for other staff members suggested, besides a complex developmental plan, an ambivalence about belonging to something of which the agency was an example.

I examined such themes in a second context, psychoanalytic theory and case material, to see what general principles of conscious or unconscious thinking they might represent. Latham's ambivalence suggested the broader hypothesis that a conflict about intimacy could interfere with becoming a member of a work organization. Erikson, for example, speaks of organizational membership as one expression of intimacy and describes a developmental conflict between intimacy and isolation. Comfort with adult intimacy, he and others observe, depends on a lifetime of relatively unconflicted experiences with loved ones such as parents. The psychoanalytic literature pointed to more specific questions to ask in analyzing the interview.

Sometimes I had answers for these questions; often I did not. Still, I examined hypotheses further in a third context, all fifty interviews. For example, I looked for other interviews where someone seemed to have difficulty becoming a psychological member of an organization and where the person made mixed or negative comments about closeness with coworkers, family members, or other associates.

In formulating an account of Latham's organizational career, I came to consider two tentative narrative truths. I rejected a third possibility, suggested by the sociological and managerial literature on organizational socialization. That perspective would see Latham's career as a conscious, deliberate, continuous, even if very slow, effort to learn what the organization expected and to adjust to it. This interpretation simply did not fit the evidence. It implies unconflicted, more or less steady progress toward organizational membership, and Latham's case involves not only considerable hesitation about becoming a member, but also unwillingness to take apparently available opportunities to join.

The first narrative truth I considered is the account of Latham's partly conscious, partly unconscious developmental agenda, presented in the book. The second would portray his ambivalence about joining the organization as an expression of lifelong conflicts about authority and belonging to groups. These two versions, both consistent with the evidence and psychoanalytic theory, are compatible with one another. They involve possible truths of different orders. The first concerns a sequence of tests one may pursue in order to grow. The second concerns conflicts about authority and intimacy that may affect the way one encounters such tests.

The interview material supports the story of a developmental plan. The story is not complete; it would be helpful to know more about Latham's thoughts, actions, and decisions. Further discussion could supply some information, as well as test the general truthfulness of this account. Nevertheless, the theme of a developmental agenda gives coherence to what he said. At the same time, even though what he said raises the question whether concerns about authority and intimacy affected his reactions to organizational membership, he did not say enough for me to construct a coherent story about this. Not only are his early life experiences unclear, but the interview did not sufficiently cover these issues in the organization to support a dynamic description of their contemporary meanings. Thus this interview raises the question about conflicts over authority and intimacy and organizational membership for future investigation but cannot settle it.

Even if Latham had said enough to support the construction of both narrative truths, there would still be other, compatible accounts of his career. Some would emphasize conscious calculations, others, different unconscious aims and conflicts. In research, as in psychoanalysis, every interpretation is inevitably partial. I have emphasized these two lines of explanation because they shed light on a conflict prominent in the events Latham reports. Moreover, Latham's concerns and experiences are not uncommon, and these analyses help understand others' efforts to find organizational membership as well.

THE PEOPLE STUDIED

The 50 people interviewed were selected randomly from Maryland public agency lists of professional and administrative personnel. Their organizations range in size from 60 to 15,000 and are located at all levels of government. Some of these organizations carry out staff functions for elected executives, others deliver services, and some do both. Table 1 shows some of the interviewees' characteristics.

A little over half are professional staff. Local workers are largely professional specialists; the proportion of interviewees who are administrators increases with each level of government. Nearly everyone has a college education, with the main variation being a significantly higher proportion of local workers with advanced degrees. This is consistent with their professional specialization, in contrast with the general educations of those who have advanced into administration at other levels. Salaries are, if anything, inversely related to years of education; most clearly, they increase with level of government and with advancement into administration. In general, the group is a reasonable sample of well-educated, relatively well-paid professionals and administrators in large organizations.

Few of these people are working in their first place of employment. Local workers have worked in the fewest organizations, probably because they are the youngest. Perhaps their professional specialization keeps them in their organizations, though with time many of them, too, may become administrators. On average, people in the sample entered their organization at age thirty and have spent thirteen years there. Federal workers are a little older than others, apparently because many have remained in their organizations longer.

Table 1. Characteristics of People Interviewed

	Level of Government			
	Local (*N* = 18)	State (*N* = 18)	Federal (*N* = 14)	Total (*N* = 50)
Sex				
Male	67%	50%	71%	62%
Female	33%	50%	29%	38%
Race				
White	67%	83%	100%	82%
Black, other	33%	17%	—	18%
Education				
No degree	11%	11%	7%	10%
A.A. only	6%	—	7%	4%
Bachelor's only	22%	56%	57%	44%
Master's	61%	28%	14%	36%
Doctorate	—	6%	14%	6%
Age				
Range	23-53	31-61	38-57	23-61
Average	40	44	46	43
Age at Organizational Entry				
Range	18-35	24-52	18-36	18-52
Average	27	32	30	30
Years in Organization				
Range	1-35	2-18	8-23	1-35
Average	13	12	16	13
Order of Organization in Career				
1st	28%	11%	7%	16%
2nd-3rd	50%	6%	57%	36%
4th-7th	22%	83%	36%	48%
Average	2.7	4.2	3.4	3.4
Position				
Professional	78%	67%	21%	57%
Administrative	22%	33%	79%	43%
Income				
Range	$15,000-$45,000	$20,000-$70,000	$30,000-$70,000	$15,000-$70,000
Average	$31,400	$36,900	$54,600	$39,900

Thus, this is a group who, when talking about entering their present organizations, are describing issues related to joining specific organizations, and not general problems of starting out in the world of work. Moreover, most have been in their organizations long enough to see whether their initial expectations could be satisfied. If they have been disappointed with their organizations, the reason (except for those with few years in) is probably (though not certainly) that their expectations do not fit, not that they have not had enough time to negotiate entry.

What can be generalized from this sample of public workers to professionals and managers in the private sector? The structure of their experiences—going through a three-part initiation, for example—is clearly comparable. Most studies of organizational socialization that find this sequence of stages, in fact, involve people in private corporations. There is no inherent reason to believe workers' reactions to the initiations differ because their employers earn profits or not.

Perhaps the content of workers' expectations differs between the public and private sectors. The study data here do not lead to strong generalizations about the distribution of expectations. However, it is difficult to imagine that private sector workers are uninterested in work abilities and identity, for example. Perhaps there are differences in other expectations, such as identifying with the organization or mentoring. Or maybe similar expectations result in different relationships with organizations. If researchers found such differences, they could try to determine whether they reflect differences in the types of people entering organizations, differences in the structure and culture of organizations, or some combination of the two. Such empirical findings would go a long way to replace largely anecdotal "evidence" on these questions.

THOSE WHO WOULDN'T TALK

In asking people for interviews, I met many more refusals than in similar past studies. Part of the explanation may be that in the past I identified myself as a member of the professional group to which the other person belonged, whereas here I was an outsider asking them about their organizational experience. Still, the anxiety and occasional hostility with which people declined, including in organizations where I had freely talked with people in the past, raise questions. Do people feel less sure about their work than before? Are they less secure in their organizational positions? Have top managers told subordinates to draw in the wagons?

No one has an obligation to participate in research projects, but the terms in which many people refused speak about the quality of their work lives. One midlevel manager declined with the reasonable explanation that he had just gone through a lengthy General Accounting Office (GAO) study of agency management. However, he did not intimate that the GAO reported the following gloomy picture of managers' perceptions. Many feel that the organization does not learn and is only moderately receptive to new ideas. Middle managers have insufficient freedom to make decisions. Top managers have given little consideration to human factors when making a series of major structural changes. There is no stable leadership, federal employees have a poor image, units in the organization are worried about their future, the agency has poor management, and the potential for promotion is poor. Although there is effort to maintain a teamwork spirit, morale is low, and the administration has shown only moderate commitment to providing a favorable work climate. When I called a supervisor in this agency, she said she would not talk to me because she did not want to add to any of the prevailing adverse publicity about the agency.

Several people said their time belonged to the government and they could not waste it in an interview. This is fair enough, though often others in similar positions in the same departments gave interviews without referring to the time involved. People identify with the organization when they express concern about the time, but sometimes their pride is desperate. One manager offered the following lengthy explanation: she would have to see me on her own time, but she had only thirty minutes for lunch, which she usually worked through. To make up the rest, she would have to take leave, and she was reluctant to do this, though a twenty-year-old, just starting out in the agency, without any of the sense of responsibility this manager had developed over twenty years, would certainly spend the time without taking leave. Generational differences, she said, mattered; when women entered the work force also mattered. To add emphasis before declining, she said she still had patriotism as part of her work ethic, even though this had declined in others lately.

A number of people asked to talk with or get a letter from someone who would corroborate my identity. Sometimes checking out my "*bona fides*," as one analyst put it, persuaded people to be interviewed. Several, including some who eventually talked with me, cited a need to get their boss' permission to talk. Many people wanted me to get authorization from someone before they would talk with me, though usually these people had no idea who should grant permission. Sometimes people suggested several possibilities, and when two people in the same organization raised this question, they never mentioned the same person or unit. They just felt, as one said, "organizational approval" protected them from the consequences of talking to an outsider.

A few people declined interviews with various explanations to the effect that they wouldn't tell the truth. Some argued that, as single individuals, they couldn't give an impartial, comprehensive view of the organization and, therefore, shouldn't be interviewed. One state employee said, simply, she wouldn't know enough to talk about her experiences and would only hem and haw.

Sometimes fear was a direct part of a refusal. One state employee reported that he had checked with a "legal specialist" and declined because of "repercussions" and "ramifications." Another said he was interested in talking but checked "on the office level" and found that there was "a policy" against such interviews. He didn't know what the policy was, but because he was new, he wanted to abide by it. Along the same lines, a federal worker said he wasn't sure I was supposed to be interviewing people and he wasn't sure workers were allowed to talk with me, because they were "not allowed to do this and not allowed to do that." A midlevel manager, who eventually agreed to an interview, spoke for several people in her department when she explained her wariness with the comment that "a certain air of paranoia pervades the place since the new governor came in." An analyst in a federal agency began his response to my request for an interview by asking if the phone conversation was being taped. He went on to ask whom I had already talked with and who had said what. He finally declined with the explanation that I should have permission from someone in "management."

Too many people made such comments to discount them simply as especially troubled people. Certainly some of the people who granted interviews were themselves anxious. At the least, these statements say something about people's connections to their organizations. They are afraid of doing something not clearly prescribed. How must this fear affect their initiative in everyday work? Moreover, how must they feel about an organization where they are afraid of taking initiative? Furthermore, how must they feel about themselves working in such an organization?

These responses to requests for an jnterview suggest that the sample may be biased toward those who consider themselves courageous. Perhaps, too, they have relatively positive ties to their organizations, or else they feel sufficiently detached that they do not worry about what will happen if they talk to outsiders. If these considerations affect participation in a study such as this, they certainly affect the responses to other organizational research. These are important questions for study themselves.

SELECTION OF CASE EXAMPLES

The examples presented in the text—both stories of whole careers and brief quotations—represent typical themes in workers' descriptions of their efforts to join organizations. After completing the interviews,

I analyzed them for common experiences and for significant variations. In general, there are differences in expectations, the nature of the initiation-self-initiation process, and outcomes. Although other choices are possible, I have organized the material by workers' expectations, which have some consistent relations with outcomes. In presenting the material, I have selected the stories of individuals who exemplify particular expectations and perhaps also certain ways of negotiating them or certain results.

In this sense, the case examples are "specimens." They represent significant types of organizational experience, even though it is difficult to speak about the absolute distribution of the experiences. There are other specimens not included here, some experiences that are more or less idiosyncratic within the sample. Perhaps further research would show them to be more common than they appear here.

THE FUTURE OF PSYCHOANALYTIC
RESEARCH ON ORGANIZATIONS

All social research is exploratory in the sense that findings are never certain. The study of organizational behavior may draw less confidently on accepted theory than a number of other fields (though this is different from saying that we know less about organizational behavior than other social behavior). Probably psychoanalysis charts territory still less understood than the objects of other social investigations. These conditions should encourage us to be careful about what we do and cautious in drawing conclusions. And yet, because psychoanalysis offers explanations where other frameworks do not, we should be willing to take risks, experimenting with imperfect but promising methods and speculating explicitly even where firm conclusions are not warranted. Those of us interested in unconscious organizational life should recognize that social research will never have the duration, intensity, or rigor of the traditional psychoanalytic method, itself imperfect.

We can adapt psychoanalytic methods to the constraints of social research. We should look for situations where we can talk at length with people who are willing and able to spend extended time with us. The relationship may involve simply a series of interviews, or it may include interviews as part of an organizational consultation or field research. We may include projective techniques to elicit unconscious imagery. The approach depends partly on the research questions—for example, whether they are primarily intrapsychic or interpersonal. It depends, also, on the relationships available to us. When we have choices, we should try to study fewer persons or social units in depth, rather than more people superficially.

Comprehensiveness and systematic sampling are also illusory, though this does not mean we should not be concerned about representativeness and generalizability. We should be willing to settle for samples of convenience: those who will talk with us. They will be biased in the direction of persons who will speak relatively openly about relatively private matters, but the thoughts and wishes they share are certainly representative of many others. Class, culture, and gender affect people's experiences and willingness to talk about them. In listening, we should be sensitive to both differences among groups and similarities among individuals. Over time, we can learn better whom to consider representative of whom else.

When we so briefly examine the manifestations of unconscious thinking in conscious life, we must be as careful as in any research to explicate our assumptions and check our inferences. But, furthermore, because of the subject matter, we must be still more careful than other researchers to avoid projecting our own wishes and conflicts onto those with whom we talk. We will never conduct psychoanalyses with our research subjects, and we will end up with more hypotheses and questions than firm conclusions. But that is the purpose—and virtue—of exploratory research: to identify new hypotheses for puzzling actions.

Psychoanalysis offers robust hypotheses about the foundations and structure of organizational life. It argues that researchers must understand actions in the same ways the actors themselves do: in terms of both conscious contemporary intentions and unconscious, often seemingly ancient aims. These hypotheses demand testing against alternatives, to construct the most coherent, comprehensive, truthful accounts of organizational—and other—experience.

Notes

Chapter 1.

1. For an additional discussion of psychological contracts, see Baum 1987; Kotter 1973; and Schein 1978.

2. The categories in this list are not mutually exclusive, and a number of the publications cover several different categories. The list is meant to illustrate the interests of psychoanalytic organizational researchers.

3. I have used pseudonyms for everyone and have changed details about place of employment or job responsibilities that might identify people.

4. See the case study of Mr. Smith in Baum (1987) for elaboration of this complaint against the mediated character of bureaucracy and analysis of the psychological meanings of the complaint.

Chapter 2.

1. Actually, even so simple a statement as this is not unambiguous. Freud (1957 [1915]) held that individuals are primarily concerned with relieving instinctual (e.g., sexual) tension and that they turn to relations with other persons only as a means toward this end. In contrast, Fairbairn (1952) and others have argued that individuals are concerned with establishing social relations for their intrinsic rewards. Thus, each of these perspectives differently interprets what it is that individuals express in social relations. In order to concentrate on interpreting workers' relations with organizations, I will generally avoid distracting excursions into this metapsychological realm. For succinct reviews of the issues, the reader is referred to Klein (1976); and Eagle (1984).

2. For a review of psychoanalytic writings on work, see Neff (1985). Some of these writings, in addition to Erikson, are discussed in chapter 4.

3. Weiss, Sampson, and the Mount Zion Psychotherapy Research Group (1986) present empirical research from psychoanalysis to show that individuals have combined conscious-unconscious plans to solve problems and grow.

4. Klein (1976) argues similarly that human actions are motivated by an interest in "integration." He observes that the traditional psychoanalytic emphasis

on conflict-resolution recognizes the importance of integration, but he, as Erikson, emphasizes the role of integration as a positive developmental aim.

5. How much the individual regresses in the ways described here depends on the individual's prior development. For example, an adult who has had a secure sense of identity for many years is less susceptible to regression than an infant or child who is only beginning to master early relational tasks. For a discussion of regression, see A. Freud (1946) and S. Freud 1963 [1936]). For Erikson's thinking about regression, see, for example, Erikson (1963, and 1975, both *passim*).

6. For a full presentation of Erikson's developmental framework the reader is referred to Erikson (1963, and 1968).

7. Elsewhere (Baum 1987) I have described this plight as the predicament of autonomous bureaucratic authority. See that book for a description of the psychological dynamics of a relationship between a subordinate and an inaccessible supervisor.

8. Psychoanalysts call this analogizing "transference": people unconsciously transfer feelings and assumptions from one relationship to another that resembles the earlier one and then act in the second situation as if it were the first. Feeling that the boss is "paternalistic" may be an example of this. For a discussion of transference in clinical situations, see Fenichel (1945); Orr (1954); Greenson (1967); Racker (1968); and Brenner (1976). Hodgson, Levinson, and Zaleznik (1965) provide a compelling study of transference in organizational relationships.

9. For a discussion of the ego ideal, see Chasseguet-Smirgel (1985).

10. For a discussion of the phenomenology and psychodynamics of shame, see Piers and Singer (1953); Lynd (1958); and Lewis (1974).

11. For an analysis of the ways in which bureaucratic subordinacy engenders shame and doubt, see Baum (1987, chap. 4).

12. Although most descriptions of the Oedipal complex emphasize its sexual content, the fact that it involves conflict reflects the participants' aggression as well. Rangell asks: "Is not anxiety over sexual transgression due basically to the fear of aggressive retaliation?" (1972:4)

13. For a description of the formation and activity of the superego, see S. Freud (1962 [1923], and 1964 [1938]); and Schafer (1960, and 1968).

14. For a discussion of the bureaucratic predicament of exercising responsibility without sufficient authority where both are ambiguous, see Baum (1987, chap. 3).

15. The structure of bureaucracy encourages subordinates to experience supervisors and bosses as parentlike moral authorities. Administrators, like parents, are high up and powerful; they set rules; and they reward and punish for conformity to the rules. In ways reminiscent of childhood aims, subordinates

want to move up and take over their bosses' positions. Thus, it is possible that reasonable work and career concerns become distorted, that legitimate interests in promoting projects become transformed into simply challenges of others with authority.

16. When Freud was old, an interviewer is said to have asked him what he had concluded a normal person should expect to be able to do. Freud answered succinctly, "to love and to work."

17. For a lucid discussion of caring, see Myeroff (1971).

18. Two good studies of mentoring are Levinson, *et al.* (1978), and Kram (1985). Levinson pioneered work on adult male development and discusses interests in mentoring during a "settling down period." Kram studied and describes the dynamics of mentoring relationships.

19. Numbers in parentheses refer to the sequence of Erikson's developmental stages. In case examples later in the book, these numbers will identify the Eriksonian stages represented by particular actions or wishes.

20. His conflict about membership undoubtedly has other meanings as well. From the interview alone it is difficult to know what these meanings are, or what their importance is, relative to the developmental issues. See the Appendix for a discussion of Latham's interview as an example of general methodological challenges.

21. These concerns commonly return to people in "midlife transition" (Levinson, *et al.*, 1978), but Landsdowne appears not to have resolved them firmly earlier either.

22. McClelland (1975) shows that being a loyal advisor brings the satisfaction of being strengthened by a powerful other. Consistent with Erikson's analysis, McClelland considers this pleasure a derivative of earlier gratifying oral dependence on a trustworthy mother. Chapter 9 examines the developmental meanings of this and other power orientations in detail.

23. For an analysis of the experience of power associated with developmental interests in initiative, see Baum (1987, chap. 4); McClelland (1975); and chapter 9.

24. The type of organizational politics Ryan reports is widespread, but it is not the only possible politics. For example, a politics of collaboration could give greater support to personal development. The final section of the book discusses the possibilities of alternative politics.

Chapter 3.

1. Van Maanen (1976) has labeled these stages (1) anticipatory socialization, (2) encounter, and (3) metamorphosis.

2. Gustafson and Cooper (1985) point to the methodological limitations of studies that conclude that groups have invariable stages of development. Most groups observed, they argue, are therapy or group relations training groups whose leaders have common implicit models in mind. In contrast, relatively few natural groups have been observed. Tuckman, for example, suggests that the first three stages of group development correspond to Bion's (1961) basic assumptions of dependency, fight-flight, and pairing, respectively, and the last stage represents what Bion calls a work group. Gustafson and Cooper would respond, first, that it is an empirical question whether Tuckman's three stages are the same as Bion's three states of group delusion, and, second, that this sequence may be more likely in some settings than in others. Nevertheless, even if there is some variation in sequence, one may argue that these "stages" at least represent tasks that normally must be completed in order for groups to develop. The order of the tasks may vary, some may be engaged in several times, and some may be carried out simultaneously. The same may be true of stages of organizational socialization, although this book offers a psychoanalytic explanation for why it should follow a specific order.

3. This effort is similar to the infant's individual project of establishing whether the world is basically trustworthy. The stages of group development resemble the stages of infants' actions to separate and differentiate themselves from the mother, as described in the next chapter. For an analysis of group development in terms of infants' separation and individuation, see Cooper and Gustafson (1981).

4. Members of new groups begin with mental images of the ideal group they would like to form. Indeed, they feel some security in dealing with strangers by imagining they are already part of this ideal organization, as if they are, in fact, proprietors of an existing group. See Jacobson (1987).

5. Wallace (1983) carefully discusses issues raised in drawing conclusions about mental processes from practices in different cultural contexts. For other discussions of parallels between van Gennep's accounts and contemporary organizational rituals, see Trice, Belasco, and Alutto (1969); and Trice and Beyer (1984).

6. For a discussion of these issues, see Toennies (1957 [1887]); Berger, Berger, and Kellner (1973); and Weick (1979).

7. An exceptional effort to examine the implications of these parallels for the meanings of modern organizational rituals is that of Trice, Belasco, and Alutto (1969).

8. When certain organizational sociologists conceptualize the new member as a *tabula rasa*, they implicitly endorse and participate in this stripping.

9. These two views of why initiates become members or not represent basic contrasting approaches to interpreting worker turnover (Louis 1980). The first approach, corresponding to traditional societies' views of reasons for failed

initiations, considers the realism of workers' expectations. The resultant explanations for turnover, however, are uselessly tautological. Wanous (1980), for instance, cites "unrealistic expectations." The second approach looks at whether workers' reasonable expectations can be met in a particular organization. Observers with this point of view consider the course of entry negotiations between newcomer and veterans a strong influence on whether workers stay or leave. Still, some of these writers also offer tautological explanations for weak fit, such as "low job satisfaction" (e.g., Porter and Steers 1973; Mobley, Griffeth, Hand, and Meglino 1979; and Muchinsky and Tuttle 1979). Job leavers offer better explanations.

10. For expressions of managers' interests in "corporate culture," see, for example, Deal and Kennedy (1982); and Peters and Waterman (1982). For sociological treatments of organizational culture and organizational symbolism, see Pettigrew (1972); Martin (1982); Martin, Feldman, Hatch, and Sitkin (1983); Pondy, Frost, Morgan, and Dandridge (1983); and Smircich (1983). For critical analysis of the psychological functions served by organizational culture, see Schneider and Shrivastava (1984); and, especially, Schwartz (1985). For a psychoanalytic description of organizational "identity," which exists prior to, and often in spite of, explicit attempts at cultural creation, see Diamond (1988). See also chapter 9.

Chapter 4.

1. See Klein (1976) for a summary of the development of these "metapsychological" assumptions.

2. On the metapsychology of aggression, see Róheim (1943b); S. Freud (1962 [1923]); Hartmann, Kris, and Loewenstein (1964); Brenner (1971); A. Freud (1972); Solnit (1972); Panel on the Role of Aggression in Human Adaptation (1973); Winnicott (1975); and Schafer (1976).

3. Holt (1976) offers a metapsychological argument for speaking of "wishes" in place of "drives" or "instincts."

4. See Schafer (1976) on the translation of traditional energic concepts into action language. The id, ego, and superego, from being nouns (containers of energy) become adverbs (ways of acting and of wanting to act).

5. See Eagle (1984) for a distinction between ego and id that turns on this experiential difference. As he makes clear, however, traditional psychoanalysts regard the ego and id as dynamically separate entities.

6. For stylistic convenience, the text may occasionally refer to "aggression" as a noun, with pronoun referents, but this does not imply that aggression is a biological drive or substance. Rather, it is a way of acting. The adverb "aggressively" most accurately expresses the meaning of aggression. See Schafer (1976) for a discussion of the grammar of motives.

256 Notes

7. Although sexual satisfaction ends sexual wishes, this cessation is only temporary.

8. On the metapsychology of sublimation, see Kris (1955); Hartmann (1964); Schafer (1968); and Klein (1976).

9. The Panel on the Role of Aggression in Human Adaptation (1973) examines the range of ways in which people act aggressively. McClelland offers an insightful analysis of social expressions of aggression in terms of "power." He identifies Erikson's developmental stages with different "power orientations." Chapter 9 discusses McClelland's framework.

10. The difficulty of satisfying this work requirement is compounded by the tendency of bureaucratic organizations to engender anxiety about retribution. See Baum (1987).

11. Clawson and Kram (1984) summarize the dangers of libidinal intrusion into working relations. Spruell (1985) offers the opposite view that sexuality and work are generally compatible.

12. This is the essence of infantile anxiety, in which abandonment by a loving parent seems to threaten annihilation of life itself. See, for example, Fenichel (1945); and Freud 1963 (1936).

13. For a discussion of how current anxiety situations unconsciously recall infantile trauma and anxiety situations, see Freud (1963 [1936]) and Furst (1967).

14. For a general discussion of the influence of past anxiety on present efforts to defend against the dangers that anxiety signals, see Fenichel (1945).

15. Freud (1977 [1920], 1963 [1936], and 1964 [1938]) presents a concept of the ego as the means through which the mind attempts to master environmental (or internal) threats. Klein (1976) elaborates this view. Weiss, Sampson, and the Mount Zion Psychotherapy Research Group (1986) emphasize how the ego may unconsciously plan actions to preserve the self. These capacities develop over time, and the initial abilities of the early infantile ego are limited.

16. Klein (1952) describes this development as the infant moving into the "depressive position."

17. Winnicott (1965) characterizes these conditions as the requirements of "good enough mothering."

18. For a discussion of how adults respond to work situations reminding them of infancy, see Baum (1987, esp. chap. 4).

19. Some psychoanalysts (e.g., Klein 1975b [1932]; and Sharpe 1930) consider sublimation to include a variety of unconscious compromises with reality and morality beginning in infancy. Whether this designation of infantile activities is valid or not, the major sublimatory work shaping adulthood takes place during latency, following the establishment of the mature superego, or conscience, in the resolution of the Oedipal conflict.

20. Bergler (1945) is one of several psychoanalysts who suggest that sublimation is still more complex, comprising five stages. Sharpe (1930) depicts sublimation similarly. Bergler's five-stage model, derived from observations of his patients, differs from the three-stage model in regarding the search for a compromise as more complex. Briefly, Bergler argues that an individual first responds to superego reproach by aggressively defending himself and prosecuting the original intentions. In turn, the superego finds such aggression also reprehensible and insists that the individual find another course of action. The individual then seeks a compromise with this second reproach, now choosing a solution that includes the original wish, recognition of social reality, and obedience to the superego. This compromise is sublimation. The number of stages sublimation follows is an empirical question. Still, at the center of the process is an effort to find a compromise between a wish, social reality, and conscience.

21. The *bau a* ritual appears to be a socially organized counterpart to individual efforts to resolve the Oedipal conflict. However, it is difficult to compare the meanings of father-mother-son relationships in the Kaluli and contemporary Western cultures, as well as to be certain of the conscious and unconscious meanings of the *bau a* ritual among the Kaluli.

22. For a discussion of changes in the conceptualization of trauma, see Furst (1967); Cooper (1986); and Yorke (1986).

23. For a discussion of repression, see Fenichel (1945); A. Freud (1946); S. Freud (1957 [1915]); and Klein (1976).

24. Weiss, Sampson, and the Mount Zion Psychotherapy Research Group (1986) believe this is the basic aim of most problem-solving plans. Klein (1976) argues that "self-initiated active reversal of passive experience" is (with repression) one of the two basic ways through which an individual pursues the universal human aim of integration. All these writers link the discovery of "reversal of voice" to Freud's (1977 [1920]) observations that, for some reason, people repeat unpleasant experiences. Freud concluded that such actions could not be serving the "pleasure principle" of doing whatever reduces pain. Instead, he determined, they were efforts to master painful experiences.

25. Consistently, activities will be characterized in the text as "playful" on the basis of their intentions, not their success or accompanying emotions.

26. Specifically, Winnicott says the transitional object "symbolizes the union of two now separate things, baby and mother, *at the point of the initiation of their state of separateness*" (1967:369).

27. Mahler, Pine, and Bergman (1975) observe that infants create transitional objects in the practicing phase of separation and individuation.

28. Erikson (1977) characterizes play as "the ritualization of experience."

29. Gustafson and Cooper do not use the term *play*. Instead, as noted earlier, they speak of an individual or group *plan*. This term, referring to

intentions and efforts to preserve or protect oneself from injury, conveys a meaning similar to that of play.

30. Roman numerals will be used in the text to designate stages in socialization, initiation, or self-initiation. As noted previously, Arabic numbers identify Eriksonian stages of identity development.

31. The excerpt quoted earlier from Cooper and Gustafson's (1981) account of separation and individuation activities in a mental health organization vividly portrays just such practicing activities. Again, they report that

> individuals began to reorient themselves within their work roles to seek other avenues for their personal development. During this period ... individual plans were pursued in the job context: if, for whatever reason, individuals could not manage to incorporate their individual plans in the job, new careers were pursued—in fact or fantasy. (1981:717)

32. Human relations organization theorists (e.g., Mayo 1933; Roethlisberger and Dickson 1939; Argyris 1957 and 1964; McGregor 1960; Likert 1961 and 1967; and Schein 1965) were the first to acknowledge workers' informal activities—those not ordered or sanctioned by management—as meaningful, more than simply insubordination or laziness. They recognized that people may want both to be productive (an organizational goal) and to be friendly with coworkers. However, human relations theorists do not recognize that such "informal" "socialization" activity represents unconsciously well-organized efforts to express salient, insistent unconscious aims.

Chapter 5.

1. As noted earlier, the book examines three groups of work expectations: "prework" expectations of recognition, autonomy, and power; "work" expectations of work ability, work identity, and organizational affiliation; and "postwork" expectations of mentoring and making sense. These labels will appear without quotation marks, with the exception of "work" expectations, where quotation marks will be used to distinguish the specific expectations of work ability, work identity, and organizational affiliation from expectations of work organizations in general.

2. Abraham Zaleznik has suggested considering psychoanalytically informed cases from organizational life "specimens." In the organizational field, where the range and variety of phenomena are unknown, a primary scientific task is to collect as many specimens as possible. Each specimen represents a group of phenomena of some size, which further research may measure. An alternative way of proceeding, namely, to insist on the presentation of only broadly representative phenomena (specimens of large species), is certain to lead to uninformed closure on inquiry. The Appendix says more about specimens.

3. There are obviously other possibilities. Someone with past relations to some staff members but not others, promoted from the outside over insiders, may evoke resentment. Furthermore, a newcomer may use the authority of a high position to control the formal terms of entry while in the process arousing hostility.

4. Again there are exceptions. Schein (1978) portrays the conflicts of graduates of management programs taking their first jobs out of school, finding or being shown that the work world is different from the university.

5. Davis' description of his experience suggests that it could be considered traumatic in the strict sense that his ego was overwhelmed and, he felt helpless. He reports being anxious and feeling inadequate in many ways.

6. For a discussion of workers' fantasies of escape and compensation as means of reconciling themselves to painful organizational situations, see Baum (1987, chap. 5).

Chapter 6.

1. All the literature on sexuality in mentoring relationships deals with male-female relationships (e.g., Kanter 1977; Levinson, Darrow, Klein, Levinson, and McKee 1978; Shapiro, Haseltine, and Rowe 1978; Fitt and Newton 1981; Missirian 1982; Phillips-Jones 1982; Collins 1983; Clawson and Kram 1984; Kram 1985; and Bowen 1986). The explanation for this focus, despite the fact that male-male mentoring relationships are more numerous, is that heterosexuality may be more acceptably expressed and discussed. Nevertheless, homosexual attraction also contributes to the motivation to mentor others. In discussions of heterosexual mentoring relationships, different authors acknowledge sexual attraction in motivating relationships but disagree whether overt sexual relationships are compatible with the open exchange and independence mentoring requires. Because homosexuality is socially much less acceptable and arouses much greater anxiety, it is highly unlikely to be openly expressed or acted on in mentoring relationships. In addition, any sign of it may arouse sufficient anxiety to lead to some of the abrupt breakups of male-male mentoring relationships described in the literature (e.g., Levinson, *et al.*, 1978).

2. Much of the mentoring literature emphasizes the organizational benefits. A number of organizations have established formal "mentoring" programs, in which senior staff members take on responsibility for new arrivals. The purpose of these programs is both to train and to socialize people for future leadership. See, for example, "Everyone Who Makes It Has a Mentor" (1978); and Klauss (1981). Because the relationships that develop in these programs are usually not voluntary and follow formal regulations, only a few of them have the intensity discussed here. In addition, few of them become subversive. The relationships described here are voluntary and exclusive.

3. For an extended discussion of the motive to repair the objects of imagined aggression, see Klein and Riviere (1964 [1937]).

4. Diminishing bodily abilities may make it difficult to act overtly in unsub-limated ways, but mental commitments to sublimation, nevertheless, may decline.

5. Winnicott (1965), speaking of a child's requirements of a mother when separating and individuating, observes that the mother need not be perfect, but must only provide "good enough mothering." In the same way, an organization does not have to make perfect sense—as none does—but must simply offer meaningful enough material.

6. This is an example of what Weick (1979) calls the "loose coupling" of organizations. Here, people use organizations for generally unrecognized and unauthorized purposes. What is important about the psychoanalytic perspective is that it shows that developmental needs, often unconscious, make it difficult for individuals to invest more deeply in organizations and preserve their identity.

Chapter 7.

1. Again, see the survey results in the U.S. Department of Health, Educa-tion, and Welfare (1973); and Yankelovich and Immerwahr (1983).

2. The unfolding relationship between Hartley and others in the analysis section can be seen as his tacit assignment to an informal group role of scape-goat. The majority seem to attribute to him all the characteristics of a strictly by-the-letter worker and ridicule and punish him as a way of vindicating their own lapses: if the alternative to their socializing were simply such rigidity, no one could expect them to act differently. At the same time, he fits this stereo-type. He is a good volunteer for this informal group role. This is an example of a general condition. Certain informal roles typically emerge in groups, with the consequence that members have a limited "choice" of informal roles; however, individuals typically "choose" certain roles. In Hartley's account, the bad work habits of many of the analysts created a situation ripe for scapegoating someone, and his work expectations made him a first-rate candidate for the position. Thus his confrontation with the section was poisonous. See Baum (1987, chaps. 7 and 8) for a discussion of scapegoating in organizations.

3. In this respect, he resembles what Shapiro (1981) has called "the rigid character," stuck on establishing autonomy.

4. His thoughts about aggression resemble what Klein (1952) has called the "paranoid-schizoid position," a way in which infants normally think about the good and bad aspects of themselves. They mentally split the bad from the good and project the bad onto someone in the environment, thus preserving the good in themselves from the bad "outside" them. The cost of this maneuver is wariness about attack from bad persons in the environment. In normal development, the infant moves on to the "depressive position," in which it acknowledges that both good and bad are part of itself and concludes that it must act in an ambiguous world. Adults may resort to the paranoid-schizoid

position either when they have not fully mastered the depressive position earlier in life, or when they find the paranoid-schizoid position an efficient defense against moral ambiguities.

5. If Hartley's problems acting autonomously are in part a defense against guilt-laden dangers in taking initiative, the compromises he must make are still more complex. In that case, hesitations to assert himself involve efforts to avoid guilt associated with aggression. In his conscience he would have to accept a broader range of action as moral or, at least, mete out punishments short of total annihilation. If, as a result, he no longer thought of action as destruction—which he feared at others' hands, which he wanted to direct against them preemptively or punitively, which he again feared from them in retaliation, and which, finally, his conscience directed against him for his impulses—he could regard acting aggressively as a matter of calculated choice.

6. See Blos (1962) on adolescents' rebellion against the superego.

7. For diverse examples of leaders' personalities, see Lasswell (1948); Maccoby (1976); Kets de Vries and Miller (1984); and LaBier (1986).

8. In this respect they differ from Bender, for example, who does not identify with the organization, but who is accepted by others.

Chapter 8.

1. Ms. Jones is discussed at length elsewhere (Baum 1987, chap. 5).

2. For another example of plans for escape for a private business, see the case of Mr. Smith in Baum (1987, chap. 5).

3. For example, 84 percent of the people interviewed in this study said they were somehow different at work than on the outside. The generalizations that follow come from their statements.

4. Arendt (1965) explains "the banality of evil" in Adolf Eichmann's work in just these terms. Eichmann seems to have succeeded in convincing himself that he was "just doing his job," and that it was the job, and not he personally, which directed Jews to extermination.

5. For a discussion of this process of projective identification, see Klein (1952).

6. Hoch (1988) reports an interesting example among city planners. When asked to describe occasions when they have become involved in threatening conflicts, they offer contrasting explanations for their victories and defeats. They win, they say, because they act professionally, convincing others with honest, disinterested, insightful analysis. In short, they overcome others by being authentically good planners. On the other hand, they lose when their adversaries muster superior, unfair political force. Their opponents reject the convention

that right should govern and turn, instead, to might. Planners rarely consider the alternative possibilities—that thay win because of their own political strategies or that they lose because their analysis is poor. Thus they portray their world as one in which they win because they are good and lose because others are bad. Many professionals reason in this way.

7. Less metapsychologically, one might say that the ego's activities here include consciously and unconsciously judging potential consequences of contemplated actions, as well as consciously and unconsciously deciding how to defend against dangers.

8. For examples of how transferences become self-fulfilling prophecies in organizations, see Hodgson, Levinson, and Zaleznik (1965).

9. Although a variety of people might offer these interpretations, a classical management theorist would be particularly likely to think of organizational behavior as rebellious, and a human relations theorist is likely to view organizational behavior as adjustments to the requirements of collaboration.

Chapter 9.

1. Erikson (1963, 1968, and 1977) emphasizes the psychological meaning of institutional divisions. Modern social institutions, he observes, are specialized not only by their societal function, but also by the developmental aims they support. The emerging person, once he outgrows absolute dependence on parents, turns to different institutions for mastering each of the developmental challenges or reinforcing responses to them.

For example, although infantile relations with the mother or her surrogate shape basic feelings of trust and mistrust toward the world (1), later on organized religion takes over these concerns. Early childhood tests determine the balance of autonomy and doubt (2), but in the larger society the law delineates autonomous domains. Childhood experiences show how much initiative is possible without guilt (3), but subsequently the theater becomes the arena for examining these questions. School and the workplace are the places to establish a sense of industry against feelings of inferiority (4). Ideology serves needs for bounding identity against confusion (5). Friendships, dating, and marriage are the normal spheres for practicing intimacy and avoiding isolation (6). The family is the conventional realm for satisfying generative wishes and avoiding stagnation (7). Finally, philosophy, or perhaps religion once again, is the institution for establishing integrity against despair (8).

In traditional societies these institutions involve overlapping sets of people, spaces, and meanings, whereas in modern societies they are only weakly or tacitly connected. Over a lifetime, a person in traditional society confronts many of the same people in each of these institutions, and these encounters reinforce one another cognitively and emotionally. Concretely, the society resides in each of the institutions. In modern society, the connections, where they exist, are impersonal and abstract. Because growth requires passage from one institution to another, no institution can command more than limited loyalty. This is a weakness of contemporary organizational initiations. At the same time, establishing a personal identity becomes especially difficult because of the need to work out so many discrete relationships. As a result, individuals can make only limited commitments to any one institution. This is one source of workers' detached relations with their organizations.

2. Some concern with "culture" is a reaction to Japanese economic success and recognition that Japanese managers and workers think differently about working in organizations. See, for example, Ouchi (1981).

3. For various reasons, Yankelovich and Immerwahr (1983) find, 26 percent of American workers are ashamed of the quality of goods they produce.

4. This is males' unconscious fear. Females have related concerns about reencountering the Oedipal mother.

5. See Baum (1983, 1986, and 1987) for other studies of complaints about "politics."

6. This is a conventional definition. See, for example, Dahl (1961); and Lasswell (1958).

7. For diverse expressions of this view, see French and Raven (1959); Dahl (1961); Kipnis (1974); Salancik and Pfeffer (1974 and 1977); Bacharach and Lawler (1980); and Wrong (1980).

8. To say, for example, that someone who enjoys drawing on the strength of a client may get gratifications analogous to those of a suckling infant is not the same as calling the advisor a baby. Everyone to some degree continues to seek reassurance of nurturance in later life; adults differ in their need for such confirmation. People who hold the Type I power orientation may be among those who especially need or take pleasure from such reassurance. However, the motives for becoming an advisor are infinitely more complex than those of the infant who wants just to be fed. Moreover, nothing in any unconscious connection between certain advising roles and earlier oral interests diminishes the validity and value of the activity. Indeed, as noted, this power orientation may especially suit someone for advising work. These observations are true for the other three power orientations as well. See Baum (1987, chap. 4) for a discussion of the strengths and dangers of each of the power orientations at work.

9. Indeed, McClelland is least clear empirically or conceptually about this orientation.

10. For a more extensive discussion of how these power orientations manifest themselves in professional practice, see Baum (1987, chap. 4).

11. Earlier (Baum 1987), I have shown how the psychological structure of bureaucracy frustrates workers from mastering the Type II power orientation and thus hinders them from asserting themselves in Type III actions and politics.

12. Argyris and Schön (1974, and 1978; Argyris 1982; and Schön 1983) identify these assumptions with the norms of "Model I" behavior. From their research, they conclude that these norms are nearly universal. Although they do not use McClelland's terms, their research suggests that most who claim to be practicing a Type IV power orientation (which they call "Model II") end up practicing some variation of a Type III or prior orientation.

Argyris and Schön's explanation is cognitive: people enact a Type III politics, for example, because it is consistent with ways of thinking learned in infancy. These mental habits encourage thinking of others as competitors for scarce resources, against whom strategizing and defense are necessary. This chapter examines the dominance of Type III politics in terms of unconscious concerns underlying conscious political thought, as well as developmental relations among types of politics. This view emphasizes the centrality of Oedipal issues and conflicts about aggression in people's lives. See Diamond (1986) for a psychoanalytic critique of Argyris and Schön's cognitive perspective.

13. Yankelovich and Immerwahr (1983) find that one-fourth of American workers are ashamed of the quality of the goods they produce. See Hirschhorn (1988) on workers' feelings about repairing others for acting aggressively against them.

14. For a discussion of these and other defenses, see Fenichel (1945); and A. Freud (1946).

15. See Baum (1987) for a description of the pseudo-Type IV orientation.

16. For a discussion and examples of this process of splitting, denial, and projection in organizations, see Hodgson, Levinson, and Zaleznik (1965) See also Hirschhorn (1988).

Chapter 10.

1. People at one developmental stage can understand others at that stage and all previous stages. In addition, they understand the meaning of the next stage. However, in general, they have difficulty understanding the tasks and tests of stages more than one stage beyond where they are. This general rule does not apply without exception at work for the following reason. Someone may be concerned at work with the tasks of a stage developmentally inferior to his accomplishments on the outside. For example, a woman who is a successful mother may be concentrating on developing an organizational work identity. In this case, she would have some idea of the meaning of mentoring, as analogous to the generative activities of mothering. Nevertheless, developmental differences between newcomers and veterans are often a source of misunderstanding and consequent rejection.

2. Torbert (1974/1975), drawing on Erikson, argues that bureaucracy is intrinsically hostile to advanced development. Different forms of social organi-

zation, he observes, correspond to different personal developmental objectives. Bureaucracy fits closest with individual interests in a sense of industry. Its norm of "predefined productivity," he argues, encourages individual development to this level but discourages anything beyond. More advanced personal development, he suggests, is more likely in different forms of organization. For example, identity can be most richly elaborated in an "openly chosen structure," intimacy is most likely in a yet more advanced "foundational community," and generativity is most possible in a "liberating discipline." Torbert has never seen an organization concerned with integrity.

3. It is important to avoid drawing simple analogies between cultural activities in traditional societies and unconscious mental processes in modern individuals. At the same time, an understanding of one domain offers hypotheses about the other.

4. Hate may seem an incongruously strong emotion in this situation, but the ego ideal—and its derivative, the organization ideal—powerfully harness all the infant's expectations of rediscovering a loving world. Adults unconsciously may react to disappointments just as infants do: by hating the world that lets them down.

5. For a discussion of workers' search for immortality in organizations, see Denhardt (1981); and Schwartz (1987a and 1987b).

6. The examples of organizational reform strategies mentioned here are discussed at length in Baum (1987, chap. 10). That analysis emphasizes the goal of helping workers develop realistic and responsible views of their interests in organizations. It is consistent with the goal of promoting personal development through Type IV politics. See also Argyris and Schön (1978), who present strategies for moving an organization from Type III politics (in their terms, a Model O[rganizational]-I theory of action) to Type IV politics (Model O-II). Using case examples, they describe the consequences of Type III politics and experiments in creating Type IV. They concede that they have seen few examples of Model O-II organizations. They concur with the perspective here that organizational change requires affecting deeply held shared beliefs and that experimentation is necessary to discover paths to new organizational patterns.

7. Schein (1978) identifies some of the ways in which managers can think of workers' developmental needs and match them with organizational resources.

8. See Baum (1987) for a discussion of the psychological effects of organizational social structures and the arousal of shame anxiety, and for a discussion of psychological, as well as political, constraints on reform.

References

Arendt, Hannah. 1958. *The Human Condition*. Chicago, Ill.: University of Chicago Press.

―――. 1965. *Eichmann in Jerusalem*. New York: Penguin Books.

Argyris, Chris. 1957. *Personality and Organization*. New York: Harper & Row, Publishers.

―――. 1964. *Integrating the Individual and the Organization*. New York: John Wiley & Sons.

―――. 1982. *Reasoning, Learning, and Action*. San Francisco, Calif.: Jossey-Bass.

―――, and Schön, Donald A. 1974. *Theory in Practice*. San Francisco, Calif.: Jossey-Bass.

―――. 1978. *Organizational Learning*. Reading, Mass.: Addison-Wesley Publishing Co.

Ariès, Philippe. 1962. *Centuries of Childhood*. New York: Vintage.

Bacharach, Samuel B., and Lawler, Edward J. 1980. *Power and Politics in Organizations*. San Francisco, Calif.: Jossey-Bass.

Baum, Howell S. 1983. *Planners and Public Expectations*. Cambridge, Mass.: Schenkman Publishing Company.

―――. 1986. "Politics in Planners' Practice." In *Strategic Perspectives on Planning Practice*, edited by Barry Checkoway. Lexington, Mass.: Lexington Books.

―――. 1987. *The Invisible Bureaucracy*. New York: Oxford University Press.

Bell, Daniel. 1973. *The Coming of Post-Industrial Society*. New York: Basic Books, Inc., Publishers.

Bellah, Robert N.; Madsen, Richard; Sullivan, William M.; Swidler, Ann; and Tipton, Steven M. 1986. *Habits of the Heart*. New York: Harper & Row, Publishers.

Berger, Peter; Berger, Brigitte; and Kellner, Hansfried. 1973. *The Homeless Mind*. New York: Random House.

Bergler, Edmund. 1945. "On a Five-Layer Structure in Sublimation." *Psychoanalytic Quarterly* 14:76-97.

Bion, Wilfrid R. 1961. *Experiences in Groups*. New York: Basic Books, Inc., Publishers.

Blos, Peter. 1962. *On Adolescence*. New York: The Free Press.

Bowen, Donald D. 1986. "The Role of Identification in Mentoring Female Protégés." *Group and Organization Studies* 11:61-74.

Brenner, Charles. 1971. "The Psychoanalytic Concept of Aggression." *International Journal of Psycho-Analysis* 52:137-44.

———. 1976. *Psychoanalytic Technique and Psychic Conflict*. New York: International Universities Press.

Buchanan, Bruce, II. 1974. "Building Organizational Commitment: The Socialization of Managers in Work Organization." *Administration Science Quarterly* 19:533-46

Chasseguet-Smirgel, Janine. 1985. *The Ego Ideal: A Psychoanalytic Essay on the Malady of the Ideal*. Translated by Paul Burrows. New York: W.W. Norton & Company.

———. 1986. *Sexuality and Mind*. New York: New York University Press.

Cherrington, David J. 1980. *The Work Ethic*. Washington,D.C.: AMACOM.

Clawson, James G., and Kram, Kathy E. 1984. "Managing Cross-Gender Mentoring." *Business Horizons* 27:22-32.

Collins, Nancy W. 1983. *Professional Women and Their Mentors: A Practical Guide to Mentoring for the Woman Who Wants to Get Ahead*. Englewood Cliffs, N.J.: Prentice-Hall.

Cooper, Arnold M. 1986. "Toward a Limited Definition of Psychic Trauma." In *The Reconstruction of Trauma; Its Significance in Clinical Work*. Edited by Arnold Rothstein. Workshop Series of the American Psychoanalytic Association, Monograph no. 2. Madison, Conn.: International Universities Press.

Cooper, Lowell, and Gustafson, James P. 1981. "Family-Group Development: Planning in Organizations." *Human Relations* 34:705-30.

Dahl, Robert. 1961. *Who Governs?* New Haven, Conn.: Yale University Press.

Dalton, Gene W.; Thompson, Paul H.; and Price, Raymond L. 1977. "The Four Stages of Professional Careers—A New Look at Performance by Professionals." *Organizational Dynamics* 6:19-42.

Deal, Terrence E., and Kennedy, Allan A. 1982. *Corporate Cultures; The Rites and Rituals of Corporate Life*. Reading, Mass.: Addison-Wesley Publishing Co.

Denhardt, Robert B. 1981. *In the Shadow of Organizations*. Lawrence: Regents Press of Kansas.

Diamond, Michael A. 1984. "Bureaucracy as Externalized Self-System: A View from the Psychological Interior." *Administration and Society* 16:195-214.

_____. 1985. "The Social Character of Bureaucracy: Anxiety and Ritualistic Defense." *Political Psychology* 6:663-79.

_____. 1986. "Resistance to Change: A Psychoanalytic Critique of Argyris and Schon's Contributions to Organization Theory and Intervention." *Journal of Management Studies* 23:543-62.

_____. 1988. "Organizational Identity; A Psychoanalytic Exploration of Organizational Meaning." *Administration and Society* 20:166-90.

Dunnette, Marvin D.; Arvey, Richard D.; and Banas, Paul A. 1973. "Why Do They Leave?" *Personnel* 50:25-39.

Eagle, Morris N. 1984. *Recent Developments in Psychoanalysis*. New York: McGraw-Hill Book Company.

Ebaugh, Helen Rose Fuchs. 1988. *Becoming an EX; The Process of Role Exit*. Chicago, Ill.: University of Chicago Press.

Erikson, Erik H. 1963. *Childhood and Society*. 2d ed. New York: W.W. Norton & Company.

_____, ed. 1965. *The Challenge of Youth*. Garden City, N.Y.: Doubleday Anchor.

_____. 1968. *Identity; Youth and Crisis*. New York: W.W. Norton & Company.

_____. 1975. *Life History and the Historical Moment*. New York: W.W. Norton & Company.

_____. 1977. *Toys and Reasons; Stages in the Ritualization of Experience*. New York: W.W. Norton & Company.

_____. 1984. "Reflections on the Last Stage—and the First." *Psychoanalytic Study of the Child* 39:155-65.

"Everyone Who Makes It Has a Mentor." 1978. *Harvard Business Review* 56:89-101.

Fairbairn, W.R.D. 1952. *An Object-Relations Theory of the Personality*. New York: Basic Books, Inc. Publishers.

Feldman, Daniel Charles. 1976. "A Contingency Theory of Socialization." *Administrative Science Quarterly* 21:433-52.

Fenichel, Otto. 1945. *The Psychoanalytic Theory of Neurosis*. New York: W.W. Norton & Company.

Fitt, Lawton Wehle, and Newton, Derek A. 1981. "When the Mentor Is a Man and the Protégée a Woman." *Harvard Business Review* 59:56, 58, 60.

French, John R.P., Jr., and Raven, Bertram. 1959. "The Bases of Social Power." In *Studies in Social Power*, edited by Dorwin Cartwright. Ann Arbor: University of Michigan, Institute for Social Research.

Freud, Anna. 1946. *The Ego and the Mechanisms of Defense*. Translated by Cecil Baines. New York: International Universities Press.

_____. 1972. "Comments on Aggression." *International Journal of Psycho-Analysis* 53:163-71.

Freud, Sigmund. 1963. "Observations on 'Wild' Analysis." 1910. Translated by Joan Riviere. In *Therapy and Technique*, edited by Philip Rieff. New York: Crowell-Collier Publishing Company.

_____. 1957. "On Narcissism: An Introduction." 1914. In *The Standard Edition of the Complete Psychological Works of Sigmund Freud*, 14:73-102. London: The Hogarth Press.

_____. 1957. "Instincts and Their Vicissitudes." 1915. *Standard Edition*, 14:117-140.

_____. 1959. *Group Psychology and the Analysis of the Ego*. 1921. Translated and edited by James Strachey. New York: W.W. Norton & Company.

_____. 1962. *Civilization and Its Discontents*. 1930. Translated and edited by James Strachey. New York: W.W. Norton & Company.

_____. 1962. *The Ego and the Id*. 1923. Translated by Joan Riviere. Revised and edited by James Strachey. New York: W.W. Norton & Company.

_____. 1963. *The Problem of Anxiety*. 1936. Translated by Henry Alden Bunker. New York: Psychoanalytic Quarterly Press and W.W. Norton & Company.

_____. 1964. "An Outline of Psychoanalysis." 1938. *Standard Edition*, 23:139-207. London: The Hogarth Press.

_____. 1965. *New Introductory Lectures*. 1933. Translated and edited by James Strachey. New York: W.W. Norton & Company.

_____. 1977. *Beyond the Pleasure Principle*. 1920. Translated by James Strachey. New York: Bantam Books.

Furst, Sidney S., ed. 1967. *Psychic Trauma*. New York: Basic Books.

Graen, George. 1976. "Role-Making Processes Within Complex Organizations." In *Handbook of Industrial and Organizational Psychology*. Edited by Marvin P. Dunnette. Chicago, Ill.: Rand-McNally.

Greenson, Ralph R. 1967. *The Technique and Practice of Psychoanalysis*. Vol. 1. New York: International Universities Press.

Guest, R.H. 1955. "A Neglected Factor in Labour Turnover." *Occupational Psychology* 29:217-31.

Gustafson, James P., and Cooper, Lowell. 1979. "Unconscious Planning in Small Groups." *Human Relations* 32:1039-64.

_____. 1985. "Collaboration in Small Groups: Theory and Technique for the Study of Small-Group Processes." In *Group Relations Reader II*, edited by Arthur D. Colman and Marvin H. Geller. Washington, D.C.: A.K. Rice Institute.

Hage, Jerald, ed. 1988. *Futures of Organizations*. Lexington, Mass.: Lexington Books.

Hartmann, Heinz. 1964. "Notes on the Theory of Sublimation." In *Essays on Ego Psychology*, edited by Heinz Hartmann. New York: International Universities Press.

_____; Kris, Ernst; and Loewenstein, Rudolph M. 1964. "Notes on the Theory of Aggression." In *Papers on Psychoanalytic Psychology*, edited by Heinz Hartmann; Ernst Kris; and Rudolph M. Loewenstein. *Psychological Issues*, vol. 4, monograph no. 14. New York: International Universities Press.

Hendrick, Ives. 1943a. "The Discussion of the 'Instinct to Master.'" *Psychoanalytic Quarterly* 12:561-65.

_____. 1943b. "Work and the Pleasure Principle." *Psychoanalytic Quarterly* 12:311-29.

Hirschhorn, Larry. 1988. *The Workplace Within: Psychodynamics of Organizational Life*. Cambridge, Mass.: The M.I.T. Press.

_____, and Krantz, James. 1982. "Unconscious Planning in a Natural Work Group: A Case Study in Process Consultation." *Human Relations* 35:805-44.

Hoch, Charles. 1988. "Conflict at Large: A National Survey of Planners and Political Conflict." *Journal of Planning Education and Research* 8:25-34.

Hodgson, Richard C.; Daniel J. Levinson; and Abraham Zaleznik. 1965. *The Executive Role Constellation*. Boston, Mass.: Harvard University, The Graduate School Of Business Administration.

Holt, Robert R. 1976. "Drive or Wish? A Reconsideration of the Psychoanalytic Theory of Motivation." In *Psychology Versus Metapsychology*, edited by M.M. Gill and P.S. Holzman. *Psychological Issues*, vol. 9, monograph no. 36. New York: International Universities Press.

Hughes, Everett C. 1958. *Men and Their Work*. Glencoe, Ill.: The Free Press.

Jacobson, Lawrence. 1987. "Basic Assumption Groups as Transitional Phenomena, and Their Relevance to the Therapeutic Group." New York: Albert Einstein College of Medicine.

Jaques, Elliott. 1951. *The Changing Culture of a Factory*. London: Tavistock Publications.

_____. 1955. "Social Systems as Defense Against Persecutory and Depressive Anxiety." In *New Directions in Psycho-Analysis: The Significance of Infant Conflict in the Pattern of Adult Behavior*, edited by Melanie Klein; Paula Heimann; and R.E. Money-Kyrle. London: Tavistock Publications.

Kanter, Rosabeth Moss. 1977. *Men and Women of the Corporation*. New York: Basic Books, Inc., Publishers.

Kets de Vries; Manfred F.R.; and Miller, Danny. 1984. *The Neurotic Organization*. San Francisco, Calif.: Jossey-Bass.

Kipnis, David. 1974. "The Powerholder." In *Perspectives on Social Power*. Edited by James T. Tedeschi. Chicago, Ill.: Aldine.

Klauss, Rudi. 1981. "Formalized Mentor Relations for Management and Executive Development in the Federal Government." *Public Administration Review* 48:489-96.

Klein, George S. 1976. *Psychoanalytic Theory; An Exploration in Essentials*. New York: International Universities Press.

Klein, Melanie. 1952. "Notes on Some Schizoid Mechanisms." In *Developments in Psycho-Analysis*. Edited by Joan Riviere. London: The Hogarth Press and the Institute of Psychoanalysis.

_____. 1952. *Developments in Psycho-Analysis*. Edited by Joan Riviere. London: The Hogarth Press.

_____. 1975a. *Envy and Gratitude and Other Works, 1946-1963*. New York: Dell.

_____. 1975b. *The Psycho-Analysis of Children*. 1932. Translated by Alix Strachey. Revised by Alix Strachey and H.A. Thorner. New York: Dell.

_____, and Riviere, Joan. 1964. *Love, Hate and Reparation*. 1937. New York: W.W. Norton & Company.

Kotter, John Paul. 1973. "The Psychological Contract: Managing the Joining-Up Process." *California Management Review* 15:91-99.

Kram, Kathy E. 1985. *Mentoring at Work; Developmental Relationships in Organizational Life*. Glenview, Ill.: Scott, Foresman and Company.

_____, and Isabella, Lynn A. 1985. "Mentoring Alternatives: The Role of Peer Relationships in Career Development." *Academy of Management Journal* 28:110-32.

Kris, Ernst. 1955. "Neutralization and Sublimation; Observations on Young Children." *Psychoanalytic Study of the Child* 10:30-46.

References

273

LaBier, Douglas. 1986. *Modern Madness*. Reading, Mass.: Addison-Wesley Publishing Co.

Lasswell, Harold. 1948. *Politics: Who Gets What, When, How*. New York: Meridian Books.

Levinson, Daniel J.; Charlotte N. Darrow; Edward B. Klein; Maria H. Levinson; and Braxton McKee. 1978. *The Seasons of a Man's Life*. New York: Ballantine Books.

Levinson, Harry. 1968. *The Exceptional Executive: A Psychological Conception*. Cambridge, Mass.: Harvard University Press.

———; Price, Charlton R.; Munden, Kenneth J.; Mandl, Harold J.; and Solley, Charles M. 1962. *Men, Management and Mental Health*. Cambridge, Mass.: Harvard University Press.

Lewin, Kurt. 1951. *Field Theory in Society Science; Selected Theoretical Papers*. Edited by Dorwin Cartwright. New York: Harper and Brothers.

Lewis, Helen Block. 1974. *Shame and Guilt in Neurosis*. New York: International Universities Press.

Likert, Rensis. 1961. *New Patterns of Management*. New York: McGraw-Hill Book Company.

———. 1967. *The Human Organization*. New York: McGraw-Hill Book Company.

Louis, Meryl. 1980. "Surprise and Sense Making: What Newcomers Experience in Entering Unfamiliar Organizational Settings." *Administrative Science Quarterly* 25:226-51.

Lynd, Helen Merrell. 1958. *On Shame and the Search for Identity*. New York: Harcourt, Brace, and World.

Maccoby, Michael. 1976. *The Gamesman*. New York: Bantam Books.

Mahler, Margaret S.; Pine, Fred; and Bergman, Anni. 1975. *The Psychological Birth of the Infant*. New York: Basic Books, Inc., Publishers.

Martin, Joanne. 1982. "Stories and Scripts in Organizational Settings." In *Cognitive Social Psychology*. Edited by Albert Hastorf and Alice M. Isen. New York: Elsevier/North-Holland.

———; Feldman, Martha S.; Hatch, Mary Jo; and Sitkin, Sim B. 1983. "The Uniqueness Paradox in Organizational Stories." *Administrative Science Quarterly* 28:439-53.

Mayo, Elton. 1933. *The Human Problems of an Industrial Culture*. New York: Macmillan Publishing Co.

McClelland, David C. 1975. *Power: The Inner Experience*. New York: Irvington Publishers.

McGregor, Douglas. 1960. *The Human Side of Enterprise*. New York: McGraw-Hill Book Company.

Menzies, Isabel E.P. 1975. "A Case-Study in the Functioning of Social Systems as a Defense Against Anxiety." In *Group Relations Reader*. Edited by Arthur D. Colman and W. Harold Bexton. Sausalito, Calif.: GREX.

Miller, Eric J., and Rice, A.K. 1969. *Systems of Organization*. London: Tavistock Publication.

Missirian, Agnes K. 1982. *The Corporate Connection; Why Executive Women Need Mentors to Reach the Top*. Englewood Cliffs, N.J.: Prentice-Hall.

Mowday, Richard T.; Porter, Lyman W.; and Steers, Richard M. 1982. *Employee-Organization Linkages; The Psychology of Commitment, Absenteeism, and Turnover*. New York: Academic Press.

Mobley, W.M.; Griffeth, R.W.; Hand, H.M.; and Meglino, R.M. 1979. "Review and Conceptual Analysis of the Employee Turnover Process." *Psychological Bulletin* 86:493-522.

Mowday, Richard T.; Porter, Lyman W.; and Steers, Richard M. 1982. *Employee-Organization Linkages; The Psychology of Commitment, Absenteeism, and Turnover*. New York: Academic Press.

Myeroff, Milton. 1971. *On Caring*. New York: Harper & Row Publishers.

Naisbitt, John, and Aburdene, P. 1985. *Reinventing the Corporation*. New York: Warner Books.

Neff, Walter S. 1985. *Work and Human Behavior*. 3rd ed. New York: Aldine Publishing Company.

Organ, Dennis W. 1988. *Organizational Citizenship Behavior: The Good Soldier Syndrome*. Lexington, Mass.: D.C. Heath & Company.

Orr, Douglass W. 1954. "Transference and Countertransference: A Historical Survey." *Journal of the American Psychoanalytic Association* 11:621-70.

Ouchi, William. 1981. *Theory Z; How American Business Can Meet the Japanese Challenge*. Reading, Mass.: Addison-Wesley Publishing Co.

"Panel on the Role of Aggression in Human Adaptation." 1973. *Psychoanalytic Quarterly* 42:178-238.

Peller, Lili E. 1954. "Libidinal Phases, Ego Development, and Play." *Psychoanalytic Study of the Child* 9:178-98.

Peters, Thomas J., and Austin, Nancy K. 1985. *A Passion for Excellence*. New York: Harper & Row Publishers.

Peters, Thomas J., and Waterman, Robert H., Jr. 1982. *In Search of Excellence: Lessons from America's Best-run Companies*. New York: Harper & Row Publishers.

Pettigrew, Andrew M. 1979. "On Studying Organizational Cultures." *Administrative Science Quarterly* 24:570-81.

Phillips-Jones, Linda. 1982. *Mentors & Protégés*. New York: Arbor House Publishing Company.

Piers, Gerhart, and Milton B. Singer. 1971. *Shame and Guilt*. 1953. New York: W.W. Norton & Company.

Pondy, Louis R.; Frost, Peter J.; Morgan, Gareth; and Dandridge, Thomas C. 1983. *Organizational Symbolism*. Monographs in Organizational Behavior and Industrial Relations, vol. 1. Greenwich, Conn.: JAI Press.

Poole, Fitz John Porter. 1982. "The Ritual Forging of Identity; Aspects of Person and Self in Bimin-Kuskusmin Male Initiation." In *Rituals of Manhood; Male Initiation in Papua New Guinea*. Edited by Gilbert H. Herdt. Berkeley: University of California Press.

Porter, Lyman W.; Crampon, W.J.; and Smith, F.J. 1976. "Organizational Commitment and Managerial Turnover: A Longitudinal Study. *Organizational Behavior and Human Performance* 15:87-98.

Porter, Lyman W., Lawler, E.E., III; and Hackman, J.R. 1975. *Behavior in Organizations*. New York: McGraw-Hill Book Company.

Porter, Lyman W., and Steers, Richard M. 1973. "Organizational Work, and Personal Factors in Employee Turnover and Absenteeism." *Psychological Bulletin* 80:151-76.

Porter, Lyman W.; Steers, Richard M.; Mowday, Richard T.; and Boulian, Paul V. 1974. "Organizational Commitment, Job Satisfaction, and Turnover Among Psychiatric Technicians." *Journal of Applied Psychology* 59:603-609.

Racker, Heinrich. 1968. *Transference and Countertransference*. New York: International Universities Press.

Rangell, Leo. 1972. "Aggression, Oedipus, and Historical Perspective." *International Journal of Psycho-Analysis* 53:3-11.

Reichers, Arnon E. 1985. "A Review and Reconceptualization of Organizational Commitment." *Academy of Management Review* 10:465-76.

Rice, A.K. 1958. *Productivity and Social Organization: The Ahmedabad Experiment*. London: Tavistock Publications.

———. 1963. *The Enterprise and Its Environment*. London: Tavistock Publications.

Roethlisberger, Fritz J., and Dickson, William J. 1939. *Management and the Worker*. Cambridge, Mass.: Harvard University Press.

Róheim, Géza. 1942. "Transition Rites." *Psychoanalytic Quarterly* 11:336-74.

———. 1943b. "Sublimation." *Psychoanalytic Quarterly* 12:338-52.

_____. 1971. *The Origin and Function of Culture*. 1943a. Garden City, N.Y.: Doubleday Anchor.

Ross, Ian C., and Zander, Alvin. 1957. "Need Satisfaction and Employee Turnover." *Personnel Psychology* 10:327-38.

Salancik, Gerald R., and Pfeffer, Jeffrey. 1974. "The Bases for Use of Power in Organizational Decision-Making: The Case of a University." *Administrative Science Quarterly* 19:453-73.

_____. 1977. "Who Gets Power—and How They Hold On to It: A Strategic-Contingency Model of Power." *Organizational Dynamics* 3-21.

Schafer, Roy. 1960. "The Loving and Beloved Superego in Freud's Structural Theory." *The Psychoanalytic Study of the Child* 15:163-88.

_____. 1968. *Aspects of Internalization*. New York: International Universities Press.

_____. 1976. *A New Language for Psychoanalysis*. New Haven, Conn.: Yale University Press.

Schein, Edgar H. 1965. *Organizational Psychology*. Englewood Cliffs, N.J.: Prentice-Hall.

_____. 1968. "Organizational Socialization and the Profession of Management." *Industrial Management Review* 9:1-16.

_____. 1978. *Career Dynamics; Matching Individual and Organizational Needs*. Reading, Mass.: Addison-Wesley Publishing Co.

_____. 1985. *Organizational Culture and Leadership*. San Francisco: Jossey-Bass.

Schieffelin, Edward L. 1982. "The *Bau A* Ceremonial Hunting Lodge; An Alternative to Initiation." In *Rituals of Manhood; Male Initiation in Papua New Guinea*. Edited by Gilbert H. Herdt. Berkeley: University of California Press.

Schneider, Susan C., and Shrivastava, Paul. 1984. "Interpreting Strategic Behavior: The Royal Road to Basic Assumptions." Working Paper, no. 28. New York: Pace University, Lubin School of Business.

Schön, Donald A. 1983. *The Reflective Practitioner*. New York: Basic Books, Inc., Publishers.

Schwartz, Howard S. 1985. "The Usefulness of Myth and the Myth of Usefulness: A Dilemma for the Applied Organizational Scientist." *Journal of Management* 11:31-42.

_____. 1987a. "Anti-social Actions of Committed Organizational Participants: An Existential Psychoanalytic Perspective." *Organization Studies* 8:327-40.

_____. 1987b. "On the Psychodynamics of Organizational Totalitarianism." *Journal of Management* 13:41-54.

Shapiro, David. 1981. *Autonomy and Rigid Character*. New York: Basic Books, Inc., Publishers.

Shapiro, Eileen C.; Haseltine, Florence P.; and Rowe, Mary P. 1978. "Moving Up: Role Models, Mentors, and the 'Patron System.'" *Sloan Management Review* 19:51-58.

Sharpe, Ella. 1930. "Certain Aspects of Sublimation and Delusion." *International Journal of Psycho-Analysis* 11:12-23.

———. 1935. "Similar and Divergent Unconscious Determinants Underlying the Sublimations of Pure Art and Pure Science." *International Journal of Psycho-Analysis* 16:186-202.

Simmel, George. 1950. "The Stranger." 1906. In *The Sociology of Georg Simmel*. Translated and edited by Kurt H. Wolff. New York: The Free Press.

Smircich, Linda. 1983. "Concepts of Culture and Organizational Analysis." *Administrative Science Review* 28:339-58.

Solnit, Albert J. 1972. "Aggression: A View of Theory Building in Psychoanalysis." *Journal of the American Psychoanalytic Association* 20:435-50.

Spence, Donald P. 1982. *Narrative Truth and Historical Truth; Meaning and Interpretation in Psychoanalysis*. New York: W.W. Norton & Company.

Spruell, Geraldine Romano. 1985. "Daytime Drama: Love in the Office." *Training and Development Journal* 39:20-23.

Sullivan, Harry Stack. 1953. *The Interpersonal Theory of Psychiatry*. New York: W.W. Norton & Company.

Taylor, K.E., and Weiss, R.J. 1972. "Prediction of Individual Job Termination from Measured Job Satisfaction and Biographical Data." *Journal of Vocational Behavior* 2:123-32.

Terkel, Studs. 1975. *Working*. New York: Avon Books.

Toennies, Ferdinand. 1957. *Community and Society*. Translated by C.P. Loomis. 1887. New York: Harper & Row, Publishers.

Torbert, William R. 1974-1975. "Pre-Bureaucratic and Post-Bureaucratic Stages of Organization Development," *Interpersonal Development* 5:1-25.

Trice, Harrison M.; Belasco, James; and Alutto, Joseph A. 1969. "The Role of Ceremonials in Organizational Behavior." *Industrial and Labor Relations Review* 23:40-51.

———, and Beyer, Janice B. 1984. "Studying Organizational Cultures Through Rites and Rituals." *Academy of Management Review* 9:384-99.

Tuckman, Bruce W. 1965. "Developmental Sequence in Small Groups." *Psychological Bulletin* 63:384-99.

Turner, Victor. 1969. *The Ritual Process; Structure and Anti-Structure*. Ithaca, N.Y.: Cornell University Press.

U.S. Department of Health, Education, and Welfare. Special Task Force. 1973. *Work in America*. Cambridge, Mass.: The M.I.T. Press.

Van Gennep, Arnold. 1960. *The Rites of Passage*. Translated by Monika B. Vizedom and Gabrielle L. Caffee. 1908. Chicago, Ill.: University of Chicago Press.

Van Maanen, John. 1976. "Breaking In: Socialization to Work." In *Handbook of Work, Organization and Society*. Edited by Robert Dubin. Chicago: Rand McNally & Company.

Waelder, Robert. 1933. "The Psychoanalytic Theory of Play." *Psychoanalytic Quarterly* 2:208-24.

Wallace, Edwin R., IV. 1983. *Freud and Anthropology; A History and Reappraisal. Psychological Issues*, monograph no. 55. New York: International Universities Press.

Wanous, John P. 1980. *Organizational Entry; Recruitment, Selection and Socialization of Newcomers*. Reading, Mass.: Addison-Wesley Publishing Co.

———; Reichers, Arnon E.; and Malik, S.D. 1984. "Organizational Socialization and Group Development: Toward an Integrative Perspective." *Academy of Management Review* 9:670-83.

Waters, L.K., and Roach, D. 1971. "Relationship Between Job Attitudes and Two Forms of Withdrawal From the Work Situation." *Journal of Applied Psychology* 55:92-94.

———. 1973. "Job Attitudes as Predictors of Termination and Absenteeism: Consistency Over Time and Across Organizational Units." *Journal of Applied Psychology* 57:341-42.

Weber, Max. 1967. *From Max Weber*. Edited and translated by Hans H. Gerth and C. Wright Mills. New York: Oxford University Press.

Weick, Karl E. 1979. *The Social Psychology of Organizing*. 2d ed. Reading, Mass.: Addison-Wesley Publishing Co..

Weiss, Joseph; Harold Sampson; and the Mount Zion Psychotherapy Research Group. 1986. *The Psychoanalytic Process; Theory, Clinical Observations, and Empirical Research*. New York: The Guilford Press.

White, Robert W. 1963. *Ego and Reality in Psychoanalytic Theory. Psychological Issues*. vol. 3, monograph no. 11. New York: International Universities Press.

Winnicott, D.W. 1953. "Transitional Objects and Transitional Phenomena." *International Journal of Psycho-Analysis* 34:89-97.

_____. 1965. *The Maturational Processes and the Facilitating Environment; Studies in the Theory of Emotional Development*. New York: International Universities Press.

_____. 1967. "The Location of Cultural Experience." *International Journal of Psychoanalysis* 48:368-72.

_____. 1971. *Playing and Reality*. New York: Basic Books, Inc., Publishers.

_____. 1975. *Through Paediatrics to Psycho-Analysis*. New York: Basic Books, Inc., Publishers.

Wrong, Dennis H. 1980. *Power, Its Form, Bases, and Uses*. New York: Harper Colophon.

Yankelovich, Daniel, and Immerwahr, John. 1983. *Putting the Work Ethic to Work*. New York: Public Agenda Foundation.

Yorke, Clifford. 1986. "Reflections on the Problem of Psychic Trauma." *Psychoanalytic Study of the Child* 41:221-36.

Zaleznik, Abraham. 1965. "The Dynamics of Subordinacy." *Harvard Business Review* 43:119-31.

_____. 1967. "Management of disappointment." *Harvard Business Review* 45:59-70.

Index